D1421527

Essential
Japanese

2nd Edition

by Lynne Strugnell
2nd edition text by Kayo Nonaka

Berlitz Publishing
New York   Munich   Singapore

Essential Japanese, 2nd Edition

Contacting the Editors
Every effort has been made to provide accurate information in this publication, but changes are inevitable. The publisher cannot be responsible for any resulting loss, inconvenience, or injury. We would appreciate it if readers would call our attention to any errors or outdated information by contacting Berlitz Publishing, 193 Morris Avenue, Springfield, NJ 07081, USA. email: comments@berlitzbooks.com

First Printing: November 2008
Printed in Singapore

Publishing Director: Sheryl Olinsky Borg
Project Manager/Editor: Eric Zuarino
1st Edition Text: Lynne Strugnell
2nd Edition Japanese Writer: Kayo Nonaka
Japanese Proofreader: Nobuo Ogawa
Production Manager: Elizabeth Gaynor
Cover Design: Claudia Petrilli
Interior Design: Claudia Petrilli and Datagrafix, Inc.

Cover Photo: © ImageGap/Alamy

TABLE OF CONTENTS

INTRODUCTION

Whether you're a beginner who's never studied a foreign language or a former student brushing up on old skills, Berlitz *Essential Japanese* will provide you with all the tools and information you need to speak a foreign tongue easily and effectively. Furthermore, the book is designed to permit you to study at your own pace, based on your level of expertise.

* Lively bilingual dialogues describe actual, everyday situations in which you might find yourself when traveling in a foreign country.
* Basic grammar is taught through actual phrases and sentences, which help you develop an instinctive sense of correct grammar without having to study long lists of rules and exceptions.
* An exercise section in each lesson gives you the opportunity to pinpoint your strengths and weaknesses, and enables you to study more efficiently.
* Internet activities at the end of each lesson expose you to the target language and culture in action.
* The glossary at the end of the book gives you an easy reference list of all the words used in the book.
* The audio CD features native Japanese speakers in all dialogues and vocabulary sections, exposing you to the sound of spoken Japanese to help perfect your pronunciation skills.
* Download free bonus audio versions of all vocabulary sections at our website, http://www.berlitzpublishing.com for more pronunciation practice.

HOW TO USE THIS BOOK

The best way to learn any language is through consistent daily study. Decide for yourself how much time you can devote to the study of *Essential Japanese* each day – you may be able to complete two lessons a day or just have time for a half-hour of study. Set a realistic daily study goal that you can easily achieve, one that includes studying new material as well as reviewing the old. The more frequent your exposure to the language, the better your results will be.

THE STRUCTURE OF THE BOOK

* Listen to the dialogue at the beginning of each lesson. Follow along slowly and carefully, using the translation and the pronunciation guide.

* You will also find the vocabulary sections of this book on our website. Just go to http://www.berlitzpublishing.com for free MP3 downloads. Listen along and repeat to perfect your Japanese pronunciation.
* When you have listened to and read the dialogues and vocabulary sections enough times to get a good grasp of the sounds and sense of the language, read the grammar section, paying particular attention to how the language builds its sentences. Then go back and listen to and read the dialogue again.
* When studying the vocabulary list, it is useful to write the words down in a notebook. This will help you remember both the spelling and meaning as you move ahead. You might also try writing the word in a sentence that you make up yourself.
* Try to work on the exercise section without referring to the dialogue, then go back and check your answers against the dialogue or by consulting the answer key at the end of the book. It's helpful to repeat the exercises.
* The last activitiy in each chapter includes an online-based opportunity to apply your knowledge of Japanese to complete real tasks using the foreign language. The sites have been selected to help you use the vocabulary and expressions that you already know, while introducing you to new cultural or grammatical concepts. Visit our website at http://www.berlitzpublishing.com and go to the downloads section for bonus activities.

By dedicating yourself to the lessons in the *Berlitz Essential Japanese* course, you will quickly put together the basic building blocks of Japanese, which will help you to continue at your own pace. You will find in this book all you need to know in order to communicate effectively in a foreign language; and you will be amply prepared to go on to master Japanese with all the fluency of a native speaker.

GUIDE TO PRONUNCIATION

One great advantage of learning Japanese over other languages is that the pronunciation is easy for English speakers. It is straightforward, regular, and does not have the complications of different tones, strong stress patterns or unfamiliar sounds that some languages have. Each letter is pronounced in one way only, so you do not have to learn complex rules for combinations of letters. In fact, you probably already know how to pronounce most of the sounds if you are familiar with such words as kimono, Honda, sumoo, Yokohama, sushi, karate, geisha and Zen.

1. THE VOWELS

"a" is pronounced as in Kawasaki.
"e" is pronounced as in Zen.
"i" is pronounced as in kimono.
"o" is pronounced as in Hiroshima.
"u" is pronounced as in sumoo.

Remember that each vowel is always said in the same way, so the two "o" sounds at the end of kimono, for example, should be the same. Also, there is much less stress on individual syllables in Japanese than there is in English, so instead of saying kiMOno or YokoHAma, you should try saying the words evenly, without any particular stress.

The rule about vowels always being pronounced the same still holds when two vowels come together. Take them one by one, and pronounce them as in the guide above. For example, think of geisha as ge-i-sha, rather than "gay-sha."

Sometimes you will see the same vowel in a row (e.g. oo, uu). This means that the sound is twice as long as a single vowel. In the place name Kyooto, for example, the "oo" lasts twice as long as the second one, so lean slightly on the first one as you say it.

There are a few cases where the vowel sound almost disappears. One of the most common of these is the final "u" at the end of present tense verbs. These all end in -masu, but in practice it sounds more like "-mass". Another example is desu ("is/are"), which is pronounced rather like "dess".

2. CONSONANTS

Most of the consonant sounds are the same as in English, so pronounce them as they look. There are only a few differences, as follows:

The letter "g" is always pronounced hard as in "gain", not soft as in "gem".

The letter "f" represents a sound somewhere between "f" and "h". To make the sound, try saying Fuji without letting your top teeth touch your bottom lip, and you'll get the idea.

The letter "r" represents a sound which is halfway between "l" and "r". Try saying Narita (the name of Tokyo's international airport), but flick the tip of your tongue on the roof of your mouth on all three consonants, that is, on "r" as well as on "n" and "t".

Sometimes you will see words with double consonants in the middle (e.g. a<u>tt</u>a, ki<u>pp</u>u, ga<u>kk</u>oo, za<u>ss</u>hi). As with the vowels, these doubled sounds should be held for twice the length of a single sound. For example, atta ("had") is pronounced like the middle part of "th<u>at tap</u>". Other than those double consonants, only one consonant appears without a vowel; that is "n", as in "konban". The "n" has the length of a sigle sound. When this "n" appears before a vowel or "y", "n" will be presented as "n'" as in "kin'yoobi" or "han'en" to distinguish from other single sounds such as "ny + vowel" or "n + vowel" combination.

Japanese written in the roman alphabet is phonetic, in other words it is written almost exactly as it sounds, so it isn't necessary to provide you with a phonetic guide to pronouncing each line in the text. However, just to make sure you're on the right track, here are some words taken from Lesson 1, along with a guide to how to pronounce them. Try saying them aloud.

arigatoo (thank you): ah-ree-gah-toe
Nihon (Japan): nee-hon
hajimemashite (How do you do?): hah-jee-meh-mash-teh
shitsurei (excuse me): she-tsoo-reh-ee
iie (no): ee-ee-eh
hai (yes): hah-ee

THE WRITING SYSTEM

Although spoken Japanese is relatively easy to learn, the written language is one of the most complex in the world (which is one reason why this book uses the Roman alphabet!). It is made up of three quite different writing systems, kanji, hiragana and katakana characters, which are used in combination.

Some examples of kanji characters and the way they are pronounced have been given in each lesson. In addition, you will find some more information on kanji, hiragana and katakana in Appendix 2.

NIHON E YOOKOSO!
WELCOME TO JAPAN!

Mike Nelson has just arrived at Narita airport, outside Tokyo. He will be met there by Ikuo Watanabe, a teacher at the high school where Mike will be teaching. Ikuo Watanabe arrives late and talks to Mike.

Watanabe	**Sumimasen, Neruson san desu ka.** Excuse me, are you Mr. Nelson?
Nelson	**Hai, soo desu. Neruson desu.** Yes, that's right. I'm Mr. Nelson.
Watanabe	**Hajimemashite, Watanabe desu. Yokohama Gakuin Kookoo no Watanabe desu. Nihon e yookoso!** How do you do? I'm Mr. Watanabe, Mr. Watanabe from Yokohama High School. Welcome to Japan!
Nelson	**Aa, Watanabe san, hajimemashite.** Ah, Mr. Watanabe, how do you do?
Watanabe	**Watashi no meishi desu. Doozo.** Here's my business card. Here it is.

Nelson   (Doomo) arigatoo gozaimasu.
         Thank you.

Watanabe (pointing to suitcases) Neruson san no suutsukeesu
          desu ka.
          Are these your suitcases, Mr. Nelson?

Nelson   Hai, soo desu.
          Yes, they are.

Watanabe Ja, doozo, kochira e.
          Well, this way, please.

Mr. Watanabe grabs a suitcase, which belongs to someone else.

Nelson   Iie, Watanabe-san, chigaimasu.
          No, Mr. Watanabe, that's not my suitcase!

Stranger Watashi no suutsukeesu desu.
          This is my suitcase.

Watanabe (To a stranger) A, doomo sumimasen.
          Oh, I'm very sorry.

It's a long drive to Yokohama, but they finally get there. Mike has been trying hard to stay awake.

Watanabe Hai, Neruson san, Yokohama desu. Neruson san.
          Neruson san.
          Well, this is Yokohama! Mr. Nelson? Mr. Nelson?

But all he gets in response is a gentle, peaceful snoring.

STRUCTURE AND USAGE NOTES

1. SAN – MR., MRS., MISS AND MS.

The word san is used as a term of respect after all names, so this one word is the equivalent of Mr., Ms., Mrs. and Miss. It is even used after first names, so don't be surprised if you are called Tom san or Susan san. Remember that, as san is a term of respect to other people, you never use it with your own name. Notice how Mr. Watanabe used san in his first line in the dialogue, but Mike didn't use it in his reply.

Watanabe Neruson san desu ka.
          Are you Mr. Nelson?

Nelson   Hai, soo desu. Neruson desu.
          Yes, that's right. I'm Mr. Nelson.

2. DESU – "TO BE"

In Japanese it is not necessary to learn long lists of different verb endings, because the verb does not change with the person, and so desu can mean "I am/you are/he is/she is/it is/we are/they are". It is usually obvious from the situation which of these meanings is intended. Notice that the verb always comes at the end of a Japanese sentence.

Gakusei desu.
(I) am a student.

Enjinia desu.
(He) is an engineer.

Amerikajin desu.
(I) am an American.

Watanabe san desu ka.
Are (you) Mr. Watanabe?

3. KA – FORMING QUESTIONS

To form a question, simply add ka to the end of the sentence with a rising intonation. You don't need to make any other changes.

Gakusei desu.
I am/He is a student.

Gakusei desu ka.
Are you/Is he a student?

Yokohama desu.
(This) is Yokohama.

Yokohama desu ka.
Is (this) Yokohama?

Kanadajin desu.
I am/She is Canadian.

Kanadajin desu ka.
Are you/Is she Canadian?

Sometimes you may hear an exchange like this:

Mike   Shitsurei desu ga, Kanadajin desu ka.
Excuse me, but are you a Canadian?

Stranger   Kanadajin? Iie, chigaimasu. Watashi wa Amerikajin desu.
Canadian? No, I'm not. I'm an American.

In this case, the question marker ka is dropped, but the intonation still goes up.

4. THE PARTICLE NO

You will come across a number of small words in Japanese which do not have a meaning in themselves, but which serve to show the relationship between different parts of a sentence, or the function of a word or phrase within a sentence. These small words are called "particles", and usually come *after* the word to which they refer. One such word is no, which acts rather like the English "-'s" to show belonging or possession. It links the owner to the owned.

Takahashi san no suutsukeesu
Ms. Takahashi's suitcase

Suzuki san no meishi
Mr. Suzuki's business card

watashi no gakkoo
my school

gakkoo no namae
the school's name

However, the usage of no is much wider than simply possession, and it can be used to connect any two nouns (or more) where the first one describes, or gives more information about, the second one.

Amerika no kaisha
an American company

Nihon no kuruma
Japanese cars

Yokohama no gakkoo
schools in Yokohama [Lit: Yokohama's schools]

You can use no more than once in the same phrase.

watashi no gakkoo no sensei
the teachers at my school [Lit: my school's teachers]

Nihongo no sensei no namae
the Japanese (language) teacher's name

Mr. Watanabe introduces himself as **Yokohama Gakuin Kookoo no Watanabe desu,** literally "I'm Yokohama High School's Mr. Watanabe", or more colloquially, "I'm Mr. Watanabe, of Yokohama High School".

---

5. PLURALS

Japanese does not usually differentiate between singular and plural except where absolutely necessary. You'll find that it is generally obvious from the context whether a particular noun is a singular or plural. In other situations you'll find it's not really necessary to differentiate.

Saitoo san? Enjinia desu.	Saitoo san to Katoo san?
Mr. Saitoo? He's an engineer	Enjinia desu.
	Mr. Saitoo and Mr. Katoo?
	They're engineers.
Watashi no meishi desu.	Saitoo san to Watanabe san
Doozo.	no meishi desu.
Here's my business card.	These are Mr. Saitoo's and
	Mr. Watanabe's business cards.

6. ARTICLES – "THE" AND "A"

Unlike English, there are no articles ("a/an/the") in Japanese.

Gakusei desu ka.
Are you (a) student?

Amerika no kaisha desu.
It's (an) American company.

Sumimasen ga, Nihongo no sensei desu ka.
Excuse me, but are you (the) Japanese language teacher?

7. THE PARTICLE E

The particle e can often be translated as "to" or "towards", as it indicates the direction of movement towards something. Unlike English, a Japanese particle comes after a noun.

Tookyoo e yookoso.
Welcome to Tokyo.

Kochira e, doozo.
This way, please.

8. NUMBERS

Generally, this is how you count from 1 to 10 in Japanese.

1	ichi
2	ni
3	san
4	yon, shi

5	go
6	roku
7	shichi, nana
8	hachi
9	kyuu, ku
10	juu

There are two different ways to say four, seven and nine. One way is used over the other depending on the context, but just for counting, you can use either one.

After 10, it goes like this. Think of them as "ten one", "ten two" and so on.

11	juuichi
12	juuni
13	juusan
14	juushi, juuyon
15	juugo
16	juuroku
17	juushichi, juunana
18	juuhachi
19	juukyuu, juuku
20	nijuu

For 20, 30, and so on, think of them as "two ten", "three ten" and so on.

20	nijuu
30	sanjuu
40	yonjuu
50	gojuu
60	rokujuu
70	nanajuu

80	hachijuu
90	kyuujuu
100	hyaku

VOCABULARY

Amerika: the United States of America
Amerikajin: an American
arigatoo: thank you [more informal than doomo arigatoo]
chigaimasu: that's incorrect, wrong [from the verb chigau]
desu: I am, you are, he is, she is, it is, we are, they are
doomo: very much, thank you (casual)
(doomo) arigatoo gozaimasu: thank you (very much)
(doomo) sumimasen: I'm sorry, I apologize
doozo: please (go ahead), here you are (when giving something)
e: to, towards
enjinia: engineer
ga: but
gakkoo: school
gakuin: institute, school, place of learning
gakusei: student
go: five
gojuu: fifty
hai: yes
hajimemashite: How do you do?
hachi: eight
hachijuu: eighty
hyaku: one hundred
ichi: one
iie: no
ja: well, in that case
...jin: person (of a country)
juu: ten
juugo: fifteen
juuhachi: eighteen
juuichi: eleven
juuku: nineteen
juukyuu: nineteen
juunana: seventeen
juuni: twelve
juuroku: sixteen
juusan: thirteen
juushi: fourteen

juushichi: seventeen
juuyon: fourteen
ka: [sentence ending to indicate a question]
kaisha: company, office
Kanada: Canada
Kanadajin: a Canadian
kochira: this way
kookoo: high school [short for kootoo gakkoo]
kuruma: car
kyuu: nine
kyuujuu: ninety
meishi: business card
namae: name
nana: seven
nanajuu: seventy
ni: two
Nihon, Nippon: Japan [Both are used equally in Japan.]
Nihongo: Japanese language
nijuu: twenty
no: [particle showing possession, similar to English "-'s"]
roku: six
rokujuu: sixty
san: Mr., Mrs., Ms., Miss
san: three
sanjuu: thirty
sensei: teacher, professor (This word is also used when addressing medical doctors and lawyers.)
shichi: seven
shichijuu: seventy
shitsurei desu ga: I'm sorry to trouble you, but...; Excuse me, but...
soo desu: that's right, that's so
soo desu ka: I see, is that so?
sumimasen: excuse me, I'm sorry
suutsukeesu: suitcase
to: and [to connect nouns]
watashi: I, me
watashi no: my
yon: four
yonjuu: forty
yookoso: welcome

TEST YOURSELF

Read through the dialogue at the beginning of the lesson again, and then say if the following statements are true or false.

1. Watanabe san wa sensei desu. T/F
2. Watanabe san no gakkoo wa Yokohama Gakuin Kookoo desu. T/F
3. Maiku san no namae wa Maiku Neruson desu. T/F

Exercise A

Answer the questions about yourself with Hai, soo desu or Iie, chigaimasu.

1. Shitsurei desu ga, Neruson san desu ka.

   _____

2. Amerikajin desu ka. _____
3. Gakusei desu ka. _____
4. Sensei desu ka. _____

Exercise B

How would you say the following sentences in Japanese?

1. How do you do? _____
2. I'm American. _____
3. Is this a Japanese car? _____
4. Yes, that's right. _____
5. (A: Is it Mr. Watanabe's suitcase?)   B: No, it's not.

   _____   _____

Exercise C

Exercise D

Make up some questions and answers, using the pictures and cues given below. (Notice that in Japan, a small circle (O) is generally used instead of a check mark as a symbol for "yes" or "correct", and (X) is used to mean "no" or "incorrect".) Here is an example to help you.

X

Example: Yokohama High School?

A. Yokohama Gakuin Kookoo desu ka.

B. Iie, chigaimasu.

O

O

1. Mike's suitcase?

_____

_____

2. A student?

_____

_____

X

O

3. A teacher?

_____

_____

4. Mr. Watanabe's car?

_____

_____

X

O

5. An engineer?

6. An American?

Introduce yourself to Mr. Tanaka, of Fujimura Company, by filling in the blanks in the conversation below with the appropriate words. (If you don't belong to a company, college, or other organization, then just give your name.)

You   Shitsurei _____, Tanaka _____.
       Excuse me. Are you Mr. Tanaka?

Tanaka Hai, soo desu.
        Yes, I am.

You   _____, _____ no _____
       desu.
       How do you do? I'm... of....

Tanaka _____, Fujimura no Tanaka desu.
        How do you do? I'm Tanaka of Fujimura.

You   Watashi no _____ desu. Doozo.
       Here is my business card. Please.

 日本

Nihon/Nippon is the Japanese word for "Japan". It is made up of the kanji characters for "sun" and "source/origin", giving the meaning "sourse of the sun".

Visit www.berlitzpublishing.com for a bonus internet activity—go to the downloads section and connect to the world in Japanese!

2

MINASAN, OHAYOO GOZAIMASU.
GOOD MORNING, EVERYONE.

It's Mike Nelson's first day of work at Yokohama High School, and Ikuo Watanabe is introducing him to some of the staff.

Watanabe **Mina san, ohayoo gozaimasu.**
Good morning, everyone.

Everyone **Ohayoo gozaimasu.**
Good morning.

Watanabe **Neruson sensei, kochira wa jimu no Takahashi san desu.**
Mr. Nelson, this is Ms. Takahashi from the administration office.

Takahashi **Hajimemashite. Takahashi desu. Doozo yoroshiku.**
How do you do? I'm Ms. Takahashi. Nice to meet you.

Nelson **Maiku Neruson desu. Yoroshiku onegai shimasu.**
I'm Mike Nelson. Nice to meet you.

Mr. Watanabe shows Mike around the office.

Watanabe	Kore wa watashi no tsukue desu. Kore wa Takahashi san no tsukue desu. This is my desk. This is Ms. Takahashi's desk.
Nelson	Watashi no tsukue wa doko ni arimasu ka. Where's my desk?
Watanabe	Neruson sensei no wa koko ni arimasu. Yours is there.
Takahashi	Watanabe sensei, chigaimasu. Sore wa Neruson sensei no tsukue ja arimasen. Saitoo san no desu. Mr. Watanabe, that's not (so). That's not Mr. Nelson's desk. It's Ms. Saitoo's.
Watanabe	Saitoo san. Saitoo san wa dare desu ka. Ms. Saitoo? Who's Ms. Saitoo?
Takahashi	Atarashii paato no hito desu. Kyoo kara desu. She's the new part-time worker. From today.
Watanabe	Soo desu ka. Atarashii paato desu ka. Ja, Neruson sensei no tsukue wa? I see. The new part-time worker. Well, what about Mr. Nelson's desk?
Takahashi	Wakarimasen. Aa, ano tsukue ja arimasen ka. I don't know. Isn't it that desk?
Watanabe	A, are desu ka. Neruson sensei, are desu. Ah, is it that one? Mr. Nelson, it's that one.
Nelson	Wakarimashita. Doomo arigatoo gozaimasu. I see. Thank you.

STRUCTURE AND USAGE NOTES

1. OHAYOO GOZAIMASU – "GOOD MORNING" AND OTHER GREETINGS

Here are some useful phrases for greetings and partings.

Ohayoo gozaimasu.
Good morning.

Konnichiwa.
Good day/Hello.

Konbanwa.
Good evening.

Shitsurei shimasu.
Goodbye. [Lit: Excuse me.]

Oyasumi nasai.
Good night.

Jaa mata.
See you later.

Sayonara.
Goodbye.

2. THE PARTICLE WA

The job of the particle wa is to point out the main topic of a sentence and, like all particles, it comes after the word or phrase to which it refers. You can think of it as meaning "As for…" or "Regarding…"

Maiku san wa Amerikajin desu.
Mike is an American. [Lit: As for Mike, he's an American.]

Yokohama Gakuin Kookoo wa ookii desu.
Yokohama High School is big.

Ogawa san wa Nihongo no sensei desu.
Ms. Ogawa is a Japanese teacher. [Lit: As for Ms. Ogawa, she's a Japanese teacher.]

Saitoo san wa dare desu ka.
Who's Ms. Saitoo? [Lit: With regard to Ms. Saitoo – who is she?]

Watanabe san no uchi wa ookii desu ka.
Is Mr. Watanabe's house big? [Lit: Regarding Mr. Watanabe's house – is it big?]

Ano sensei no namae wa Ogawa desu ka.
Is that teacher's name Ms. Ogawa?

3. KORE, SORE, ARE AND DORE – "THIS", "THAT" AND "WHICH ONE?"

In English, we divide things into the two groups of "this" and "that", but in Japanese there are three groups: kore, meaning "this thing" or "these things" near me; sore, meaning "that thing" or "those things" near you; and are meaning "that thing" or "those things" over there, away from both of us. (Don't pronounce that last one like the English "are". Remember that it should be pronunced more like "ah-reh".)

Kore wa atarashii purintaa desu ka.
Is this a new printer?

A: Neruson san no suutsukeesu wa kore desu ka.
Your suitcase, Mr. Nelson – is it this one?

B: Iie, chigaimasu. Sore wa Watanabe san no desu.
No, it's not. That's Mr. Watanabe's.

Sore wa paato no hito no tsukue desu.
That's the part-time worker's desk.

Itoo san no uchi wa are desu.
Mr. Itoo's house is that one over there.

The corresponding question word is dore.

A: Itoo san no kuruma wa dore desu ka.
Which is your car, Mr. Itoo?

B: Sore desu.
It's that one near you.

4. KOKO, SOKO, ASOKO AND DOKO – "HERE", "THERE" AND "WHERE?"

Another set of words beginning with ko-, so-, a- and do- relate to location: koko means "here", near me; soko means "there", near you; and asoko means "over there", away from both of us. The question word doko means "where".

Asoko no kuruma wa dare no kuruma desu ka.
That car over there – whose (car) is it?

A. Johnson san no okuni wa doko desu ka.
Where are you from, Mr. Johnson?

B. Shikago desu.
I'm from Chicago.

5. ...NI ARIMASU

Sentences describing the location of something usually use the verb arimasu ("to be/exist"), and the particle ni follows the word or phrase showing the place where something exists, so it can often be translated as "at" or "in".

Kyoo no shinbun wa koko ni arimasu.
Today's newspapers are over here.

Denwa wa soko ni arimasu. Doozo.
The telephone's there. Please (go ahead and use it).

Eki wa asoko ni arimasu ka.
Is the station over there?

Ginkoo wa doko ni arimasu ka.
Where's the bank?

---

6. ARIMASU VS. DESU – "TO BE", "TO BE LOCATED", "TO EXIST"

Both arimasu and desu mean "is/are", but there is a difference in the way they are used. Desu is used when one thing is, or equals, another.

Koko wa Yokohama eki desu.
This is Yokohama station.

Neruson san wa atarashii sensei desu.
Mr. Nelson is a new teacher.

Kore wa watashi no meishi desu. Doozo.
This is my business card. Please (take it).

The verb arimasu means that something exists, so it is often used to describe the location of something. As we saw above, in this case it is preceded by ni, a particle pointing out place or location.

Daigaku wa Oosaka ni arimasu.
(My) university is (located) in Osaka.

Ogawa san no kaisha wa Tookyoo ni arimasu.
Mr. Ogawa's company is (located) in Tokyo.

Denwa wa doko ni arimasu ka.
Where's the telephone (located)?

When describing the location of something, ni arimasu can often be replaced by desu. The nuance is slightly different, but the English translation is usually the same.

Ginkoo wa doko desu ka.
Where's the bank?
[Lit: What place is the bank?]

Ginkoo wa doko ni arimasu ka.
Where's the bank?
[Lit: In what place is the bank located?]

Gakkoo wa asoko desu.
The school is over there.
[Lit: The school is that place over there.]

Gakkoo wa asoko ni arimasu.
The school is over there.
[Lit: The school is located in that place over there.]

The verb arimasu can often be translated as "there is/are", or "have".

Denwa wa arimasu ka.
Do you have a telephone?/Is there a telephone?

Answers to this kind of "yes or no" question are **Hai, arimasu** ("Yes, I have."/Yes, there is".), **Iie, arimasen** ("No, I haven't./No, there isn't".), or **Wakarimasen** ("I don't know".).

A. **Denwa wa arimasu ka.**
Do you have a telephone?/Is there a telephone?

B. **Iie, arimasen.**
No, we don't./No, there isn't.

A. **Saitoo san, kyoo no shinbun wa arimasu ka.**
Ms. Saito, do you have today's paper?

B. **Hai, arimasu. Doozo.**
Yes, I do. Here you are.

A. **Koko ni daigaku ga arimasu ka.**
Is there a university here?

B. **Wakarimasen.**
I don't know.

7. JA ARIMASEN – "ISN'T", "AREN'T"

Ja arimasen is the negative of **desu,** so it means "isn't", or "aren't". **Ja** is a contraction of **de wa.** (You may also hear the alternative forms **de wa arimasen, ja nai desu** and **de wa nai desu,** which all mean "isn't" or "aren't".)

Amerikajin ja arimasen. Igirisujin desu.
I'm not American. I'm British.

Sensei ja arimasen. Jimu no hito desu.
I'm not a teacher. I am an office worker.

Ookii kookoo ja arimasen.
It's not a big high school.

A. **Kore wa atarashii konpyuutaa desu ka.**
Is this a new computer?

B. **Iie, atarashii konpyuutaa ja arimasen.**
No, it isn't a new computer.

Are wa Watanabe san no kuruma ja arimasen ka.
Isn't that Mr. Watanabe's car?

8. SAITOO SAN NO DESU – "IT'S MS. SAITO'S"

The word **no** can be used in place of a noun when it is obvious what you are talking about, in much the same way as "one" or simply "...'s" is used in English.

Kaisha no kuruma desu. It's the company's car.	Kaisha no desu. It's the company's.
Dare no shinbun desu ka. Whose newspaper is it?	Dare no desu ka. Whose is it?
Atarashii purintaa wa arimasu ka. Do you have a new printer?	Atarashii no wa arimasu ka. Do you have a new one?
Oosaka no daigaku wa ookii desu. The university in Osaka is big.	Oosaka no wa ookii desu. The one in Osaka is big.

9. "YOU" AND "YOURS"

Although there is a word for "you" in Japanese (anata), you won't hear it used very often. Instead, the person's name is generally used, even when you are talking to him or her directly.

Neruson san no tsukue wa soko ni arimasu.
Your desk is there (Mr. Nelson).

Kore wa Neruson san no shinbun desu ka.
Is this your newspaper (Mr. Nelson)?

Maiku san no gakkoo wa Yokohama ni arimasu ka.
Is your school in Yokohama (Mike)?

VOCABULARY

anata: you [not used as much]
are: that thing over there [noun]
arimasen: there isn't/aren't, don't have [from aru]
arimasu: be, exist, there is/are, have [from aru]
asoko: over there
atarashii: new
daigaku: university
dare: who?
denwa: telephone
doko: where?
dore: which one?
Doozo yoroshiku.: Nice to meet you.
eki: train station
ginkoo: bank
hito: person, people
Igirisu: England, Great Britain
Igirisujin: an English/British person
ja arimasen: isn't, aren't
jimu: office work, administration office

18

kara: from
kochira: this person [used with introductions]
koko: here
konbanwa: good evening
konnichiwa: good day, hello [not used early in the morning]
konpyuutaa: computer
kore: this thing near me [noun]
kyoo: today
mina san: everyone
ni: in, at [particle indicating location]
ohayoo gozaimasu: good morning
ookii: big
(o)kuni: (your) country
oyasumi nasai: good night
paato: part-time worker
purintaa: printer
sensei: professor, doctor [used when addressing teachers, professors, and doctors, etc. instead of san]
shinbun: newspaper
shitsurei shimasu: excuse me, goodbye
soko: there
sore: that thing near you [noun]
tsukue: desk
uchi: house, home
wa: [particle to indicate main topic of sentence]
wakarimasen: I don't know, I don't understand [from wakaru]
Yoroshiku onegai shimasu.: Pleased to meet you.

TEST YOURSELF

Read through the dialogue at the beginning of the lesson again, and then say if the following statements are true or false.

1. Takahashi san wa sensei ja arimasen. T/F

2. Atarashii paato wa kyoo kara desu. T/F

3. Paato no namae wa Takahashi san desu. T/F

Exercise A

Exercise B

Answer the following questions about yourself.

1. **Kyoo no shinbun wa arimasu ka.**

   _____

2. **Anata no kaisha [OR gakkoo, daigaku] wa doko ni arimasu ka.**

   _____

   _____

3. **Anata no uchi wa ookii uchi desu ka.**

   _____

4. **Atarashii kuruma wa arimasu ka.**

   _____

5. **Okuni wa doko desu ka.**

   _____

Exercise C

Provide the Japanese word for the following words.

1. person _____

2. business card _____

3. desk _____

4. telephone _____

5. part-time worker _____

6. printer _____

7. computer _____

Exercise D

How would you say the following sentences in Japanese?

1. What country are you from?

   _____

2. My company is in New York.

   _____

3. Excuse me, but where's the bank?

   _____

4. The telephone's over there – please go ahead (and use it).

   _____

5. That isn't my house.

   _____

Fill in the blanks with an appropriate word from the lists below. Each word can only be used once. Note that there are more words than you need. Mark X if no word is necessary.

no	kara	arimasen
dare	soo	asoko
ni	ja	wa
ka	are	namae

1. Saitoo san no daigaku wa doko _____ arimasu ka.

2. Sumimasen ga, kyoo no shinbun wa _____.

3. Denwa wa _____ ni arimasu.

4. Iie, watashi wa Amerikajin _____ arimasen.

5. Watanabe san _____ uchi wa atarashii desu ka.

6. Nihongo no sensei no _____ wa Itoo sensei desu.

7. Tanaka san _____ enjinia desu ka.

8. Neruson san no okuni wa doko _____ desu ka.

横浜 The name of the port of Yokohama, just south of Tokyo, combines the characters for "next to/side" and "beach".

Visit www.berlitzpublishing.com for a bonus internet activity—go to the downloads section and connect to the world in Japanese!

3

NANI O TABEMASU KA.
WHAT ARE YOU GOING TO HAVE (EAT)?

Ikuo Watanabe has invited Mike out for lunch at a small Japanese restaurant near the school. The menu is all in Japanese, which Mike Nelson can't read yet, so Watanabe asks him what he would like.

Watanabe	**Neruson san wa nani o tabemasu ka.** What are you going to eat?
Nelson	**Hmm, wakarimasen. Kono resutoran wa, nani ga oishii desu ka.** Hmm, I don't know. What's good at this restaurant?
Watanabe	**Sakana ga oishii desu. Sakana ga suki desu ka.** The fish is good. Do you like fish?
Nelson	**Hai, dai-suki desu.** Yes, I like it very much.
Watanabe	**Ja, yaki-zakana teishoku wa doo desu ka.** Well, how about the grilled fish set meal?
Nelson	**Yaki-zakana teishoku? Sore wa nan desu ka.** Yaki-zakana teishoku? What is it?

Watanabe	Yaki-zakana to gohan to tsukemono to miso shiru desu.
	That's grilled fish, rice, pickles and miso soup.
Nelson	Sore wa ii desu ne. Hai, watashi wa yaki-zakana teishoku ni shimasu. Watanabe san wa?
	That's good. Yes, I'll have the grilled fish dinner. And you?
Watanabe	Watashi wa sashimi teishoku ni shimasu. (to waitress) Sumimasen!
	I'll have the sashimi [raw fish] dinner. Excuse me!
Waitress	Hai, nani ni shimasu ka.
	Yes, what would you like?
Watanabe	Yaki-zakana teishoku to sashimi teishoku o onegaishimasu.
	The grilled fish dinner and the sashimi dinner, please.

The waitress soon comes back with a tray of food each for Watanabe and Mike.

Nelson	Itadakimasu.
	Enjoy your meal.
Watanabe	Itadakimasu.
	Enjoy your meal.
Nelson	Kono miso shiru wa oishii desu ne. (noticing something decorating Mr. Watanabe's raw fish) E? Sore wa nan desu ka. Hana ja arimasen ka.
	This miso soup is good, isn't it. Eh? What's that? Isn't it a flower?
Watanabe	Hai, soo desu. Kono hana wa kiku desu.
	Yes, that's right. That flower's a chrysanthemum.
Nelson	E? Nan desu ka? Kiku desu ka. Kiku o tabemasu ka.
	Eh? What? It's a chrysanthemum? You eat chrysanthemums?
Watanabe	Hai, tokidoki tabemasu! A, o-cha ga arimasen ne. O-cha o nomimasu ka.
	Yes, sometimes we do! Ah, there isn't any green tea, is there? Do you drink green tea?
Nelson	Sumimasen ga, o-cha wa amari suki ja arimasen. Mizu ga sukidesu.
	I'm sorry, but I don't really like green tea. I like water.

> *Watanabe*   Hai, mizu desu ne. (to waitress) Sumimasen, o-cha to mizu o onegai shimasu.
> Yes, water – right. Excuse me, some green tea and some water, please.

STRUCTURE AND USAGE NOTES

1. SIMPLE PRESENT TENSE VERBS

As we have seen with desu, Japanese verbs do not change to agree with the person or persons doing the action, and there is usually no need even to mention any words for "you", "I", etc. So tabemasu, for example, can mean "I eat/you eat/he eats/she eats/we eat/they eat". Likewise, the negative, tabemasen, can mean "I/you/he/she/we/ they don't eat". Here are some more present tense verbs for you to learn, with the negative forms. (Note that the final -u is almost silent, so the first word in the list, for example, is pronounced like nomimass.)

Present positive		Present negative	
nomimasu	drink	nomimasen	don't drink
ikimasu	go	ikimasen	don't go
kimasu	come	kimasen	don't come
wakarimasu	understand	wakarimasen	don't understand
arimasu	there is, have	arimasen	there isn't, don't have
kikimasu	listen, hear, ask	kikimasen	don't listen, don't hear, don't ask
yomimasu	read	yomimasen	don't read
oshiemasu	tell, teach	oshiemasen	don't tell, don't teach
mimasu	see, watch	mimasen	don't see, don't watch
shimasu	do	shimasen	don't do
hanashimasu	talk, speak	hanashimasen	don't talk, don't speak
tabemasu	eat	tabemasen	don't eat

Because this form of the present tense verb always ends in -masu in the positive, it is generally referred to as "the -masu form". There is another form, known as the plain form, or dictionary form, because it is the one used to list words in dictionaries (rather like the infinitive is used in English). The plain form of tabemasu, for example, is taberu. Both have exactly the same meaning, but the tone of taberu is much more informal, and the -masu form is the one used in everyday polite conversation. We will do some work with the plain form later in the book, but for the moment we will concentrate only on the -masu form, although you will find the plain form of new verbs given in the vocabulary lists at the end of each lesson. When you are learning a new verb, you should try to learn both the -masu form and the plain form.

2. THE OBJECT PARTICLE o

Before we go any further with verbs, we need another particle, o, because this points out the direct object of the verb by following directly after it. In other words, it shows what the action of the verb is affecting.

Nihongo o hanashimasu.
I speak Japanese.

Tokidoki eiga o mimasu.
I sometimes watch movies.

Watanabe san wa Eigo o hanashimasen.
Mr. Watanabe doesn't speak English.

Mainichi rajio o kikimasu ka.
Do you listen to the radio every day?

Takahashi san wa sakana o tabemasen.
Ms. Takahashi doesn't eat fish.

Tokidoki sashimi o tabemasu.
I sometimes eat raw fish.

Nihongo no shinbun o yomimasu ka.
Do you read Japanese (language) newspapers?

Takahashi san wa mainichi Eigo no shinbun o yomimasu.
Ms. Takahashi reads an English (language) newspaper every day.

3. THE FUTURE

The -masu form is also used to refer to events happening in the future. If it is not clear from the context whether a present or future meaning is intended, then a time word such as "tomorrow/next week/at 2:00" can be used.

Watanabe san wa ashita Tookyoo e ikimasu.
Mr. Watanabe will go to Tokyo tomorrow.

Tomodachi wa asatte Igirisu kara kimasu.
The day after tomorrow, a friend is coming from Britain.

Nani o nomimasu ka.
What will you drink? [This sentence is also used to mean "What would you like to drink?"]

Konban nani o tabemasu ka.
What are you going to eat tonight?

Ashita, oshiemasen.
I'm not teaching tomorrow.

Konban eiga o mimasu ka.
Are you going to see a movie tonight?

Kyoo nani o shimasu ka.
What are you going to do today?

Watashi wa kyoo kaisha e ikimasen.
I won't be going to the office today.

---

4. "KONO", "SONO", "ANO" AND "DONO" – THE ADJECTIVES "THIS", "THAT" AND "WHICH?"

In English, the words "this", "that" and "which" can be used as pronouns or adjectives, but this is not the case in Japanese. We came across kore, sore, are and dore in Lesson 2, but these are used only as pronouns. In other words, they stand by themselves to represent something. There is another set of ko-, so-, a- and do- words to use as adjectives: kono, sono, ano and dono. These words are always accompanied by a noun. Compare the pairs of sentences below.

Kono wain wa doko no desu ka.
Where is this wine from?

Kore wa doko no desu ka.
Where is this from?

Sono konpyuuta wa atarashii desu.
That computer's new.

Sore wa atarashii desu.
That's new.

Sono shinbun o yomimasu ka.
Are you going to read that newspaper?

Sore o yomimasu ka.
Are you going to read that?

Ano hito wa dare desu ka.
Who's that person?

Are wa dare desu ka.
Who's that?

Itoo san no kuruma wa dono kuruma desu ka.
Which car is Mr. Itoo's car?

Itoo san no kuruma wa dore desu ka.
Which is Mr. Itoo's car?

Dono teishoku ni shimasu ka.	Dore ni shimasu ka.
Which set meal are you going to have?	Which are you going to have?

5. THE TAG QUESTION NE

The particle ne at the end of a sentence plays the same role as tag questions in English, such as "isn't it?", "didn't he?", "aren't they?", "don't you?", "am I right?", etc. Such questions may be asking for confirmation, in which case they have rising intonation, or they may just be asking for agreement, in which case they have falling intonation.

Maiku san wa Amerikajin desu ne.
Mike is an American, isn't he?

Neruson san wa Eigo o oshiemasu ne.
Mr. Nelson will teach English, won't he?

Mainichi Nihongo no shinbun o yomimasu ne.
You read a Japanese newspaper every day, don't you?

Kono wain wa oishii desu ne.
This wine is good, isn't it!

Sono hito wa Itoo san desu ne.
That person's Mr. Itoo, right?

Kaigi wa asatte desu ne.
The meeting's the day after tomorrow, right?

Tomodachi no namae wa Fukuda san desu ne.
Your friend's name is Ms. Fukuda, isn't it?

6. THE SUBJECT PARTICLE GA

The particle ga marks the subject of a sentence, especially when the information is being introduced for the first time. When the information is already known, and so is already the topic of conversation, then the topic marker wa is used.

Asoko ni atarashii resutoran ga arimasu ne. Sono resutoran wa oishii desu.
There's a new restaurant over there, right? That restaurant is really good.

Konban Takahashi san no tomodachi ga kimasu ne. Sono tomodachi wa doko no hito desu ka. Kanadajin desu ka.
This evening Ms. Takahashi's friend is arriving, right? Where's the friend from? Is he Canadian?

A. Koko ni denwa wa arimasu ka.
Is there a telephone here?

B. Hai, denwa wa asoko ni arimasu.
   Yes, the phone's over there.

Question words like nani, doko and dare by their very nature are asking about unknown information, so they can't be topics. Therefore, they always take ga, not wa, when they are the subject of a sentence.

Dare ga ashita Yokohama e ikimasu ka.
Who's going to Yokohama tomorrow?

Wain wa, nani ga arimasu ka.
What (kind of) wine do you have?

Resutoran wa doko ga ii desu ka.
Where is there a good restaurant?

There are certain verbs which usually take the subject particle ga, and one of these is wakarimasu, "to understand/know". The person understanding or knowing is marked by wa, and the thing understood or known is marked by ga.

Watanabe san wa Eigo ga wakarimasu ka.
Does Mr. Watanabe understand English?

Watashi wa Maiku san no tomodachi no namae ga wakarimasen.
I don't know Mike's friend's name.

Another verb which takes ga is arimasu when it indicates possession or the meaning "have".

Kono daigaku ni atarashii konpyuuta ga arimasu.
This university has some new computers.

Maiku san wa kyoo kaigi ga arimasu ne.
You have a meeting today, don't you, Mike?

---

7. SUKI DESU/KIRAI DESU – I LIKE IT/I HATE IT

Unlike English, the Japanese words for "like" and "hate" (and the various shades in between) are not verbs, but adjectives. The subject of such a sentence is the thing or person liked or disliked, and so is followed by wa or ga. Here are some sentences to show how to say the various degrees of like and dislike, which are dai suki desu ("I like very much"), suki desu ("I like"), amari suki ja arimasen ("I don't like very much"), kirai desu ("I dislike"), and dai-kirai desu ("I loathe").

Watashi wa sashimi ga dai-suki desu.
I love raw fish.

Hana ga suki desu ka.
Do you like flowers?

Maiku san wa eiga ga suki desu ne.
Mike likes (going to) movies, doesn't he?

Watashi wa ano resutoran ga amari suki ja arimasen.
I don't like that restaurant very much.

Sakana wa kirai desu ka.
Don't you like fish? [Lit: Do you dislike fish?]

Ano sensei ga dai-kirai desu.
I loathe that teacher.

---

8. ...O ONEGAI SHIMASU – ASKING FOR SOMETHING

The word onegai shimasu means "please give me", although it sounds more polite than that in Japanese, and can be translated into English in several different ways. When you want someone to give you something – for example in a restaurant, or when shopping – simply say what you want and add o onegai shimasu. Often times, kudasai is used instead of onegai shimasu. Kudasai sounds a little casual and direct compared to onegai shimasu.

Sumimasen, mizu o onegai shimasu.
Excuse me, could I have some water, please?

A. Nani o nomimasu ka.
   What would you like to drink? [Lit: What will you drink?]
B. Wain o onegai shimasu.
   Wine, please.

Mainichi Shinbun o kudasai.
I'd like the Mainichi Newspaper please.

Sashimi teishoku o kudasai.
I'd like the sashimi (raw fish) set meal, please.

CULTURAL NOTE

ITADAKIMASU – TABLE MANNERS

The expression itadakimasu is usually said just before eating or drinking something, and it literally means "I receive food/drink". Make sure you say this expression because it shows appreciation of what you are receiving. After a meal, the phrase go-chisoo sama deshita is also said. This is a set phrase of thanks for the meal, whether you are at home, in a restaurant, or at someone's house.

VOCABULARY

amari: not very [+ negative form of verb]
ano: that...over there [adjective]
asatte: the day after tomorrow
ashita: tomorrow
dai-kirai desu: hate, detest, loathe
dai-suki desu: like very much, love
doo: how?
...wa doo desu ka: how about...?, how is...?
dono: which? [adjective]
eiga: movie, film
Eigo: English language
ga: [particle indicating the subject of a verb]
go-chisoo sama/go-chisoo sama deshita: Thank you for the meal.
gohan: cooked rice
hana: flower
hanashimasu: speak, talk [from hanasu]
ii desu: good, fine
ikimasu: go [from iku]
itadakimasu: [I receive food/drink] ritual expression before a meal
kaigi: a meeting
kikimasu: hear, listen, ask [from kiku]
kiku: chrysanthemum
kimasu: come [from kuru]
kirai desu: dislike
konban: this evening
kono: this [adjective]
mainichi: every day
miso shiru: miso soup
mizu: water
nan/nani: what?
ne: isn't it, aren't they, don't you
...ni shimasu: I'll have [decide on]...
nomimasu: drink [from nomu]
...o kudasai/...o onegai shimasu: Could I have..., please?
o: [particle to indicate object of verb]
(o)cha: green tea
oishii: tasty, delicious
oshiemasu: tell, teach [from oshieru]
rajio: radio
resutoran: restaurant
sakana: fish
sashimi: raw fish
shimasu: do [from suru]
sono: that [adjective]

suki desu: like
suki ja arimasen: don't like
sumimasen ga…: I'm sorry, but…
tabemasu: eat [from taberu]
teishoku: set meal
tokidoki: sometimes
tomodachi: friend
tsukemono: pickles
wain: wine
wakarimasu: understand [from wakaru]
yaki-zakana: grilled fish
yomimasu: read [from yomu]

TEST YOURSELF

Read through the dialogue at the beginning of the lesson once more, and then say if the following statements are true or false.

1. Kono resutoran wa, sakana ga oishii desu. T/F

2. Maiku san wa sashimi teishoku ni shimasu. T/F

3. Maiku san wa miso shiru ga kirai desu. T/F

4. Nihonjin wa tokidoki kiku o tabemasu. T/F

5. Maiku san to Watanabe san wa o-cha o nomimasu. T/F

Exercise A

If you were in a restaurant, how would you ask for:

1. some water? _____

2. some green tea? _____

3. the grilled fish dinner? _____

4. some wine? _____

5. raw fish? _____

6. that [pointing to what someone else is having]?
   _____

Exercise B

Exercise C

Look at the following pictures and use them to make up questions and answers, as in the example. (Remember that a small circle means a positive answer, and a cross means a negative answer.) If you are working with a partner, ask each other the questions and get true answers, then try to make up some new examples.

Example:
Every day?
Q. **Mainichi shinbun o yomimasu ka.**
A. **Hai, mainichi (shinbun o) yomimasu.**

1. Tomorrow?
   Q: _____
   A: _____

2. Every day?
   Q: _____
   A: _____

3. Today?
   Q: _____
   A: _____

4. Sometimes?
   Q: _____
   A: _____

X

5. Every day?

Q: _____

A: _____

Choose the appropriate particle – wa, ga, o, no or e – to complete the following sentences.

Exercise D

1. Maiku san _____, nani _____ nomimasu ka.

2. Watashi _____ eiga _____ dai-suki desu.

3. Mainichi Eigo _____ shinbun _____ yomimasu ka.

4. Nihongo _____ wakarimasu ka.

5. Tanaka san _____ ashita Tookyoo _____ ikimasu ne.

6. Are _____ dare _____ kuruma desu ka.

How would you say these sentences in Japanese?

Exercise E

1. Do you understand English?

   _____

2. What are you doing this evening?

   _____

3. I don't really like raw fish.

   _____

4. What are you going to teach, Ms. Tanaka?

   _____

5. Which movie are you going to see this evening?

   _____

6. This university's big, isn't it?

_____

大好き **Daisuki** is made up of the characters for "big/great" and "like", so the two together mean "like very much/love".

 Visit www.berlitzpublishing.com for a bonus internet activity—go to the downloads section and connect to the world in Japanese!

ROKU-JI NI AIMASHOO.
LET'S MEET AT 6:00.

Ms. Takahashi calls Mr. Saito, who is a part-time worker at the school to see if he would like to go to a movie.

Saito	**Moshi moshi, Saitoo desu ga.** Hello, this is Saito.
Takahashi	**Moshi moshi. Saitoo san? Takahashi desu ga.** Hello. Mr. Saito? This is Takahashi.
Saito	**Aa, Takahashi san, konbanwa.** Ah, Ms. Takahashi, good evening.
Takahashi	**Saitoo san, konban uchi ni imasu ka.** Saito-san, are you going to be at home this evening?
Saito	**Hai, imasu. Doo shite desu ka.** Yes, I am. Why?
Takahashi	**Ja eiga o mimasen ka. Konban ii eiga ga arimasu.** Then, would you like to see a movie? There's a good movie tonight.

Saito   **Eiga desu ka.**
A movie?

Takahashi   **Hai, eiga no namae wa *Anata No Ashita* desu.**
Hachi-ji han ni hajimarimasu. Ikimasen ka.
Yes, the name of the movie is *Your Tomorrow*. It starts at 8:30. Would you like to go?

Saito   **Ii desu ne. Sono eiga wa SF (ess efu) desu ne. SF ga suki desu. Ikimashoo. Tokorode, Takahashi san wa bangohan o tabemashita ka.**
Sounds good. That's science fiction, right? I like science fiction. By the way, did you have dinner already?

Takahashi   **Mada desu.**
Not, yet.

Saito   **Jaa, sono mae ni bangohan o tabemasen ka.**
Well then, would you like to have dinner before that (movie)?

Takahashi   **Ii desu ne. Soo shimashoo. Nani o tabemashoo ka.**
Sounds good. Let's do that. What shall we eat?

Saito   **Takahashi san wa nani ga sukidesu ka. Niku ga suki desu ka.**
What do you like, Ms. Takahashi? Do you like meat?

Takahashi   **Niku desu ka. Amari suki ja arimasen. Demo, sakana wa daisuki desu yo.**
Meat? I don't like meat much. But, I like fish (you know).

Saito   **Ja, sakana o tabemashoo ka. Watashi no uchi ni kimasen ka. Koko de gohan o tabemashoo. Watashi ga ryoori shimasu yo.**
Then, shall we have fish? Would you like to come to my house? Let's eat here. I'll cook. Okay?

Takahashi   **E. Ii desu ka.**
Oh? Would that be okay?

Saito   **Doozo doozo.**
Please, by all means.

Takahashi   **Ja, takushii de Saitoo san no uchi made ikimasu. Nanji ga ii desu ka.**
Then, I'll go to your house by taxi. What time would be good?

Saito   **Soo desu ne. Ja, rokuji goro wa doo desu ka.**
Let's see. How about 6:00 then?

Takahashi	Hai, wakarimashita. Jaa sugu ikimasu.
	Okay. I'll be over there soon.
Saito	Hai, roku ji ni aimashoo.
	Okay, see you at 6:00.
Takahashi	Jaa mata.
	See you then.
Saito	Hai, jaa mata.
	Okay, see you.

STRUCTURE AND USAGE NOTES

1. MOSHI MOSHI – TELEPHONE PHRASES

Here are some commonly-used sentences that you might need if you make a telephone call in Japanese.

Moshi moshi.
Hello? [This is usually said by both parties, and is a phrase used almost exclusively on the telephone.]

Tanaka san desu ka.
Is this Mr. Tanaka?

Tanaka san wa irasshaimasu ka.
Is Mr. Tanaka there? [The verb irasshaimasu is a very polite form of imasu, "to be".]

Tanaka san onegai shimasu.
Mr. Tanaka, please.

Harisu desu.
This is (Mr.) Harris.

Sumisu Enjiniaringu no Harisu desu.
This is (Mr.) Harris, from Smith Engineering.

The following phrases are all polite ways of finishing a telephone conversation. You can say any combination or all of these phrases to end the conversation.

Shitsurei shimasu.
Excuse me.

Gomen kudasai.
Pardon me for any inconvenience. [very polite]

2. IMASU AND ARIMASU – "TO BE"

The verbs imasu (from iru) and arimasu (from aru) both mean "to be/ exist", but there is a very important difference between them. Imasu is used only to refer to the existence or location of animate objects, such as people, animals and fish, whereas arimasu is used only to refer to inanimate objects, such as tables, chairs and buildings. Compare the following pairs of sentences.

Kyoo no shinbun wa doko ni arimasu ka.
Where's today's newspaper?

Watanabe san wa doko ni imasu ka.
Where's Mr. Watanabe?

Uchi ni terebi ga arimasen.
We don't have a television at home.

Uchi ni inu wa imasen.
We don't have a dog at home.

Tookyoo ni wa, ii resutoran ga takusan arimasu.
In Tokyo, there are a lot of good restaurants.

Tookyoo ni wa, gaijin ga takusan imasu.
In Tokyo, there are a lot of foreigners.

3. MADA – "STILL" OR "NOT YET"

When mada is followed by a positive verb, it can be translated as "still" in the sense of something remaining as it was some time ago.

Gohan wa mada takusan arimasu.
There's still a lot of rice.

Maiku san wa mada gakkoo ni imasu ka.
Is Mike still at the school?

Koohii wa mada arimasu.
I still have some coffee.

When mada is followed by a negative verb, it can usually be translated as "(not) yet".

Nihongo ga mada wakarimasen.
I don't understand Japanese yet.

Takushii wa mada kimasen ne.
The taxi hasn't come yet, has it?

Kaigi wa mada hajimarimasen.
The meeting hasn't started yet.

The phrase Mada desu by itself means "Not yet".

---

4. ISSHO NI SHIMASEN KA – INVITATIONS, USING A NEGATIVE VERB

When you want to invite someone to do something, a polite way of doing
so is to use a negative question, in other words, one ending in -masen ka.

Ashita eiga e ikimasen ka.
Would you like to go to a movie tomorrow?

Konban wain o nomimasen ka.
Would you like to drink wine tonight?

Asatte tenisu o shimasen ka.
Would you like to play tennis the day after tomorrow?

---

5. MAKING SUGGESTIONS USING -MASHOO

If you want to suggest doing something, then the way to express it is to
change the final -masu of the verb to -mashoo. This usually corresponds
to "Let's…" in English.

Ashita Yokohama e ikimashoo.
Let's go to Yokohama tomorrow.

Rajio o kikimashoo.
Let's listen to the radio.

Nihongo o benkyoo shimashoo.
Let's study Japanese.

Nihongo de hanashimashoo.
Let's talk in Japanese.

Koohii o nomimashoo.
Let's have [Lit: drink] some coffee.

If you turn it into a question, then it becomes the equivalent of "Shall we…?"
or "Shall I…?"

Kyoo wa nani o shimashoo ka.
What shall we do today?

Nani o tabemashoo ka. Sakana ni shimashoo ka.
What shall we eat? Shall we have fish?

Terebi o mimashoo ka.
Shall we watch television?

6. TELLING THE TIME

To say the hours, first you'll need to remember the numbers up to twelve.

1 ichi	5 go	9 kyuu/ku
2 ni	6 roku	10 juu
3 san	7 shichi/nana	11 juu-ichi
4 yo/yon/shi	8 hachi	12 juu-ni

As you can see, there are different ways of saying the numbers 4, 7 and 9, and which one you use depends on what you are counting. In the case of saying the hour when telling the time, use the yo (4), shichi (7) and ku (9) alternatives. The hour is indicated by adding -ji to the number.

Ichi-ji desu.
It's one o'clock.

Yo-ji desu.
It's four o'clock.

Ima nan-ji desu ka. Shichi-ji desu ka.
What time is it now? Is it seven o'clock?

Next, the minutes. First, let's look at how to say plain numbers up to 99, then we'll add the word for "minutes". Here are the numbers from 11 to 19. Remeber that they are simply the equivalents of "ten-one", "ten-two", "ten-three", etc.

11 juu-ichi	14 juu-yon/shi	17 juu-shichi/nana
12 juu-ni	15 juu-go	18 juu-hachi
13 juu-san	16 juu-roku	19 juu-kyuu/ku

To count in tens, think of the numbers as corresponding to "two tens", "three tens", "four tens", etc.

10 juu	40 yon-juu	70 shichi/nana-juu
20 ni-juu	50 go-juu	80 hachi-juu
30 san-juu	60 roku-juu	90 kyuu/ku-juu

Finally, counting in between numbers is simply a matter of building up from what you already know. For example, think of the number twenty-one as "two-tens, one", or ni-juu ichi. Here are some more examples.

23 ni-juu-san	57 go-juu-nana
34 san-juu-yon	68 roku-juu-hachi
45 yon-juu-go	89 hachi-juu-kyuu

The word for "minutes" is fun, although this often changes to pun depending on the sound which precedes it. Here is a list of how to say the minutes up to ten.

1 minute ip-pun	6 minutes rop-pun
2 minutes ni-fun	7 minutes nana-fun
3 minutes san-pun	8 minutes hap-pun
4 minutes yon-pun	9 minutes kyuu-fun
5 minutes go-fun	10 minutes jup-pun

When telling the time, the particle ni is used as an equivalent of "at". Here are some examples of times.

go-ji jup-pun ni at 5:10	san-ji ni-jup-pun ni at 3:20
roku-ji ni-juu-go-fun ni at 6:25	hachi-ji yon-juu-go-fun ni at 8:45

The word han, or "half", is often used instead of san-jup-pun.

juu-ji han ni at 10:30	juu-ni-ji han ni at 12:30

Here are some sentences to show how these time words are used.

Ni-ji han ni aimashoo.
Let's meet at 2:30.

Ichi-ji no nyuusu o mimashoo.
Let's watch the one o'clock news.

Takahashi san wa ashita no san-ji ni kimasu.
Ms. Takahashi will come at 3:00 tomorrow.

Shigoto wa hachi-ji go-jup-pun ni hajimarimasu.
Work begins at 8:50.

Nihon no ginkoo wa ku-ji kara desu.
Japanese banks (are) open from 9:00.

A. Kaigi wa nan-ji kara nan-ji made desu ka.
What time is the meeting? [Lit: From what time to what time...?]

B. Juu-ji kara juu-ichi-ji han made desu.
It's from 10:00 to 11:30.

---

7. TAKUSHII DE – BY TAXI

One use of the particle de is to show the instrument or means by which
something is done. (We will see another use of de in the next lesson.)

San-ji no densha de ikimashoo.
Let's go by the 3:00 train.

Nihongo de hanashimashoo.
Let's speak in Japanese.

Sushi o hashi de tabemasu ka.
Do you eat sushi with chopsticks?

Eiga no jikan wa, denwa de kikimasu.
I'll call and ask the time of the movie. [Lit: The time of the movie, I'll ask by
telephone.]

Mainichi nyuusu o rajio de kikimasu.
I listen to the news every day on the radio.

---

8. BENKYOO O SHIMASU AND OTHER VERBS WHICH USE SHIMASU

There are a number of verbs which are made up of a noun with shimasu.
Here are some of them. The object particle o is optional.

ryoori cooking	ryoori (o) shimasu to cook
benkyoo study, work	benkyoo (o) shimasu to study

denwa a telephone	denwa (o) shimasu to telephone, call
shigoto work, employment	shigoto (o) shimasu to work
tenisu tennis	tenisu (o) shimasu to play tennis
hanashi a talk, conversation	hanashi (o) shimasu to have a conversation

Ashita, tomodachi to tenisu o shimasu.
I'm going to play tennis with a friend tomorrow.

Ashita sakana o ryoori shimasu.
I'll cook fish tomorrow.

Itoo san wa tokidoki shichi-ji made shigoto shimasu.
Mr. Itoo sometimes works until 7:00.

Nan-ji ni denwa shimashoo ka.
What time shall I call you?

Neruson san wa ashita kara Nihongo no benkyoo o shimasu.
Mr. Nelson will be studying Japanese starting tomorrow.

---

9. KIMASU VS. IKIMASU – "COME" AND "GO"

The verbs kimasu ("come") and ikimasu ("go") are sometimes used in a slightly different way from English, as you can see in Keiko Takahashi's conversation with Mr. Saito in the dialogue. Takahashi says Takushii de ikimasu and Sugu ikimasu, where in English we would say "I'll come by taxi", and "I'll come soon". This is because ikimasu means to leave where you are now, regardless of where you're going, whereas the English "go" means to leave where you are now and go anywhere, except where the person you are speaking to is.

A. Ashita, watashi no uchi ni kimasen ka.
   Would you like to come over to my house tomorrow?

B. Hai, ikimasu. Nan-ji ni ikimashoo ka.
   Yes, I would. What time shall I come?

VOCABULARY

aimashoo: let's meet [from au]
benkyoo (o) shimasu: to study [from benkyoo suru]
benkyoo: study [noun]
de: by [particle indicating means by which something is done]
demo: however, but [at the beginning of a sentence]
densha: train
doo shite/naze: why?
doozo doozo: please do so, please go ahead
-fun/pun: minute
gaijin: foreigner
gomen kudasai: Pardon me for causing any inconvenience.
hajimarimasu: to begin [from hajimaru]
-han: half past
hanashi: a talk, conversation, chat
hanashi o shimasu: have a talk/chat [from hanashi o suru]
hanashimashoo: let's talk [from hanasu]
hashi: chopsticks
ichi: one
ikimashoo ka: Shall we go? [from iku]
ima: now, at the moment
imasu: am, is, are [used with animate objects, from iru]
inu: dog
irasshaimasu: is, are [very polite form of imasu, from irassharu]
-ji: o'clock
jikan: time, hour
jup-pun: ten minutes
mada: still, (not) yet
made: until
mata: again, once more, another time
mata ashita: until tomorrow, see you tomorrow [informal]
mimashoo: let's see [from miru]
moshi moshi: Hello? [only on the telephone]
nan-ji: what time?
ni: at [when giving the time]
ni: two
niku: meat
nyuusu: the news
...onegai shimasu: Could I speak to...?
roku-ji: six o'clock
roku: six
ryoori: cooking
ryoori shimasu: to cook

sakana: fish
SF (ess efu): science-fiction
shichi/nana: seven
shigoto shimasu: to work
shigoto: work, employment
shitsurei shimasu: goodbye [on the telephone]
sono mae ni: before that
sore kara: and also, after that
sugu: soon
takusan: a lot of, many, much
takushii de: by taxi
tenisu: tennis
terebi: television, TV
tesuto: a test

TEST YOURSELF

Read through the dialogue at the beginning of the lesson once more, and then say if the following statements are true or false.

1. Takahashi san wa ima uchi ni imasen. T/F

2. Eiga wa roku-ji kara desu. T/F

3. Saitoo san wa SF ga suki ja arimasen. T/F

4. Saitoo san to Takahashi san wa sakana o tabemasu. T/F

5. Konban Saitoo san to Takahashi san wa eiga o mimasen. T/F

6. Saitoo san wa takushii de Takahashi san no uchi e ikimasu. T/F

Exercise A

How would you say the following times in Japanese?

1. 4:00   2. 2:30   3. 9:45

_____   _____   _____

4. 11:40   5. 1:30   6. 6:15

_____   _____   _____

Exercise B

45

In tomorrow's English class, Mike will be teaching the students how to talk about their daily schedule, so he has just written out his own schedule to use as a sample. Look at the information below, and make up some sentences about what he does each day and when, as in the examples.

Example:

7:00	news on TV
10:10-12:10	teach English

Shichi-ji ni terebi no nyuusu o mimasu.
Juu-ji jup-pun kara juu-ni-ji jup-pun made Eigo o oshiemasu.

1. 7:15   coffee

_____

_____

2. 7:30 - 7:45   news on radio

_____

_____

3. 8:00   go to station

_____

_____

4. 8:45 - 4:45   work

_____

_____

5. 6:00   read paper

_____

_____

6. 7:00 - 8:30   study Japanese

_____

_____

7. 9:30 - 11:00   TV

_____

_____

How would you say the following sentences in Japanese?

1. Let's meet at 7:30.

2. I'm going to study Japanese from tomorrow.

_____

3. Shall we watch the news on TV?

_____

4. What time does tomorrow's meeting begin?

   _____

5. Let's go to the station by taxi.

   _____

6. Is there any wine left?

   _____

Mr. Watanabe calls Mike Nelson to see if he would like to see a movie with him. Complete their conversation by filling in the blanks.

Exercise E

Nelson	(Hello?) _____ _____, Neruson desu ga.
Watanabe	(Hello?) _____ _____, Neruson san? **Watanabe desu.**
Nelson	**Aa Watanabe san,** (good evening) _____.
Watanabe	(Good evening.) _____. **Ne, Neruson san,** (you like movies, don't you?) _____ _____ _____ _____ _____.
Nelson	(Yes, I do.) _____, _____ _____.
Watanabe	**Neruson san wa ashita** (do you have some time?) _____ _____ _____ _____. (Would you like to see a movie?) _____ _____ _____ _____.
Nelson	**Ii desu ne. Nani o mimashoo ka.**
Watanabe	**"Anata no Ashita" o mimasen ka.**
Nelson	(That's a good movie, isn't it.) _____ _____ _____ _____ _____ _____. SF **desu ne.**
Watanabe	(Yes, it is.) _____, _____ _____. SF **wa doo desu ka.**
Nelson	**Hai, dai-suki desu.** (What time shall we meet?) _____ _____ _____ _____.
Watanabe	**Eiga wa roku-ji han ni hajimarimasu.** (How about 6:00?) _____ _____ _____ _____ _____.
Nelson	**Ja, roku-ji ni** (let's meet) _____.
Watanabe	(See you later.) _____ _____.
Nelson	**Hai,** (see you later.) _____ _____.

 The first character is **niku,** which means "meat", and the second kanji is **sakana,** which is "fish".

 Visit www.berlitzpublishing.com for a bonus internet activity–go to the downloads section and connect to the world in Japanese!

KOKO O MIGI NI MAGATTE KUDASAI.
PLEASE TURN RIGHT HERE.

Keiko Takahashi has just taken a taxi to go to Mr. Saito's house, which is near Yamate station.

Takahashi	**Yamate eki made onegai shimasu.** To Yamate station, please.
Taxi driver	**Hai, wakarimashita.** Yes, certainly.

They arrive at Yamate station, and Ms. Takahashi gives the driver instructions from there to Mr. Saito's house.

Taxi driver	**Hai, Yamate eki desu yo.** We're here at Yamate station.
Takahashi	**Moo eki desu ka. Ja, koko o migi ni magatte kudasai.** The station already? Well, please turn right here.
Taxi driver	**Koko desu ka.** Here?
Takahashi	**Hai, soo desu. Sore kara, massugu itte kudasai. Asoko ni ookii tatemono ga arimasu ne.**

Yes, that's right. And then, please go straight ahead.
There is a large building over there, right?

Taxi driver   Hidari-gawa desu ka.
On the left-hand side?

Takahashi   Hai, soo desu. Asoko de ii desu. Asoko de tomete
kudasai. Ikura desu ka.
Yes, that's right. Over there is fine. Please stop there.
How much is it?

Taxi driver   Sen ni-hyaku en desu.
One thousand, two hundred yen.

Takahashi   Ja, kore, ni-sen en desu.
Here's two thousand yen.

Taxi driver   Hai, hap-pyaku en no o-tsuri desu. Doozo.
Right, eight hundred yen change. Here you are.

Takahashi   Doomo.
Thank you.

She gets out of the taxi, and walks the last few meters to Mr. Saito's
house. She opens the door to the house and calls out:

Takahashi   Gomen kudasai.
Hello? Excuse me!

Saito   Aa, Takahashi san. Irasshai. Doozo, agatte kudasai.
Surippa, doozo.
Ah, Ms. Takahashi. Good evening. Please come in.
Here, have some slippers.

Takahashi   (taking off her shoes, and stepping into the slippers
provided) O-jama shimasu.
Excuse me for disturbing you.

Saito   Doozo, kochira e. Koohii wa ikaga desu ka.
This way. Would you like some coffee?

Takahashi   Itadakimasu.
Yes, please.

STRUCTURE AND USAGE NOTES

1. ASKING FAVORS USING ONEGAI SHIMASU

As explained in Lesson 3, the phrase onegai shimasu is used (just like
kudasai) to ask for something.

Koohii o onegai shimasu./Koohii o kudasai.
Coffee, please.

Mizu o onegai shimasu./Mizu o kudasai.
Could I have some water, please?

It can also mean "please do that", when used in response to someone offering to do something for you.

A. Ashita denwa shimashoo ka.
Shall I phone (you) tomorrow?
B. Hai, onegai shimasu.
Yes, please.

A. Eigo de hanashimashoo ka.
Shall I speak in English?
B. Onegai shimasu.
Please.

A. Namae to juusho o kakimashoo ka.
Shall I write down my name and address?
B. Hai, onegai shimasu.
Yes, please.

2. SHOWING EMPHASIS WITH YO

The particle yo at the end of a sentence doesn't have any meaning in itself, but is used to give the sentence emphasis. The meaning is something like "you know?" or "I'm telling you". It's better not to overuse yo. Compare the following pairs of sentences.

Watashi no suutsukeesu desu.
It's my suitcase.

Watashi no suutsukeesu desu yo.
It's *my* suitcase!

Nihon no kuruma desu.
It's a Japanese car.

Nihon no kuruma desu yo.
It's a *Japanese* car!

Ii desu.
It's okay.

Ii desu yo.
It's okay, you know?

3. MOO – "ALREADY" AND "(NOT) ANYMORE"

When moo is used with a positive verb, it corresponds to the English "already", indicating that something is not in the same condition as it was a while ago.

Moo juu-ji desu.
It's already 10:00.

Moo Kyooto desu ka.
Are we in Kyoto already?

Kenji san wa moo daigakusei desu ka.
Is Kenji at university [Lit: a university student] already?

When moo is used with a negative verb, it corresponds to "(not) anymore".

Moo sono resutoran e wa ikimasen.
I'm not going to that restaurant anymore.

Mondai wa moo arimasen.
I don't have any problems anymore.

---

4. ...-TE KUDASAI – MAKING REQUESTS

So far we have only come across the -masu form of verbs, and now it is time to introduce the -te form. The -te form has many uses, and in some ways corresponds to the "-ing" form in English (and like the "-ing" form, it has no tense, and cannot exist by itself to form a sentence). In this lesson you'll learn how to use the -te form to make requests.

The formation of the -te form is very regular, but it is somewhat involved, so although we have given a brief explanation of the rules, you might prefer simply to learn the -te form of verbs by heart from the list below.

To find out how to make the -te form, first you need to know the plain form, or dictionary form, of the verb, which you have come across so far only in the vocabulary lists at the end of each lesson. Japanese verbs can be divided into two groups. One group is of verbs which end in -iru or -eru in the plain form. To make the -masu form, the -ru ending is dropped. Look at the list below showing the dictionary form, -masu form and -te form of some -iru/-eru verbs.

dictionary form	meaning	-masu form	-te form
tabe-ru	eat	tabemasu	tabete
oshie-ru	teach, tell	oshiemasu	oshiete
i-ru	be, exist	imasu	ite
mi-ru	see, watch	mimasu	mite
tome-ru	stop, halt	tomemasu	tomete

The other group is of verbs which drop the final -u from the dictionary form, and then add -imasu to make the -masu form. This group contains all verbs which do *not* end in -eru or -iru, and also a few verbs which do. As you can see from the list of -u verbs below, the -te form ending varies depending on the sound which comes before it.

dictionary form	meaning	-masu form	-te form
yom-u	read	yomimasu	yonde
nom-u	drink	nomimasu	nonde
ar-u	be, exist	arimasu	atte
hajimar-u	begin	hajimarimasu	hajimatte
wakar-u	understand	wakarimasu	wakatte
a-u	meet	aimasu	atte
chiga-u	differ	chigaimasu	chigatte
mats-u	wait	machimasu	matte
hanas-u	speak, talk	hanashimasu	hanashite
kik-u	hear, ask	kikimasu	kiite
kak-u	write	kakimasu	kaite

(Iku is an exception to the rule for -ku verbs.)

ik-u	go	ikimasu	itte

The only two irregular verbs are kuru ("come") and suru ("do").

kuru	come	kimasu	kite
suru	do	shimasu	shite

When the -te form is followed by kudasai, it is a way of asking someone to do something.

Yukkuri hanashite kudasai.
Please speak slowly.

Yukkuri itte kudasai.
Please go slowly.

Namae to juusho o kaite kudasai.
Please write your name and address.

Go-ji han ni kite kudasai.
Please come at 5:30.

Konban denwa shite kudasai.
Please call me this evening.

Sensei no hanashi o kiite kudasai.
Listen to what the teacher has to say.

Hon o mite kudasai.
Please look at your books.

---

5. ANOTHER USE OF THE PARTICLE DE – TO SHOW LOCATION

The particle de is used to indicate the place where something happens, so it can usually be translated as "at" or "in". (You may remember from Lesson 2 that the particle ni also points out location, but ni is only used to indicate the place where something or someone exists, so it is only used with the verbs iru/imasu and aru/arimasu.)

Ano atarashii resutoran de tabemashoo.
Let's eat at that new restaurant.

Doko de aimashoo ka.
Where shall we meet?

Ashita uchi de benkyoo shimasu.
I'm going to study at home tomorrow.

Koko de machimasu.
I'll wait here.

Itoo san wa Amerika de Eigo o benkyoo shimasu.
Mr. Itoo is going to study English in America.

---

6. UNDERSTANDING DIRECTIONS

It is not always easy to find your way around a city in Japan, as only the largest streets are given names, and addresses are based on numbered areas, with the numbers not always running consecutively. This means that it is almost impossible to find someone's house or office building just from the address if you are not familiar with the area, and so you will need to ask for directions. If you are going by taxi, then you will probably have to give directions to the taxi driver, unless you are going to a famous landmark that he or she is likely to know. Otherwise, you should get a friend or co-worker to draw a map or write directions in Japanese, and then you can just hand this to the taxi driver.

Here are some useful sentences for giving and understanding directions.

Koko made onegai shimasu.
(as you hand over the map and directions of where you want to go) To this place, please.

Massugu itte kudasai.
Please go straight ahead.

Moo sukoshi massugu itte kudasai.
Please go a little further ahead.

Koko de migi ni magatte kudasai.
Please turn right here.

Shingoo de hidari ni magatte kudasai.
Please turn left at the traffic lights.

Tsugi no shingoo de migi ni magatte kudasai.
Please turn right at the next traffic lights.

Tsugi no kado de tomete kudasai.
Please stop at the next corner.

Koko de ii desu.
This is fine.

Hidari-gawa ni arimasu.
It's on the left-hand side.

Gakkoo wa migi-gawa ni arimasu.
The school is on the right-hand side.

---

7. HUNDREDS AND THOUSANDS

The word for "hundred" is hyaku, although the beginning of the word changes sometimes depending on the sound which comes before it. Here's how to count in hundreds.

100 hyaku	400 yon-hyaku	700 nana-hyaku
200 ni-hyaku	500 go-hyaku	800 hap-pyaku
300 san-byaku	600 rop-pyaku	900 kyuu-hyaku

Numbers in Japanese are very regular, so to make any numbers in between, simply build up from what you already know. For example, 235 is the equivalent of "two hundreds, three tens, five", or ni-hyaku san-juu-go. Here are some more examples. See if you can work them out yourself before looking at the Japanese.

126 hyaku ni-juu-roku	491 yon-hyaku kyuu-ju-ichi
345 san-byaku yon-juu-go	633 rop-pyaku san-juu-san
810 hap-pyaku juu	505 go-hyaku go

The word for "thousand" is sen, although, like the hundreds, there are some phonetic changes depending on the sound which precedes sen.

1,000 sen	4,000 yon-sen	7,000 nana-sen
2,000 ni-sen	5,000 go-sen	8,000 has-sen
3,000 san-zen	6,000 roku-sen	9,000 kyuu-sen

Here are some more examples of large numbers.

2,350 ni-sen san-byaku go-juu
4,500 yon-sen go-hyaku
7,468 nana-sen yon-hyaku roku-juu-hachi
8,055 has-sen go-juu-go

A. Sumimasen, kore wa ikura desu ka.
   Excuse me, how much is this?
B. Sore wa ni-sen go-hyaku go-juu en desu.
   It's 2,550 yen.

A. Ii hon desu ne. Amerika no hon desu ka.
   Nice book, isn't it. Is it American?
B. Hai, soo desu. Kono hon wa Amerika de ni-juu doru desu ga,
   Nihon de wa nana-sen go-hyaku en desu.
   Yes, it is. In America this book is twenty dollars, but in Japan it's 7,500 yen.

CULTURAL NOTE

VISITING SOMEONE'S HOME

If you are lucky enough to be invited to someone's home in Japan, there are a number of set phrases of greeting and a set procedure that you should know. Just inside the door is the genkan, an area where you leave your shoes before you step up to the level of the rest of the house. As the genkan is not really considered to be a part of the inside of the house, it is acceptable to open the door and step inside (although in newer houses or apartments, you will need to ring the bell instead). Then call out:

Gomen kudasai.
Hello? Is there anyone home?

When you are invited in, step out of your shoes and up to the higher level of the house. Be careful not to put your feet down on the floor of the genkan after you have taken off your shoes. Slippers are always provided except for the floors covered with traditional tatami mats. As you step up, say:

Shitsurei shimasu.
Excuse me.

or
O-jama shimasu.
Pardon me for disturbing you.

If you are shown into a Western-style room, keep your slippers on.
But if you go into a Japanese-style room with tatami-mat flooring,
then step out of your slippers as you enter the room.

A. Doozo, o-kake kudasai. [or Doozo, suwatte kudasai.]
Please have a seat.
B. Shitsurei shimasu.
Thank you.
A. O-cha wa ikaga desu ka.
Would you like some green tea?
B. Onegai shimasu. [or Itadakimasu.]
Yes, thank you.

VOCABULARY

agatte kudasai: please come in [Lit: please come up] [from agaru]
daigakusei: university student
de: at, in [particle indicating a place where an action occurs]
doru: dollars
en: yen
...gawa: the side of...
genkan: entrance area (in a house)
gomen kudasai: Excuse me, is anyone there?
hidari: the left
hidari-gawa: the left-hand side
hon: book
hyaku: hundred
ikaga desu ka: How about some...?, Would you like some...?
  [polite form of doo desu ka]
ikura: how much (money)?
itadakimasu: yes, please [when offered food or drink]
itte kudasai: please go [from iku]
juusho: address
kado: corner
kaite kudasai: please write [from kaku]
koohii: coffee
machimasu: wait [from matsu]
made: as far as
magatte kudasai: please turn [from magaru]
massugu: straight ahead
migi ni: to the right
migi-gawa: right-hand side

moo: already, (not) any longer, another, further
mondai: problem
ni-hyaku: two hundred
O-jama shimasu.: Excuse me for disturbing you.
O-kake kudasai.: Please take a seat.
onegai shimasu: please [Lit: I have a request/favor.]
o-tsuri: the change (money)
sen: thousand
shingoo: traffic lights
suki ja nai: don't like [more informal than suki ja arimasen]
sukoshi: a little, a small amount
surippa: slippers
Suwatte kudasai.: Please sit down. [from suwaru]
tatemono: building
tokorode: by the way
Tomete kudasai.: Please stop/halt. [from tomeru]
tsugi no: the next
wakarimashita: I see, I've got it, I understand [from wakaru]
yo: [sentence ending to show emphasis]
yukkuri: slowly

TEST YOURSELF

Exercise A

Read through the dialogue at the beginning of the lesson once more, and then say if the following statements are true or false.

1. Takahashi san wa Yamate eki made takushii de ikimasu. T/F

2. Eki kara, takushii wa migi ni magarimasu. T/F

3. Hidari-gawa ni ookii tatemono ga arimasu. T/F

4. O-tsuri wa ni-sen en desu. T/F

5. Takahashi san wa koohii o nomimasen. T/F

Exercise B

Imagine you are going to visit the home of a Japanese friend, and fill in the missing lines in the conversation below. First, open the door to the genkan and see if anyone is home.

You	_____
Friend	Aa doozo, agatte kudasai. Surippa, doozo.
You	_____
Friend	Ja, kochira e. Doozo, suwatte kudasai.
You	_____
Friend	Koohii wa ikaga desu ka.
You	_____

Imagine you are standing at the points on the map marked with an X, and you want to get to the buildings which are also marked. Ask a passer-by where the places are, and give the answers too.

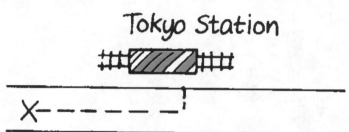

Tokyo Station

Example: You: Sumimasen ga, Tookyoo eki wa doko desu ka.
Passer-by: Massugu itte kudasai. Hidari-gawa ni arimasu.

1.

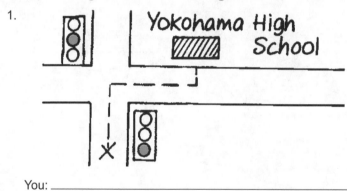

Yokohama High School

You: _____

Passer-by: _____

2.

Osaka University

You: _____

_____

Passer-by: _____

_____

3. **Yamate Station**

You: _____

_____

Passer-by: _____

_____

Exercise D

You are having a day out shopping. Ask the store assistant the price of the goods you want to buy, and give the responses too. Write the numbers out in full, as in the example.

Example:

A. **Sumimasen ga, kono hana wa ikura desu ka.**
B. **Sen go-hyaku en desu.**

1.
A. _____
_____
B. _____
_____

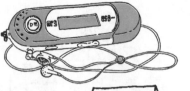

2.
A. _____
_____
B. _____
_____

3.
A. _____
_____
B. _____
_____

4.
A. _____
_____
B. _____
_____

What are the following numbers in English?

5. Has-sen ni-hyaku go-juu-go _____

6. Sen hyaku ni-juu _____

7. Go-sen kyuu-juu-san _____

8. Nana-sen san-byaku-san _____

How would you say these sentences in Japanese?

1. Please turn left at the next traffic lights.

   _____

2. I'll watch TV at home tomorrow.

   _____

3. I've got to talk to you.

   _____

4. Please write your name and address here.

   _____

5. Excuse me, but how much is that book?

   _____

6. There's a large school on the left-hand side, right?

   _____

7. By the way, what are you doing tomorrow?

   _____

8. Would you like some coffee?

   _____

Exercise E

八百円 Hap-pyaku en consists of three characters meaning "eight", "one hundred" and "yen".

 Visit www.berlitzpublishing.com for a bonus internet activity—go to the downloads section and connect to the world in Japanese!

Lesson

6

DAI IK-KA KARA DAI GO-KA MADE NO FUKUSHUU.
REVIEW OF LESSONS 1 TO 5.

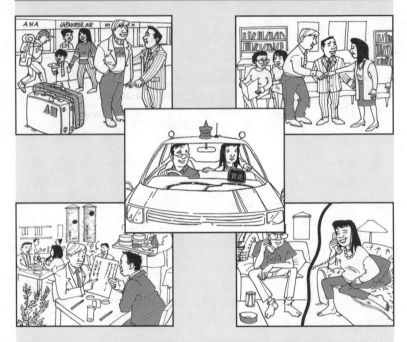

Listen to Dialogues 1 to 5 again, and answer the following questions without referring back to the English translations in previous lessons.

Dialogue 1: NIHON E YOOKOSO!

Mike Nelson has just arrived at Narita airport, outside Tokyo. He will be met there by Ikuo Watanabe, a teacher at the high school where Mike will be teaching. Ikuo Watanabe arrives late and talks to Mike.

Watanabe	Sumimasen, Neruson san desu ka.
Nelson	Hai, soo desu. Neruson desu.
Watanabe	Hajimemashite, Watanabe desu. Yokohama Gakuin Kookoo no Watanabe desu. Nihon e yookoso!
Nelson	Aa, Watanabe san, hajimemashite.
Watanabe	Watashi no meishi desu. Doozo.
Nelson	(Doomo) arigatoo gozaimasu.

Watanabe	(pointing to suitcases) Neruson san no suutsukeesu desu ka.
Nelson	Hai, soo desu.
Watanabe	Ja, doozo, kochira e.

Mr. Watanabe grabs a suitcase, which belongs to someone else.

Nelson	Iie, Watanabe-san, chigaimasu.
Stranger	Watashi no suutsukeesu desu.
Watanabe	A, doomo sumimasen.

It's a long drive to Yokohama, but they finally get there. Mike has been trying hard to stay awake.

| Watanabe | Hai, Neruson san, Yokohama desu. Neruson san. Neruson san. |

But all he gets in response is a gentle, peaceful snoring.

QUESTIONS:

1. Watanabe san no shigoto wa nan desu ka.
2. Watanabe san no gakkoo wa doko desu ka.
3. Maiku san wa doko no hito desu ka.

Dialogue 2: MINA SAN, OHAYOO GOZAIMASU.

It's Mike Nelson's first day of work at Yokohama High School, and Ikuo Watanabe is introducing him to some of the staff.

Watanabe	Mina san, ohayoo gozaimasu.
Everyone	Ohayoo gozaimasu.
Watanabe	Neruson sensei, kochira wa jimu no Takahashi san desu.
Takahashi	Hajimemashite. Takahashi desu. Doozo yoroshiku.
Nelson	Maiku Neruson desu. Yoroshiku onegai shimasu.

Mr. Watanabe shows Mike around the office.

Watanabe	Kore wa watashi no tsukue desu. Kore wa Takahashi san no tsukue desu.
Nelson	Watashi no tsukue wa doko ni arimasu ka.
Watanabe	Neruson sensei no wa koko ni arimasu.
Takahashi	Watanabe sensei, chigaimasu. Sore wa Neruson sensei no tsukue ja arimasen. Saitoo san no desu.

Watanabe	Saitoo san. Saitoo san wa dare desu ka.
Takahashi	Atarashii paato no hito desu. Kyoo kara desu.
Watanabe	Soo desu ka. Atarashii paato desu ka. Ja, Neruson sensei no tsukue wa?
Takahashi	Wakarimasen. Aa, ano tsukue ja arimasen ka.
Watanabe	A, are desu ka. Neruson sensei, are desu.
Nelson	Wakarimashita. Doomo arigatoo gozaimasu.

QUESTIONS:

1. Takahashi san no shigoto wa nan desu ka.
2. Nelson san wa, tsukue ga arimasu ka.
3. Atarashii paato no hito no namae wa nan desu ka.

 Dialogue 3: NANI O TABEMASU KA.

Ikuo Watanabe has invited Mike out for lunch at a small Japanese restaurant near the school. The menu is all in Japanese, which Mike Nelson can't read yet, so Watanabe asks him what he would like.

Watanabe	Neruson san wa nani o tabemasu ka.
Nelson	Hmm, wakarimasen. Kono resutoran wa, nani ga oishii desu ka.
Watanabe	Sakana ga oishii desu. Sakana ga suki desu ka.
Nelson	Hai, dai-suki desu.
Watanabe	Ja, yaki-zakana teishoku wa doo desu ka.
Nelson	Yaki-zakana teishoku? Sore wa nan desu ka.
Watanabe	Yaki-zakana to gohan to tsukemono to miso shiru desu.
Nelson	Sore wa ii desu ne. Hai, watashi wa yaki-zakana teishoku ni shimasu. Watanabe san wa?
Watanabe	Watashi wa sashimi teishoku ni shimasu. (to waitress) Sumimasen!
Waitress	Hai, nani ni shimasu ka.
Watanabe	Yaki-zakana teishoku to sashimi teishoku o onegai shimasu.

The waitress soon comes back with a tray of food each for Watanabe and Mike.

Nelson	Itadakimasu.
Watanabe	Itadakimasu.
Nelson	Kono miso shiru wa oishii desu ne. (noticing something decorating Mr. Watanabe's raw fish) E? Sore wa nan desu ka. Hana ja arimasen ka.
Watanabe	Hai, soo desu. Kono hana wa kiku desu.
Nelson	E? Nan desu ka. Kiku desu ka. Kiku o tabemasu ka.
Watanabe	Hai, tokidoki tabemasu. A, o-cha ga arimasen ne. O-cha o nomimasu ka.
Nelson	Sumimasen ga, o-cha wa amari suki ja arimasen. Mizu ga sukidesu.
Watanabe	Hai, mizu desu ne. (to waitress) Sumimasen, o-cha to mizu o onegai shimasu.

QUESTIONS:

1. Nelson san wa sakana ga kirai desu ka.
2. Watanabe san wa sakana teishoku ni shimasu ka.
3. "Kiku" wa nan desu ka.
4. Nelson san wa nani o nomimasu ka.

Dialogue 4: ROKU-JI NI AIMASHOO.

Ms. Takahashi calls Mr. Saito, who is a part-time worker at the school to see if he would like to go to a movie.

Saito	Moshi moshi, Saitoo desu ga.
Takahashi	Moshi moshi. Saitoo san? Takahashi desu ga.
Saito	Aa, Takahashi san, konbanwa.
Takahashi	Saitoo san, konban uchi ni imasu ka.
Saito	Hai, imasu. Doo shite desu ka.
Takahashi	Ja eiga o mimasen ka. Konban ii eiga ga arimasu.
Saito	Eiga desu ka.
Takahashi	Hai, eiga no namae wa *Anata No Ashita* desu. Hachi-ji han ni hajimarimasu. Ikimasen ka.
Saito	Ii desu ne. Sono eiga wa SF (ess efu) desu ne. SF ga suki desu. Ikimashoo. Tokorode, Takahashi san wa bangohan o tabemashita ka.

Takahashi	Mada desu.
Saito	Jaa, sono mae ni bangohan o tabemasen ka.
Takahashi	Ii desu ne. Soo shimashoo. Nani o tabemashoo ka.
Saito	Takahashi san wa nani ga sukidesu ka. Niku ga suki desu ka.
Takahashi	Niku desu ka? Amari suki ja arimasen. Demo, sakana wa daisuki desu yo.
Saito	Ja, sakana o tabemashoo ka. Watashi no uchi ni kimasen ka. Koko de gohan o tabemashoo. Watashi ga ryoori shimasu yo.
Takahashi	E. Ii desu ka.
Saito	Doozo doozo.
Takahashi	Ja, takushii de Saitoo san no uchi made ikimasu. Nan-ji ga ii desu ka.
Saito	Soo desunee. Ja, rokuji goro wa doo desu ka.
Takahashi	Hai, wakarimashita. Jaa sugu ikimasu.
Saito	Hai, roku-ji ni aimashoo.
Takahashi	Jaa mata.
Saito	Hai, jaa mata.

QUESTIONS:

1. Saitoo san wa doko ni imasu ka.
2. Eiga wa nan-ji ni hajimarimasu ka.
3. Takahashi san to Saitoo san wa nani o tabemasu ka.
4. Takahashi san wa nani de Saitoo san no uchi e ikimasu ka.

Dialogue 5: KOKO O MIGI NI MAGATTE KUDASAI.

Keiko Takahashi has just taken a taxi to go to Mr. Saito's house, which is near Yamate station.

Takahashi	Yamate eki made onegai shimasu.
Taxi driver	Hai, wakarimashita.

They arrive at Yamate station, and Ms. Takahashi gives the driver instructions from there to Mr. Saito's house.

Taxi driver	Hai, Yamate eki desu yo.
Takahashi	Moo eki desu ka. Ja, koko o migi ni magatte kudasai.

Taxi driver	Koko desu ka.
Takahashi	Hai, soo desu. Sore kara, massugu itte kudasai. Asoko ni ookii tatemono ga arimasu ne.
Taxi driver	Hidari-gawa desu ka.
Takahashi	Hai, soo desu. Asoko de ii desu. Asoko de tomete kudasai. Ikura desu ka.
Taxi driver	Sen ni-hyaku en desu.
Takahashi	Ja, kore, ni-sen en desu.
Taxi driver	Hai, hap-pyaku en no o-tsuri desu. Doozo.
Takahashi	Doomo.

She gets out of the taxi, and walks the last few meters to Mr. Saito's house. She opens the door to the house and calls out:

Takahashi	Gomen kudasai.
Saito	Aa, Takahashi san. Irasshai. Doozo, agatte kudasai. Surippa, doozo.
Takahashi	(taking off her shoes, and stepping into the slippers provided) O-jama shimasu.
Saito	Doozo, kochira e. Koohii wa ikaga desu ka.
Takahashi	Itadakimasu.

QUESTIONS:

1. Ookii tatemono wa dochira-gawa ni arimasu ka.
2. Takahashi san no uchi kara Saitoo san no uchi made takushii de ikura desu ka.
3. O-tsuri wa hap-pyaku en desu ka.
4. Takahashi san wa Saitoo san no uchi de nani o nomimasu ka.

TEST YOURSELF

Join the words in the left-hand column with their opposites on the right. Be careful – there are two words too many in the right-hand column.

Exercise A

	gakusei
migi	kimasu
kono	kara
kirai	watashi

e	tokidoki
itadakimasu	hidari
koko	ohayoo gozaimasu
iie	sono
ikimasu	sukoshi
konbanwa	hai
oshiemasu	go-chisoo sama
sensei	ookii
takusan	benkyoo shimasu
anata	suki
	soko

Exercise B

Read the following numbers out loud.

1. ¥5,650
2. $310
3. 12:25
4. ¥3,995
5. $4,500
6. 10:40

Exercise C

Which is the odd man out in each of the groups of words below? Underline the word which doesn't fit with the others, as in the example.

Example:

gakkoo

<u>takushii</u>　　　　　(the only one which is not a building)

kaisha

ginkoo

eki

1.	2.	3.	4.	5.
doko	hachi	ashita	sakana	daigaku
nani	juu	inu	gohan	jimu no hito
dare	ni	kyoo	tsukemono	enjinia
koko	nana	asatte	sushi	sensei
nan-ji	ano	konban	hashi	paato

Join up the phrases to make complete sentences.

1. Denwa de   ni shimasu.
2. Takushii de   eki made ikimasu.
3. Eiga ga   suki desu ne.
4. Nan-ji ni   desu ka.
5. Wain wa mada   aimashoo ka.
6. Ashita Yokohama   hanashimasu.
7. Doozo   e ikimashoo ka.
8. Watashi wa sashimi teishoku   suwatte kudasai.
9. Maiku san no gakkoo wa doko   takusan arimasu.

Answer the following questions about yourself.

1. Namae wa nan desu ka.

   _____

2. Sakana ga suki desu ka.

   _____

3. Ashita kaisha (gakkoo, daigaku) e ikimasu ka.

   _____

4. Tokidoki tenisu o shimasu ka.

   _____

5. Anata no uchi wa doko desu ka.

   _____

6. Nihongo ga wakarimasu ka.

   _____

7. Anata no uchi ni inu ga imasu ka.

8. Mainichi terebi o mimasu ka.

一、二、三、四、五、六

These are the characters for the numbers one to six, the lessons you have covered so far. They are pronounced ichi, ni, san, yon or shi, go, roku.

Visit www.berlitzpublishing.com for a bonus internet activity—go to the downloads section and connect to the world in Japanese!

AA ATAMA GA ITAI.
OH, I HAVE A HEADACHE.

Ikuo Watanabe had a late night out last night, and he has just woken up, feeling somewhat the worse for wear. He goes downstairs and greets his wife, Miho.

Miho	**A, ohayoo. Chooshi wa doo.**	
	Good morning. How's your head?	
Ikuo	**Itai! Atama ga itai! Ima nan-ji.**	
	It hurts! My head hurts! What time is it?	
Miho	**Osoi wa yo. Moo juu-ni-ji jup-pun mae yo. Koohii wa.**	
	It's late. It's already ten to twelve. Coffee?	
Ikuo	**A, ii ne. Tomoko to Takashi to Hiro wa doko ni iru.**	
	Ah, great. Where are Tomoko, Takashi and Hiro?	
Miho	**Tomoko wa tonari no uchi de, tomodachi to issho ni terebi o miteru. Takashi wa ni-kai de gakkoo no Eigo no shukudai o shiteru.**	
	Tomoko is watching TV with her friend next door. Takashi is doing his English homework upstairs.	

Ikuo	Hiro wa.
	And Hiro?
Miho	Hiro wa gakkoo de yakyuu no renshuu. Moo sugu kaettekuru. Hai, koohii. Atsui yo. Ki o tsukete.
	Hiro has baseball practice at school. He'll be home soon. Here's some coffee. It's hot. Be careful.
Takashi	(running downstairs) O-toosan, ohayoo!
	Morning, Dad!
Miho	Takashi, ki o tsukete. O-toosan wa koohii o nonde iru no yo.
	Takashi, be careful. Your father is drinking his coffee.
Ikuo	Takashi, Eigo no shukudai wa doo. Muzukashii.
	Takashi, how's your English homework? Difficult?
Takashi	Unn, muzukashiku nai yo. Eigo wa suki dakara.
	No, it isn't difficult. I like English so...
Miho	A, moo hiru-gohan no jikan ne. Takashi, Tomoko o yonde kite. Mada tonari ni iru no yo.
	Ah, it's time for lunch. Takashi, call Tomoko. She's still next door.
Takashi	Hai.
	Okay.
Miho	(to her husband) Ne, kyoo no gogo wa minna de Kawasaki ni ittekuru ne.
	So, we're all going to Kawasaki this afternoon, right?
Ikuo	Ee. Kawasaki. Doo shite.
	Eh? Kawasaki? Why?
Miho	Oboete nai no. Kyoo wa okaasan no tanjoobi deshoo.
	Don't you remember? Today is my mother's birthday, isn't it?
Ikuo	O-kaasan no tanjoobi. Itte (i)rasshai. A, atama ga itai! Mata neru yo.
	Your mother's birthday? Oh, my head hurts! I'm going back to bed!

STRUCTURE AND USAGE NOTES

1. ADJECTIVES ENDING IN -I

There are two types of adjectives in Japanese: those that end in -i, and those that are followed by -na when they come before nouns.

Predictably, they are generally referred to as "-i adjectives" and "-na adjectives". For now, we will concentrate on -i adjectives, and look at -na adjectives in the next lesson.

We have already come across several -i adjectives, and you will find these listed below along with some other common -i adjectives, which will be useful for you to learn.

ii	good, fine	atarashii	new, fresh
warui	bad, wrong	atsui	hot
hayai	fast, early	samui	cold (weather)
osoi	slow, late	muzukashii	difficult
takai	high, expensive	itai	painful
yasui	cheap	ookii	big
oishii	delicious, tasty	chiisai	small

Just as in English, these words can come before the word they are describing, or stand alone.

Kore wa oishii sakana desu ne.
This is delicious fish, isn't it?

Kono sakana wa oishii desu ne.
This fish is delicious, isn't it?

Kore wa muzukashii shukudai
desu.
This is difficult homework.

Kono shukudai wa muzukashii
desu.
This homework is difficult.

Here are some more examples of sentences with -i adjectives.

Kyoo wa atsui desu ne.
Hot today, isn't it?

Chotto osoi desu ne. Moo kaerimashoo.
It's a bit late, isn't it? Let's go home.

Ano atarashii resutoran no teishoku wa yasui desu yo. Soko de tabemashoo.
Hey, the set meals at that new restaurant are cheap. Let's eat there.

Kono hon wa go-sen en desu ka. Chotto takai desu ne.
This book is five thousand yen? A bit expensive, isn't it?

Sono chiisai rajio wa ikura desu ka.
How much is that small radio?

The -i group of adjectives have a different form for negatives and for past tenses, so in some ways they act more like verbs than adjectives. In fact, they can stand alone without desu and still make sentences which are complete grammatically, although the tone is pretty informal and familiar, and it is better to add desu. (For example, in the dialogue at the beginning of the lesson, Mr. Watanabe says Atama ga itai, or, literally, "My head is painful". In more formal company, he would say Atama ga itai desu.)

To make a negative sentence, that is, to say when something isn't big, or isn't expensive, or isn't good, drop the final -i and add -ku arimasen. (You may also come across the endings -ku nai desu and -ku nai n desu, which mean the same thing. Nai is the plain form of arimasen.)

Positive	Negative	Meaning
takai	takaku arimasen	isn't expensive
ookii	ookiku arimasen	isn't large
chiisai	chiisaku arimasen	isn't small
muzukashii	muzukashiku arimasen	isn't difficult
itai	itaku arimasen	isn't painful
warui	waruku arimasen	isn't bad
atsui	atsuku arimasen	isn't hot

The adjective ii ("good") has an alternative form yoi, and its negative is formed from this: yoku arimasen.

Kyoo wa amari atsuku arimasen ne.
It's not very hot today, is it?

Watashi no shigoto wa muzukashiku arimasen.
My work isn't difficult.

Atama wa moo itaku arimasen.
My head doesn't hurt anymore./I don't have a headache anymore.

Sono kaisha wa amari ookiku nai desu ne.
That company isn't very big, is it?

Kono purintaa wa yoku arimasen yo.
This printer is no good.

2. MORE ON TELLING THE TIME

Juu-ni-ji jup-pun mae, or "ten minutes before twelve", is an alternative to saying juu-ichi-ji go-jup-pun, or "eleven fifty". The word mae means "before" or "in front of", so you can use it to talk about the minutes *to* the hour. Here are some more times using mae.

Kaigi wa ku-ji juu-go-fun mae ni hajimarimasu.
The meeting starts at a quarter to nine.

Hachi-ji jup-pun mae ni denwa shimasu.
I'll call you at ten to eight.

Ni-ji chotto mae ni kite kudasai.
Please come a little before two o'clock.

In the same way, you can use sugi ("past/after") with the minutes past the hour, although the meaning is usually clear without it.

Juu-ji jup-pun sugi desu.
It's ten past ten.

Moo ichi-ji sugi desu.
It's already after one o'clock.

---

3. **PRESENT PROGRESSIVE TENSE**

Another use of the -te form of the verb is to form the present progressive tense, that is, the one we use to describe an event that's happening at the moment. Simply add the verb iru/imasu after the -te form.

Tomoko wa ima nani o shite imasu ka.
What's Tomoko doing at the moment?

Hiro wa mada nete imasu.
Hiro is still sleeping.

Kenji wa konban uchi de Eigo no benkyoo o shite imasu.
Kenji is studying English at home this evening.

Takahashi san wa ima denwa de tomodachi to hanashite imasu.
Ms. Takahashi's talking to a friend on the phone at the moment.

(on the phone) Eki no mae de matte imasu. Sugu kite kudasai.
I'm waiting in front of the station. Hurry up! [Lit: Please come soon.]

Hiro wa tenisu no renshuu o shite imasen. Kyoo wa yakyuu desu yo.
Hiro isn't at tennis practice. Today it's baseball.

The -te iru form is also used to describe actions that continue over a long period of time.

Maiku san wa Nihon no kookoo de Eigo o oshiete imasu.
Mike teaches [Lit: is teaching] English at a Japanese high school.

Sono kaisha de moo hataraite imasen. Ima ginkoo de hataraite imasu.
I don't work at that company any more. Now I work [Lit: am working] at a bank.

A. Takahashi san no tomodachi wa doko ni sunde imasu ka.
   Where does your friend live, Ms. Takahashi?
B. Yokohama ni sunde imasu.
   She lives [Lit: is living] in Yokohama.

---

4. HAHA VS. O-KAASAN – FAMILY WORDS

A clear distinction is made in Japan between people in your "in-group" and people outside the group, and this is reflected in the language used to refer to them. The in-group and out-group will differ depending on the situation. If you are talking to someone at work about your family, then naturally the family members will be your in-group, and the person you are talking to will be outside this group. However, if you are talking about colleagues at your company to someone from a different company, then you use more familiar terms to refer to them, while using more polite, formal words to refer to people from the company of the person you are talking to.

There are different ways of referring to members of someone else's family, usually by adding the polite o- or go- to the beginning of the word, but sometimes by using different words altogether. Because this makes it obvious that you are talking about the other person's family, it is not necessary to use the words for "my" or "your".

My family	Your family	
kazoku	go-kazoku	family
haha	o-kaasan	mother
chichi	o-toosan	father
kanai/tsuma	okusan	wife
shujin/otto	go-shujin	husband
ane	o-neesan	older sister
ani	o-niisan	older brother
imooto	imootosan	younger sister
otooto	otootosan	younger brother

Ani wa ginkoo de hataraite imasu ga, otooto wa mada daigakusei desu.
My older brother works in a bank, but my younger brother is still at university [Lit: is a university student].

O-neesan wa Igirisu de benkyoo shite imasu ne.
Your older sister is studying in Britain, isn't she?

Ashita haha to issho ni Tookyoo ni ikimasu.
I'm going to Tokyo (together) with my mother tomorrow.

Chichi no kaisha wa Kawasaki ni arimasu.
My father's company is in Kawasaki.

The polite forms are also used when addressing older members of one's own family. (Younger children are generally addressed by their older brothers and sisters using their names.)

O-kaasan, atama ga itai!
Mom, I have a a headache!

O-toosan, o-neesan wa mada tonari no uchi ni iru?
Dad, is my older sister still next door?

---

5. INFORMAL SPEECH LEVELS

A more informal level of speech tends to be used within the family, or with very close friends, and this is characterized by use of the plain form of the verb instead of the -masu form, and leaving off desu after -i adjectives. In everyday conversation, you will be safer using the polite -masu form of verbs, as use of the plain form can sound too familiar if used inappropriately, but it is useful for you to be able to recognize such forms. Below are some of the sentences from the main dialogue, and how they would be if spoken to someone outside the family.

Plain form	Polite -masu form
Atama ga itai. My head hurts./I have a headache.	Atama ga itai desu.
Ima nan-ji? What time is it?	Ima nan-ji desu ka.
A, ii ne. Great.	A, ii desu ne.
...doko ni iru? Where are...?	...doko ni imasu ka.
Eigo no shukudai wa doo? How's your English homework?	Eigo no shukudai wa doo desu ka.
Muzukashii? Is it difficult?	Muzukashii desu ka.
Iie, muzukashiku nai yo. No, it's not difficult.	Iie, muzukashiku arimasen yo.

Tomoko o yonde.
Please call Tomoko.

Tomoko o yonde kudasai.

Mata neru yo.
I'm going back to sleep./I'm going to sleep again.

Mata nemasu yo.

CULTURAL
NOTE

FIRST NAMES AND FAMILY NAMES

First names are not generally used in Japan except within the family, with children, or with very close friends. Even colleagues who have worked together for many years tend to call each other by their family names.

VOCABULARY

ane: (my) older sister
ani: (my) older brother
atama: head
Atama ga itai.: I have a headache./My head hurts.
atsui: hot
chichi: (my) father
chiisai: small
chotto: a little
go-kazoku: (your) family
go-shujin: (your) husband
gogo: afternoon
haha: (my) mother
hataraite imasu: is working [from hataraku]
hayai: fast, early
hiru-gohan: lunch
imooto: (my) younger sister
imootosan: (your) younger sister
issho ni: together
itai: painful
kaerimasu: return, go/come home [from kaeru]
kanai/tsuma: (my) wife
Kawasaki: industrial city near Tokyo
kazoku: family
ki o tsukete (kudasai): take care, be careful [from tsukeru]
mae: before, in front of

matte imasu: is waiting [from matsu]
minna de: altogether, everyone together
mite imasu: is watching [from miru]
muzukashii: difficult
muzukashiku nai: isn't difficult
neru: to sleep, go to bed
ni-kai: second floor, upstairs
nonde iru: is drinking [from nomu]
o-kaasan: (your) mother [or when addressing one's own mother]
o-neesan: (your) older sister [or when addressing one's own older sister]
o-niisan: (your) older brother [or when addressing one's own older brother]
o-toosan: (your) father [or when addressing one's own father]
Oboete imasen ka.: Don't you remember? [from oboeru]
okusan: (your) wife
oshiete imasu: is teaching [from oshieru]
osoi: late, slow
otooto: (my) younger brother
otootosan: (your) younger brother
otto/shujin: (my) husband
renshuu: practice
samui: cold
shukudai: homework
sugi: past, after
sunde imasu: is residing, living [from sumu]
takai: high, expensive
tanjoobi: birthday
tonari: next to, by the side
tsuma/kanai: (my) wife
warui: bad, wrong
yakyuu: baseball
yasui: cheap
yonde: call [short for yonde kudasai, from yobu]

TEST YOURSELF

Read through the dialogue at the beginning of the lesson once
more, and then say if the following statements are true or false.

1. Ima juu-ichi-ji go-jup-pun desu. T/F

2. Tomoko san to Takashi san to Hiro san wa ima uchi ni
   imasu. T/F

3. Ikuo san no koohii wa atsuku arimasen. T/F

Exercise A

4. Takashi san wa Eigo o benkyoo shite imasu. T/F

5. Miho san no o-kaasan no tanjoobi wa kyoo desu. T/F

6. Miho san no o-kaasan wa Kawasaki ni sunde imasu. T/F

Exercise B

Make a comment about the things in the first column, choosing an appropriate word from the second column, as in the example.

Example: Kono resutoran wa yasui desu ne!

Kono	sushi	wa	chiisai	desu ne!
	shukudai		yasui	
	resutoran		muzu-kashii	
	densha		takai	
	kaisha		oishii	
	inu		hayai	
	tatemono		ookii	

Exercise C

A co-worker is trying to make conversation, but you are busy, and not in the mood for a chat. Irritated, you contradict everything he says, as in the example below.

Example: A. Nyuu Yooku wa ima atsui desu ne.
          B. Iie, amari atsuku arimasen yo.

1. Nihongo wa muzukashii desu ne.

   _____

2. Anata no kuruma wa atarashii desu ne.

   _____

3. Ano atarashii resutoran wa oishii desu ne.

   _____

4. Sono konpyuutaa wa ii desu ne.

   _____

5. Ima chotto samui desu ne.

   _____

Exercise D

The principal at Yokohama High School is looking for someone to help him with some school duties at lunchtime, but discovers that all the staff seem to be busy. Using the information on the staff board below, answer his questions about what everyone is doing at the moment, as in the example.

Example:　*Principal*　Watanabe san wa imasu ka.
　　　　　　You　Iie, imasen.
　　　　　　Principal　Nani o shite imasu ka.
　　　　　　You　Watanabe san wa ima kaigi o shite imasu.

NAMAE (names)	DOKO (where?)
Watanabe	meeting
Ito	lunch
Sakai	reading students' homework
Nelson	teaching English class
Takahashi	studying English
Ogawa	doing baseball practice

How would you say these sentences in Japanese?

Exercise E

1. Today's Japanese homework is difficult, isn't it?

2. It's my mother's birthday tomorrow.

3. I'll be home before twelve o'clock.

4. Where does your older brother live?

5. Mike is teaching English in Kawasaki today.

6. I'm sorry, but Keiko isn't in at the moment. She's watching a movie on TV next door. Shall I call her?

英語 The word Eigo, combining the kanji characters for "England" and "word", means "the English language". The suffix, -go can be added to the name of any country to give that country's language.

 Visit www.berlitzpublishing.com for a bonus internet activity—go to the downloads section and connect to the world in Japanese!

IYA DESU NE.
HORRIBLE, ISN'T IT?

Ikuo Watanabe has reluctantly agreed to go shopping with his wife, Miho, as she has persuaded him that he needs a new suit. They are now in the menswear section of a large department store in Ginza, Tokyo's central shopping area.

Miho	**Suutsu wa doko kashira.** (to sales assistant) **Anoo, sumimasen, suutsu wa doko deshoo ka.** I wonder where the suits are. Uh, excuse me, where are the suits?
Clerk	**Suutsu desu ka. Koko o moo sukoshi massugu itte kudasai. Migi-gawa ni gozaimasu.** The suits? Go a little further along here. They're on the right-hand side.
Miho	**Doomo. A, koko da. Kono guree no suutsu wa ii ne.** Thank you. Ah, here they are. This gray suit is nice, isn't it?
Ikuo	**Guree wa dame. Suki ja nai yo.** Gray's no good. I don't like it.

Miho	Soo. Ja, kono buruu no wa doo. (looking inside at the label) A, kono dezainaa wa yuumei yo. Ii ne. I see. Well, how about this blue one? Ah, this designer is famous. It's nice, isn't it?
Ikuo	Yuumei-na dezainaa. Takai daro. Motto yasui suutsu ga ii na. A, kore ga ii. A famous designer? It's probably expensive. A cheaper suit is fine. Ah, this one's okay.
Miho	Sore wa ii kedo, saizu wa chotto chiisai ne. (to sales assistant) Sumimasen, motto ookii saizu wa arimasu ka. That one's nice, but it's a bit small, isn't it? Excuse me, do you have a larger size?
Clerk	Gozaimasu. Kochira e doozo. We do. This way, please.

Mr. Watanabe goes off to try on the suit, and while the rest of the family is waiting for him, Mrs. Watanabe suddenly sees one of her acquaintances.

Miho	A, Kawada san, konnichiwa! O-hisashiburi desu ne. Ah, Mr. Kawada, hello! I haven't seen you for ages!
Kawada	A, Watanabe san, konnichiwa. O-genki desu ka. Ah, Mrs.Watanabe, hello. How are you?
Miho	Hai, genki desu. O-kage sama de. Kawada san wa. I'm fine, thank you. And you?
Kawada	Hai, o-kage sama de. Watashi mo genki desu. Yes, fine, thank you. I'm fine, too.
Miho	Kyoo wa konde imasu ne. It's crowded today, isn't it?
Kawada	Soo desu ne. Iya desu ne. Kaimono wa kirai ja nai desu ga, Ginza no depaato wa itsumo konde iru deshoo. Watanabe san wa yoku Ginza e kimasu ka. Yes, it is. Horrible, isn't it! I don't dislike shopping, but the Ginza department stores are always crowded, aren't they? Do you often come to Ginza?
Miho	Tokidoki kimasu. Watashi mo kaimono wa suki desu ga, kyoo wa shujin no atarashii suutsu o mite imasu... Sometimes. I like shopping too, but today my husband is looking at new suits...
Kawada	A, soo desu ka. Go-shujin to issho desu ka. Oh, I see, you're (shopping) with your husband.

Miho	Soo desu!
	(Mr. Watanabe comes out of the fitting room where he changed suits) A, shujin desu. Doo. Saizu wa daijoobu.
	It is! Ah, there he is. How is it? Is the size all right?
Ikuo	Saizu wa daijoobu da kedo, dezain ga chotto...
	The size is okay, but the design is a bit...

STRUCTURE AND USAGE NOTES

1. USES OF DESHOO

The word deshoo has its origins in desu, but it has different nuances depending on the situation and intonation used. When it is used in a question, and followed by ka, it is the equivalent of "I wonder..." so it makes the question less direct.

Kore wa nan desu ka.
What's this?

Kore wa nan deshoo ka.
I wonder what this is?

Sono hito wa Watanabe san no o-toosan desu ka.
Is that (person) Mr. Watanabe's father?

Sono hito wa Watanabe san no o-toosan deshoo ka.
I wonder if that (person) is Mr. Watanabe's father?

Kaigi wa nan-ji desu ka.
What time is the meeting?

Kaigi wa nan-ji deshoo ka.
I wonder what time the meeting is?

When it is used with rising intonation (without ka at the end), it is asking for the agreement of the person being spoken to, so it is similar to ne, but softer and less direct.

Are wa Watanabe san no uchi deshoo.
That's Mr. Watanabe's house, right?

Asoko no kodomo wa Takashi chan deshoo.
That child over there is Takashi, isn't it?

Nihongo wa muzukashii deshoo.
Japanese is difficult, isn't it?

Kyoo wa tanjoobi deshoo.
Today is your birthday, am I right?

Sono dezainaa wa yuumei deshoo.
That designer is famous, isn't she?

When the intonation is falling at the end of the sentence, it shows that the speaker is almost, but not completely, sure of his or her facts, so is making an assumption. This kind of sentence is often translated into English using words such as "probably", "must be" and "almost certainly".

Hokkaidoo wa ima samui deshoo.
It's probably cold in Hokkaido now.

Sono saizu wa daijoobu deshoo.
I guess that size will be okay.

Paato no shigoto mo, benkyoo mo shite imasu ka. Sore wa taihen deshoo.
You're doing part-time work and studying? That must be tough.

Deshoo can also be used instead of **desu** when you want to be extra polite.

Sumimasen ga, Tanaka san deshoo ka.
Excuse me, but would you be Mr. Tanaka?

Chotto sumimasen, eki wa doko deshoo ka.
Excuse me, where might the station be?

2. VOCABULARY FOR CLOTHING

Much of the vocabulary for Western-style clothing has been taken from English, so if you want to buy an item of clothing and you don't know the word, try saying the English equivalent with Japanese pronunciation. Chances are that you will be correct.

burausu	blouse	suutsu	suit
seetaa	sweater	nekutai	necktie
sukaato	skirt	shatsu	shirt
jaketto	jacket	kooto	coat
beruto	belt	T-shatsu	T-shirt
wanpiisu	dress ("one-piece")	G-pan, jiinz	jeans ("jean pants")
kutsu	shoes	zubon, pants	pants, trousers

3. GOZAIMASU – WE HAVE

As we saw in the previous lesson when talking about family members, vocabulary can differ markedly in Japanese, depending on who you are talking to, the degree of formality of the situation and even the relative age of the people talking. In situations which demand a high degree of courtesy, such as a sales assistant in a department store talking to a customer, or staff in a prestigious hotel talking to a guest, the speaker is likely to use the very formal and humble gozaimasu instead of arimasu.

A. Kono hoteru ni wa, jimu ga arimasu ka.
   Do you have a gym in this hotel?
B. Hai, gozaimasu.
   Yes, we do.

In the same way, de gozaimasu is used in formal situations instead of desu.

A. Sumimasen, kono seetaa wa ikura desu ka.
   Excuse me, how much is this sweater?
B. Sore wa kyuu-sen en de gozaimasu.
   It's ¥9,000.

---

4. GUREE, BURUU **AND OTHER COLORS**

Some of the words for colors are -i adjectives.

kuroi	black
shiroi	white
aoi	blue, green, blue/green
akai	red
chairoi	brown

Asoko no shiroi tatemono wa hoteru desu ka.
That white building over there – is it a hotel?

Sono akai kuruma wa dare no desu ka.
Whose is that red car?

These words can be turned into nouns by dropping the final -i.

Kono kuroi sukaato wa ii desu ne. Watashi wa kuro ga suki desu.
This black skirt is nice, isn't it? I like black.

Ki o tsukete kudasai. Shingoo wa aka desu.
Be careful. The traffic lights are red.

Other color words are nouns, so when they are used in front of the word they are describing, they need to be followed by no.

kiiro	yellow
midori	green
murasaki	purple

(Kiiro also has the alternative form kiiroi, acting like an -i adjective.)

Sono chairo to midori no nekutai wa ikura desu ka.
How much is that brown and green necktie?

Kono kiiro no hana no namae wa nan desu ka.
What's the name of these yellow flowers?

A third set of color words are those that have been borrowed from English. Generally these tend to be used to describe man-made things rather than those found in nature. For example, a sweater may be guriin, but the park in spring would be midori; jeans may be buruu, but the sky is ao. These words also have to be followed by no when they are used before the word they are describing.

buruu	blue
guree	gray
orenji	orange
guriin	green
buraun	brown
pinku	pink

Mata pinku no wanpiisu o kaimasu ka.
You're going to buy another pink dress?

Kono buruu no seetaa wa doo desu ka.
How about this blue sweater?

---

5. YUUMEI-NA DEZAINAA – -NA ADJECTIVES

In the previous lesson you learned about -i adjectives. Now we will look at -na adjectives, so-called because they are always followed by -na when they come before a noun to describe it. Here are some of the most common -na adjectives.

iya-na	horrible	kirei-na	pretty, clean
dame-na	no good, useless	yuumei-na	famous
taihen-na	terrible, tough	shizuka-na	quiet, peaceful
shinsetsu-na	kind	kantan-na	simple, brief
suki-na	like	kirai-na	dislike
genki-na	healthy, cheerful	hen-na	strange, odd

Ima no shigoto wa taihen desu.
My current job is really tough.

Sono buruu no burausu wa kirei desu ne.
That blue blouse is pretty, isn't it?

Atarashii jimu no hito wa itsumo genki desu ne.
The new office worker is always cheerful, isn't she?

To make a negative statement, use ja arimasen, the negative of desu.

Ogawa san no atarashii uchi wa amari shizuka ja arimasen ne.
Mr. Ogawa's new house isn't very quiet, is it?

Tomoko san no Eigo no sensei wa amari shinsetsu ja arimasen.
Tomoko's English teacher isn't very kind.

These adjectives are followed by -na to join them to the thing they are describing.

Hen-na hito desu ne!
He's a weird person, isn't he!

Kantan-na repooto o kaite kudasai.
Please write a brief report.

Kyoo no sora wa kirei-na ao desu ne.
The sky today is a beautiful blue, isn't it?

A. Saitoo san no kaisha wa yuumei desu ka.
   Is Ms. Saitoo's company famous?
B. Hai, totemo yuumei-na kaisha desu yo.
   Yes, it's a really famous company.

Suki-na sakana wa nan desu ka.
What (kind of) fish do you like?

Takashi wa genki-na kodomo desu ne.
Takashi is an energetic child, isn't he?

The words ookii ("big") and chiisai ("small") can also become -na adjectives (drop the final -i first) when they come before a noun.

Sore wa totemo ookii/ooki-na hoteru desu ne.
That's a really big hotel, isn't it?

Tomoko chan no gakkoo wa chiisai/chiisa-na gakkoo desu ka.
Is your school a small school, Tomoko?

6. MOTTO YASUI, MOTTO OOKII – "CHEAPER" AND "BIGGER"

To describe something as "bigger", "smaller", "more expensive", "cheaper", etc. in Japanese, simply put motto ("more") in front of the appropriate word, which is the equivalent of saying "more big", "more small", "more quiet".

Sumimasen ga, motto chiisai no wa arimasu ka.
Excuse me, but do you have a smaller one?

Kono buraun no jaketto wa suki desu ga, sono kuroi no wa motto suki desu.
I like this brown jacket, but I like that black one more.

Tsugi no tesuto wa motto muzukashii deshoo.
The next test will probably be more difficult.

Sumimasen, motto yukkuri hanashite kudasai.
Excuse me, but could you please speak more slowly?

7. SORE WA II DESU GA – CONNECTING SENTENCES WITH "BUT"

The word ga can be used to join two sentences which are in contrast, so it is much like the English "but". However, remember that in Japanese ga ends the first part of the sentence before the comma, whereas the English equivalent "but" begins the second part of the sentence.

Maiku san wa kimasu ga, Takahashi san wa kimasen.
Mike is coming, but Ms. Takahashi isn't.

Kono buruu no seetaa wa suki desu ga, sono guriin no wa iya desu ne.
I like this blue sweater, but that green one is horrible, isn't it?

Tookyoo no depaato wa itsumo konde imasu ga, Chiba no wa amari konde imasen.
The department stores in Tokyo are always crowded, but the ones in Chiba aren't (very crowded).

Tomoko wa mada chiisai kodomo desu ga, mainichi shinbun o yomimasu.
Tomoko is still a small child, but she reads the newspaper every day.

Ani wa Tookyoo ni sunde imasu ga, ane wa Chiba ni sunde imasu.
My older brother lives in Tokyo, but my older sister lives in Chiba.

Sometimes ga is used to link two sentences even though there isn't a very strong element of contrast.

Watashi wa kaimono ga totemo suki desu ga, Takahashi san wa doo desu ka.
I really enjoy shopping – how about you, Ms. Takahashi?

Watashi wa ashita Yokohama e ikimasu ga, Saitoo san mo issho ni ikimasen ka.
I'm going to Yokohama tomorrow – do you want to come along too, Ms. Saitoo?

Asatte wa haha no tanjoobi desu ga, nani o kaimashoo ka.
It's Mom's birthday the day after tomorrow. What shall we buy her?

---

8. O-GENKI DESU KA – HOW ARE YOU?

This phrase, literally meaning "Are you well?", is a common greeting when seeing someone after a long while, but note that the honorific beginning o- should not be used in your answer, because you are talking about yourself. To make your response even more courteous, thank the person for asking by using the set phrase o-kage sama de.

A. O-genki desu ka.
How are you?
B. Hai, o-kage sama de, genki desu.
Thank you, I'm fine.

---

9. ITSUMO, TOKIDOKI – "ALWAYS", "SOMETIMES" AND OTHER WORDS OF FREQUENCY

Here are some of the most commonly-used words of frequency that you might find useful. They usually come before the verb, but they can also be used to begin the sentence or phrase. Both amari and zenzen need a negative ending.

itsumo	yoku	tokidoki	amari	zenzen
always	often	sometimes	not often	never, not at all

Ani wa ima daigakusei desu ga, zenzen benkyoo shimasen.
My older brother is a university student now, but he never does any work.

Rajio no nyuusu o itsumo kikimasu ga, terebi no nyuusu wa amari mimasen.
I always listen to the news on the radio, but I don't often watch it on TV.

A. **Maiku san wa gakkoo de yoku Nihongo de hanashimasu ka.**
Do you often speak in Japanese at the school, Mike?
B. **Hai, yoku hanashimasu.**
Yes, often.

Itsumo ginkoo no tonari no resutoran de hiru-gohan o tabemasu.
We always eat lunch at the restaurant next to the bank.

---

10. KASHIRA/KANA – I WONDER

Kashira and kana are used to mean "I wonder". The plain form of verbs and -i adjectives is used before them. As for -na adjectives and nouns, simply put kashira and kana after them. Kashira sounds feminine, whereas kana sounds neutral.

Watanabe-san wa moo shigoto ni itta kashira/kana.
I wonder if Mr. Watanabe went to work?

Ano terebi wa yasui kashira/kana.
I wonder if that TV is cheap?

Ano hito wa sensei kashira/kana.
I wonder if that person is a teacher?

VOCABULARY

beruto: belt
Chiba: satellite city of Tokyo
daijoobu: fine, all right
dame-na: no good, useless
de gozaimasu: is, are [formal]
depaato: department store
deshoo: I wonder if…, probably, must be
dezain: design
dezainaa: designer
G-pan: jeans
ga: but [when joining two sentences]
genki: healthy, energetic
gozaimasu: have [formal]
hen-na: odd, strange
Hokkaidoo: northernmost of the four main islands of Japan
hoteru: hotel
Ii desu ga/Ii desu kedo: It's fine, but…
itsumo: always
jiinzu: jeans
jimu: gym
iya-na: horrible

jaketto: jacket
kaimashoo ka: shall we buy? [from kau]
kaimono: shopping [noun]
…kana/kashira: I wonder…
kantan-na: brief, simple
kedo: but
kirei-na: pretty, clean
kodomo: child
konde imasu: is crowded [from komu]
kooto: coat
kutsu: shoes
mo: too, also
motto yasui: cheaper
motto: more
nekutai: necktie
O-genki desu ka.: How are you?
O-hisashiburi.: It's been a long time.
O-kage sama de.: Thank you for asking. [set phrase in response to
O-genki desu ka.]
repooto: report
saizu: size
seetaa: sweater
shatsu: shirt
shinsetsu-na: kind, gentle
shizuka-na: quiet, peaceful
sora: sky
sukaato: skirt
suki ja nai: don't like [informal]
suutsu: suit
T-shatsu: T-shirt
taihen-na: terrible, awful
tokidoki: sometimes
totemo: very, extremely
wanpiisu: dress
yoku: often
yuumei-na: famous
zenzen: never [+ negative verb]

Colors:
aka(i): red
ao(i): green
chaiiro(i): brown
kiiro(i): yellow
kuro(i): black
midori: green
murasaki: purple
shiro(i): white

buraun: brown
buruu: blue
guree: gray
guriin: green
orenji: orange
pinku: pink

TEST YOURSELF

Exercise A

Read through the dialogue at the beginning of the lesson again, and then say if the following statements are true or false.

1. Watanabe san to okusan wa ima depaato ni imasu. T/F

2. Watanabe san wa guree no suutsu wa suki ja arimasen. T/F

3. Buruu no suutsu no dezainaa wa yuumei ja arimasen. T/F

4. Okusan wa kaimono ga suki desu ga, tomodachi wa suki ja arimasen. T/F

5. Watanabe san no okusan wa yoku Ginza e ikimasu. T/F

6. Yasui suutsu no saizu wa daijoobu desu ga, Watanabe san wa dezain ga suki ja arimasen. T/F

Exercise B

Ms. Takahashi is out shopping with a friend, and at the moment she's looking at blouses. Choose the appropriate word from the parentheses to complete their conversation.

Takahashi	Suki-na burausu ga arimasen ne.
Sato	Kore wa doo desu ka. Kono (aka/akai) hana (no/na) burausu wa kirei deshoo.
Takahashi	Aka wa amari suki (desu/ja arimasen).
Sato	Soo desu ka. Tokorode (doo shite/daijoobu) atarashii burausu o (kaeru/kau) ndesu ka. A, wakarimashita. Konban Neruson san to issho ni eiga o (iku/miru) n desu ne.
Takahashi	Soo desu yo. Ima yo-ji han desu (ga/wa), roku-ji han ni Neruson san ni (aimasu/imasu). Doo shimashoo ka. Jikan ga arimasen ne.
Sato	Ja, wanpiisu wa doo desu ka.
Takahashi	Soo ne. Wanpiisu ni shimashoo. A, (kono/kore) dezainaa wa dai-suki desu. Demo takai (arimasu/deshoo).
Sato	Iie, mite kudasai yo. (Takai/takaku) arimasen.
Takahashi	Ja, kore wa ii desu ne. Kore ni shimasu.

Make comments about the items in the pictures, as in the example.

Example: like
Suki-na kuruma desu ne!

1. pretty!

2. full of energy!

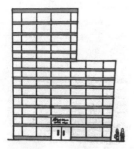

3. high!

4. famous!

5. strange!

Exercise D

Look at the three short sentences in each group below, and then choose the two which can be joined together with ga ("but") to make one long sentence, as in the example.

Example: a. Kodomo ja arimasen.
b. Hiro-chan wa mada chiisai kodomo desu.
c. Konpyuutaa ga dai-suki desu.

b+c: Hiro-chan wa mada chiisai kodomo desu ga, konpyuutaa ga dai-suki desu.

1. a. Kono guree no suutsu wa suki desu.
   b. Guree wa suki ja arimasen.
   c. Chotto ookii desu.

2. a. Sakana wa tokidoki tabemasu.
   b. O-cha wa amari suki ja arimasen.
   c. Watashi wa koohii o yoku nomimasu.

3. a. Eiga wa go-ji ni hajimarimasu.
   b. Chotto hayai deshoo.
   c. Oishii deshoo.

4. a. Asatte imasu.
   b. Asatte kimasen.
   c. Watashi wa ashita kaisha ni imasen.

5. a. Purintaa wa dame desu.
   b. Watashi no konpyuutaa wa daijoobu desu.
   c. Konpyuutaa wa daijoobu ja arimasen.

Exercise E

How would you say these sentences in Japanese?

1. I wonder if that person over there is Mr. Saitoo.

2. Could you write a briefer report, please?

3. The black jacket is probably a bit small.

4. The train is very crowded today, isn't it?

5. I don't really like Tokyo, but Yokohama is nice.

6. My mother works at a famous department store in Tokyo.

東京 The name of Japan's captital city, Tookyoo, uses a combination of the characters for "east" and "capital".

 Visit www.berlitzpublishing.com for a bonus internet activity—go to the downloads section and connect to the world in Japanese!

Lesson

9 SHUUMATSU WA DOO DESHITA KA.
HOW WAS YOUR WEEKEND?

 It's Monday morning, and as Ikuo Watanabe waits on the station platform for the train to work, he bumps into Mike Nelson.

Watanabe	**Ohayoo gozaimasu.**
	Good morning.
Nelson	**Ohayoo gozaimasu. Kyoo wa, densha wa konde imasu ne.**
	Good morning. The trains are crowded today, aren't they!
Watanabe	**Soo desu ne. Getsuyoobi wa itsumo soo desu ne. Tokorode, shuumatsu wa doo deshita ka. Dokoka e ikimashita ka.**
	Yes, they are. It's always like this on Mondays, isn't it? By the way, how was your weekend? Did you go anywhere?

Nelson	Ee, totemo tanoshikatta desu. Tomodachi futari to issho ni, yama e ikimashita. Doyoobi no asa itte, kinoo no yoru kaette kimashita. Dakara kesa chotto tsukarete imasu.
	Yes, it was extremely enjoyable. I went to the mountains together with two friends. We went on Saturday morning, and came back yesterday evening. That's why this morning I'm a bit tired.
Watanabe	Ii desu ne. Doko ni ikimashita ka.
	That's nice. Where did you go?
Nelson	Nihon Arupusu no onsen ni ikimashita. Machi no namae wa wasuremashita kedo, totemo kirei-na tokoro deshita.
	We went to a hot spring in the Japan Alps. I've forgotten the name of the town, but it was a really pretty place.
Watanabe	Onsen! Ii desu ne. Soto no onsen mo arimashita ka.
	A hot spring! Nice. Was there an outside hot spring bath too?
Nelson	Arimashita. Doyoobi no yoru mo, nichiyoobi no asa mo hairimashita. Chotto samukatta kedo, onsen no yu wa taihen atsukatta desu.
	Yes, there was. We went in Saturday evening and Sunday morning. The weather was a bit cold, but the spring water was extremely hot.
Watanabe	Ryokan ni tomarimashita ka.
	Did you stay at an inn?
Nelson	Hai, tomarimashita. Konde imashita yo. Wakai hitotachi ga takusan tomatte imashita yo. Amerikajin mo imashita.
	Yes, we did. It was crowded, but there were a lot of young people staying there. There was also an American staying there.
Watanabe	Soo desu ka. Hanashi o shimashita ka.
	I see. Did you get to talk?
Nelson	Iie, chansu ga arimasen deshita.
	No, there was no chance.
Watanabe	Sore wa zannen deshita ne.
	That was a pity!
Nelson	Ee, soo desu ne. Tokorode, Watanabe san wa nani o shimashita ka. Dokoka e ikimashita ka.
	Yes, it was. By the way, what did you do, Mr. Watanabe? Did you go anywhere?

> Watanabe Taihen deshita yo. Zenzen omoshiroku arimasen
> deshita. Kazoku to issho ni Tookyoo e itte, kaimono
> o shimashita ga, nichiyoobi no depaato wa, moo iya
> desu yo.
> It was terrible. Completely uninteresting. I went with the
> family to Tokyo, and we did some shopping –
> department stores on a Sunday are horrible!
>
> Nelson Nanika kaimashita ka.
> Did you buy anything?
>
> Watanabe Ee, atarashii suutsu o kaimashita kedo, hontoo ni
> jikan ga kakarimashita. Kyoo wa, watashi mo taihen
> tsukarete imasu yo.
> Yes, I bought a new suit, but it really took (a long) time.
> Today I'm really exhausted too!

STRUCTURE AND USAGE NOTES

1. GETSUYOOBI – "MONDAY" AND OTHER DAYS OF THE WEEK

To ask what day it is, you would say:
Nan-yoobi desu ka.

The days of the week are as follows:

getsuyoobi	Monday
kayoobi	Tuesday
suiyoobi	Wednesday
mokuyoobi	Thursday
kin'yoobi	Friday
doyoobi	Saturday
nichiyoobi	Sunday

Tokidoki doyoobi ni kaisha e ikimasu.
I sometimes go to the office on Saturdays.

Kin'yoobi no yoru ni eiga o mimashoo ka.
Shall we see a movie on Friday evening?

Getsuyoobi kara mokuyoobi made Tookyoo ni imasu ga, kin'yoobi no
asa Nagoya e kaerimasu.
I'm in Tokyo from Monday to Thursday, but I'll return to Nagoya on Friday
morning.

Raishuu no doyoobi to nichiyoobi ni umi e ikimasu ga, issho ni
ikimasen ka.
Next Saturday and Sunday we're going to the ocean – would you like to
come with us?

---

2. IKIMASHITA KA – "DID YOU GO?" AND OTHER PAST TENSE VERBS

To talk about something which happened in the past, simply end the verb
with -mashita instead of -masu. (There are also plain forms of the past
tense verbs, but we will look at those in the following lessons.) Note that
the pronunciation of this past tense ending is like -mash'ta, that is, the final
-i- is hardly sounded. Here are some examples of past tense verbs.

Plain form	-masu form	Past	Meaning
iku	ikimasu	ikimashita	went
kuru	kimasu	kimashita	came
tomaru	tomarimasu	tomarimashita	stayed
matsu	machimasu	machimashita	waited
hairu	hairimasu	hairimashita	entered
aru	arimasu	arimashita	there was/were
miru	mimasu	mimashita	saw, watched
matte iru	matte imasu	matte imashita	was waiting
mite iru	mite imasu	mite imashita	was watching
shite iru	shite imasu	shite imashita	was doing

Doyoobi no gogo ni, yakyuu o mimashita ka.
Did you see the baseball (game) on Saturday afternoon?

Mainichi kanji no benkyoo o shimashita ga, sugu wasuremashita.
I studied kanji (Chinese characters) every day, but I soon forgot them.

Itsu kaisha ni hairimashita ka.
When did you join your company?

Kinoo kono atarashii kutsu o kaimashita ga, chotto chiisai desu.
I bought these new shoes yesterday, but they're a bit small.

Doyoobi ni kaimono ni ikimashita ne. Nanika kaimashita ka.
You went shopping on Saturday, right? Did you buy anything?

Ichi-jikan machimashita yo. Doo shimashita ka.
I waited an hour! What happened?

The past form of desu is deshita ("was/were").

Takashi chan no Eigo no sensei no namae wa nan deshita ka.
What was the name of Takashi's English teacher?

Nichiyoobi wa hontoo ni iya-na tenki deshita ne.
It was really awful weather on Sunday, wasn't it?

Eiga wa doo deshita ka.
How was the movie?

Tanjoobi wa nan-yoobi deshita ka.
What day was your birthday?

Senshuu Saitoo san ni aimashita ne. Genki deshita ka.
You met Mr. Saitoo last week, right? How was he?

Saying what you *didn't* do isn't so difficult. Just add deshita to the negative -masen form.

Present negative		Past negative	
kakimasen	don't write	kakimasen deshita	didn't write
ikimasen	don't go	ikimasen deshita	didn't go
tabemasen	don't eat	tabemasen deshita	didn't eat
shimasen	don't do	shimasen deshita	didn't do
kaimasen	don't buy	kaimasen deshita	didn't buy
kaerimasen	don't return	kaerimasen deshita	didn't return
shite imasen	isn't doing	shite imasen deshita	wasn't doing
matte imasen	isn't waiting	matte imasen deshita	wasn't waiting
kaite imasen	isn't writing	kaite imasen deshita	wasn't writing

Kare no hanashi ga zenzen wakarimasen deshita.
I didn't understand what he was saying at all.

Doo shite kaigi no repooto o kakimasen deshita ka.
Why didn't you write up the report of the meeting?

Nyuu Yooku ni sunde imasen deshita yo. Rondon ni sunde imashita.
I wasn't living in New York. I was living in London.

Jikan ga amari kakarimasen deshita.
It didn't take very long.

Ichi-jikan machimashita ga, tomodachi wa kimasen deshita.
I waited an hour, but my friend didn't come.

The same principle applies to desu when making the past form of the negative ("wasn't/weren't"). In other words, find the negative (ja arimasen) and add deshita.

Sono ryokan wa amari suki ja arimasen deshita.
We didn't like that inn very much.

Kirei-na tokoro ja arimasen deshita.
It wasn't a pretty place.

Machi no namae wa Shirakawa ja arimasen deshita yo. Shirazawa deshita.
The name of the town wasn't Shirakawa. It was Shirazawa.

You may also come across the form ja nakatta desu instead of ja arimasen deshita. It means the same thing, but is derived from the plain form.

Watanabe san no tanjoobi wa kinoo ja nakatta desu yo. Ashita desu.
Mr. Watanabe's birthday wasn't yesterday! It's tomorrow.

---

3. TANOSHIKATTA – "IT WAS ENJOYABLE", AND OTHER PAST TENSE ADJECTIVES

As you know by now, Japanese adjectives conjugate like verbs. Let's see how to make past tense. -i adjectives are used when describing something that was in the past. To make the past form, drop the last -i and add -katta. Because this -katta ending already shows that it's the past tense, the final desu doesn't need to change. (If the adjective comes in the middle of a sentence, as in the first example below, then desu can be omitted.)

-i adjective	Past tense	Meaning
oishii desu	oishikatta desu	was delicious
tanoshii desu	tanoshikatta desu	was enjoyable

atsui desu	atsukatta desu	was hot
ii/yoi	yokatta desu	was good
hazukashii	hazukashikatta desu	was embarrassed, shy
ookii desu	ookikatta desu	was big

Hoteru wa yokatta (desu) ga, chotto takakatta desu.
The hotel was fine, but it was a little expensive.

Totemo oishikatta desu. Go-chisoo sama deshita.
That tasted wonderful. Thank you for the meal.

Maiku san no tanjoobi no paatii wa hontoo ni tanoshikatta desu yo.
Tomodachi ga takusan kimashita.
Mike's birthday party was really good. Lots of (his) friends came.

Bideo wa omoshirokatta desu ka.
Was the video interesting?

Sensei no namae o zenzen oboete imasen deshita. Dakara hontoo ni
hazukashikatta desu yo.
I couldn't remember the teacher's name at all. So it was really
embarrassing!

To make the negative of -i adjectives in the past, in other words to talk
about things which *weren't* hot or *weren't* expensive, etc., once again just
add deshita to the present tense negative. This, you may remember, ends
in -ku arimasen, so the past form ending is -ku arimasen deshita.

Kanji no tesuto wa amari muzukashiku arimasen deshita ne.
The kanji test wasn't very difficult, was it?

Maiku san no tanjoobi no paatii de o-sake o takusan nomimashita ga,
atama wa zenzen itaku arimasen deshita.
I drank a lot of sake at Mike's birthday party, but I didn't have a headache
at all.

Instead of the ending -ku arimasen deshita, you may also hear -ku
nakatta desu.

Sono hon wa amari omoshiroku nakatta desu ne.
That book wasn't very interesting, was it?

---

4. FUTARI – COUNTING PEOPLE

When we count things in English, we sometimes need to use special
counters, such as "two *bars* of chocolate", "one *spoonful* of sugar", "three

cartons of milk", "a *glass* of water", etc. This happens even more in Japanese, and there are, for example, special counters for things which are flat (newspapers, stamps, train tickets), things which are long and thin (bottles, rolled umbrellas, pencils), large animals (cows, horses), and many others. To count people, add the counter -nin, except in the cases of "one person" and "two people", which are irregular.

Nan-nin?	How many people?		
hitori	one person	roku-nin	six people
futari	two people	shichi-nin	seven people
san-nin	three people	hachi-nin	eight people
yo-nin	four people	ku-nin	nine people
go-nin	five people	juu-nin	ten people

Sono chiisai gakkoo de wa sensei ga juu-nin oshiete imasu.
There are ten teachers teaching at that small school.

Imooto ga hitori to otooto ga futari imasu.
I have one younger sister and two younger brothers.

Nan-nin Ogawa san no kaisha de hataraite imasu ka.
How many people are there working at Mr. Ogawa's company?

Sono ryokan ni wa hachi-nin dake tomatte imashita yo. Otoko no hito ga san-nin to, onna no hito ga san-nin to, kodomo ga hitori to watashi deshita.
There were only eight people staying at that inn - three men, three women, a child and me.

Kinoo no yoru Nihongo no kurasu ga arimashita ga, futari dake kimashita. Dakara hontoo ni tsukaremashita.
I had a Japanese class yesterday evening, but only two people came. So it was really tiring.

---

5. THE PARTICLE NI – "TO", "TOWARDS"

We have already come across the particle ni used with arimasu or imasu to show the location of something, but it can also be used like e to show movement to or towards a place.

Shuumatsu ni dokoka e/ni ikimashita ka.
Did you go anywhere on the weekend?

Takahashi san wa itsu Kyooto e/ni kaerimasu ka.
When is Ms. Takahashi going back to Kyoto?

Takashi san wa kinoo amari genki ja arimasen deshita. Dakara gakkoo e/ni ikimasen deshita.
Takashi wasn't very well yesterday. That's why he didn't go to school.

---

6. ...MO...MO – BOTH...AND...

Sentences with ...mo...mo are the equivalent of "both...and..." when in the positive, and "neither...nor..." when in the negative.

O-sake mo biiru mo nomimashita. Dakara atama ga itai desu.
I drank (both) sake and beer. That's why I have a headache.

Takahashi san wa tenisu mo gorufu mo joozu desu ga, watashi wa heta desu.
Ms. Takahashi is good at both tennis and golf, but I'm bad (at them).

Koohii mo o-cha mo nomimasen.
I don't drink (either) coffee or green tea.

---

7. CONNECTING SENTENCES WITH -TE

The -te form of verbs can be used to link two or more sentences together, and can often be translated as "and". This "and" can be just connecting two sentences, but sometimes the first part with the -te form could be a reason for the clause that comes after that. The -te form can be used in the middle of a sentence regardless of whether the event it describes happened in the past, is happening now or will happen in the future, because it is the word (predicate) at the *end* of the sentence that shows the overall tense of the sentence.

Doyoobi no asa ni Tookyoo e ikimashita. +
Atarashii suutsu o kaimashita. =
Doyoobi no asa ni Tookyoo e itte, atarashii suutsu o kaimashita.
On Saturday morning I went to Tokyo, and bought a new suit.

Shuumatsu ni tomodachi to issho ni yama e ikimasu. +
Onsen no ryokan ni tomarimasu. =
Shuumatsu ni tomodachi to issho ni yama e itte, onsen no ryokan ni tomarimasu.
On the weekend I'm going to the mountains with a friend, and staying at an inn at a hot spring.

Here are some more examples of how the -te form is used in this way.

Ashita Pari ni itte, asatte wa Roma ni ikimasu. Tsukaremasu yo!
I'm going to Paris tomorrow, and Rome the next day. I'm going to be tired!

Tanaka san wa mainichi tenisu no renshuu o shite, totemo joozu desu.
Mr. Tanaka practices tennis every day, and is really good [Lit: skillful].

Mokuyoobi ni atarashii Nihongo no kurasu ni haitte, totemo omoshirokatta desu.
On Monday I joined a new Japanese class, and it was really interesting.

Kinoo no yoru, uchi ni ite, bideo o mimashita.
Yesterday evening, I stayed at home and watched a video.

The equivalent form for desu is de.

Getsuyoobi no yoru wa yakyuu no renshuu desu. +
Kayoobi wa tenisu no renshuu desu. =
Getsuyoobi no yoru wa yakyuu no renshuu de, kayoobi wa tenisu no renshuu desu.
Monday evening is baseball practice, and Tuesday is tennis practice.

Takahashi san no imootosan wa kirei desu. +
Takahashi san no imootosan wa shinsetsu desu. =
Takahashi san no imootosan wa kirei de, shinsetsu desu.
Ms. Takahashi's younger sister is pretty and kind.

Maiku san wa sensei desu. +
Yokohama Gakuin Kookoo de oshiete imasu. =
Maiku san wa sensei de, Yokohama Gakuin Kookoo de oshiete imasu.
Mike is a teacher, and he teaches at Yokohama High School.

Watashi wa Eigo ga heta desu. +
Hazukashii desu. =
Watashi wa Eigo ga heta de, hazukashii desu.
I'm embarrassed because I'm bad at English.

8. CONNECTING SENTENCES WITH KEDO – BUT

The word kedo (and its more formal variations keredo and keredomo) is used to join sentences together with the meaning "but", and always ends the first part of the sentence, before the comma. It can sometimes be used instead of ga ("but"), but kedo sounds more casual than ga. When speaking, a plain form should not be used before ga, but kedo has no such restriction.

Tenisu wa dai-suki desu kedo, amari joozu ja arimasen.
Although I really like tennis, I'm not very good.

Shuumatsu ni umi ni ikimashita kedo, taihen samukatta desu. Dakara tanoshiku arimasen deshita.
We went to the ocean on the weekend, but it was very cold. So it wasn't much fun.

Ogawa san wa mainichi mainichi gorufu no renshuu o shimasu kedo, mada heta desu.
Although Mr. Ogawa practices golf day after day, he's still no good.

When an -i adjective is followed by kedo, the desu (which usually comes after such an adjective) can be omitted.

Atama ga chotto itai kedo, daijoobu desu.
My head hurts a little, but I'm okay.

Sono o-sake wa oishii kedo, chotto takai desu.
That sake is delicious, but it's very expensive.

---

9. A BRIEF NOTE ON THE PLAIN FORM

As you've seen in earlier lessons, all verbs have a plain form (e.g. taberu, kaeru, wakaru) which can be used in informal situations such as talking with very close friends and with your family members, and the more polite -masu form (tabemasu, kaerimasu, wakarimasu) for general use. However, when in a complex sentence, it is the predicate at the end of the sentence which determines the overall tone. So as long as this final verb is in the -masu form, any verb which occurs in the middle of the sentence can be in the plain form and still sound courteous. Here are some examples.

Takahashi san wa gorufu ga joozu da kedo, watashi wa joozu ja arimasen yo.
You're good at golf, Ms. Takahashi, but I'm not!

Watanabe san no kazoku wa ashita yama no onsen ni iku kedo, Watanabe san wa ikimasen.
Mr. Watanabe's family is going to a hot spring in the mountains tomorrow, but Mr. Watanabe isn't going.

Sushi wa tokidoki taberu kedo, amari suki ja arimasen.
Although I eat sushi sometimes, I don't really like it very much.

Oosaka kara Tookyoo made kuruma de jikan ga kakaru deshoo.
It must take a long time to go from Osaka to Tokyo by car.

We will look at the plain form of negatives and past tenses in the next few lessons.

CULTURAL
NOTE

NIHON ARUPUSU NO ONSEN / HOT SPRINGS IN THE JAPAN ALPS

There are natural hot springs (onsen) all over Japan, and staying at a nearby ryokan, or traditional Japanese-style inn, and relaxing in the hot waters of the springs is a very popular weekend pursuit. Most ryokan have several segregated baths inside the building, but also have rock pools outside which are fed by the natural hot water, and it is very pleasant to relax in the steaming water, surrounded by beautiful views of mountains, especially in the winter when snow is lying on the ground. Visiting hot springs used to be popular mainly among the older generation, but more and more young people are now beginning to enjoy this healthy pastime.

VOCABULARY

arimashita: was/were [from aru]
asa: morning
atsukatta:was hot [from atsui]
bideo: video
biiru: beer
chansu: chance, opportunity
dakara: so, therefore
dake: only
deshita: was/were [from desu]
Doo shimashita ka.: What happened?
dokoka: somewhere, anywhere
doyoobi: Saturday
ee: yes [informal]
futari: two (people)
getsuyoobi: Monday
gorufu: golf
hairimashita: went in, entered [from hairu]
heta desu: bad at, unskillful
hitori: one (person)
hitotachi: people
hontoo ni: really, truly
ikimashita: went [from iku]
itsu: when?
itte: go and... [from iku]
-jikan: — hours
joozu: skillful, good at

kaerimashita: went home [from kaeru]
kaettekimashita: came home, return home to this place
kaimashita: bought [from kau]
kakarimashita: took (time), lasted [from kakaru]
kanji: Chinese written characters
kayoobi: Tuesday
kedo: but, although
kesa: this morning
kinoo: yesterday
kin'yoobi: Friday
kissaten: coffee shop
konde imashita: was crowded [from komu]
kurasu: class
machi: town, city
...mo...mo: both...and.../neither...nor...
mokuyoobi: Thursday
nan-nin: How many people?
nan-yoobi: What day?
nanika: something, anything
ni: to, towards
nichiyoobi: Sunday
Nihon Arupusu: Japan Alps, mountain range in central Japan
...nin: [counter for people]
Nyuu Yooku: New York
o-sake/sake: sake, rice wine
omoshiroi: interesting, amusing
omoshiroku arimasen deshita: wasn't interesting [from omoshiroi]
onsen: hot spring
otoko no hito: man
paatii: party
raishuu: next week
Rondon: London
ryokan: Japanese-style inn
samukatta desu: was cold [from samui]
san-nin: three (people)
senshuu: last week
shimashita: did [from suru]
shuumatsu: weekend
soto: outside
suiyoobi: Wednesday
...tachi: [plural ending for words associated with people]
tanoshikatta desu: was fun [from tanoshii]
tenki: weather
tokoro: place
tomarimashita: stayed [from tomaru]
tomatte imashita: was/were staying [from tomaru]

tsukarete imasu: is/are tired [from tsukareru]
umi: sea, ocean
wakai: young
wasuremashita: forgot [from wasureru]
watashitachi: us, we
yama: mountain
yoru: evening
(o) yu: hot water
zannen: pity, unfortunate

TEST YOURSELF

Read through the dialogue at the beginning of the lesson again, and then say if the following statements are true or false.

Exercise A

1. Sannin ga yama e ikimashita. T/F

2. Onsen wa Nihon Arupusu no kirei-na tokoro ni arimashita. T/F

3. Tenki mo, onsen no yu mo, atsukatta desu. T/F

4. Neruson san wa, wakai hitotachi to hanashimashita. T/F

5. Watanabe san wa kaimono o shimashita ga, tanoshiku arimasen deshita. T/F

6. Watanabe san wa hitori de Tookyoo e ikimashita. T/F

Mike has decided that it's time he became more organized, so he's putting all of his appointments down on his calendar. Look at what he did last week, and then ask questions and give answers about each evening's activities, as in the example below.

Exercise B

Example: A. Getsuyoobi no yoru, nani o shimashita ka.
           B. Uchi ni ite, terebi o mimashita.

Monday	Tuesday	Wednesday	Thursday	Friday	Saturday	Sunday
stay home – watch TV	6:30–7:30 tennis practice	call Mom	6:00–8:00 Japanese class	to restaurant with Ms. Takahashi	go to ocean!	

Exercise C

Unfortunately, last week was not the success it appeared to be. In fact, something went wrong every evening. Using the notes Mike wrote on the calendar, make sentences about what went wrong each evening, as in the example. Use kedo in your answers.

Example: Getsuyoobi no yoru, uchi ni ite, terebi o mimashita kedo, zenzen omoshiroku arimasen deshita.

Monday	Tuesday	Wednesday	Thursday	Friday	Saturday	Sunday
at home – watch TV	6:30–7:30 tennis practice	call Mom	6:00–8:00 Japanese class	to restaurant with Ms. Takahashi	go to ocean!	
Completely uninteresting!	I wasn't any good!	she wasn't in!	only me!	tasted awful!	extremely cold!	

Exercise D

Ms. Takahashi is telling her friend about her visit to the movies with Mike last week. What did she say? Below are some cues to help you piece together what she said. Use the -te form to join the sentences, as in the example.

Example: (waited in front of the station – really cold!)
Eki no mae de matte, hontoo ni samukatta desu.

1. met Mike – went to Ginza – saw a movie

2. movie was SF – not interesting

3. went into coffee shop (kissaten) – drank coffee

4. we were speaking in English – difficult!

5. bad at English – was shy!

6. went home by taxi – expensive!

How would you say these sentences in Japanese?

1. When did you come back from the USA?

   _____

2. How many people went to the hot spring in the mountains?

   _____

3. It was really horrible weather.

   _____

4. We ate a lot of sushi and drank a lot of sake last night.

   _____

5. I read the paper this morning, but I've already forgotten the
   news.

   _____

6. Did you go anywhere on the weekend?

   _____

The word onsen, meaning "hot spring/
spa", is a combination of the characters
for "hot/warm" and "spring water".

Visit www.berlitzpublishing.com for a bonus internet
activity—go to the downloads section and connect to the
world in Japanese!

10

NIHON O DOO OMOIMASU KA.
WHAT DO YOU THINK OF JAPAN?

It's Friday evening, and everyone has gathered in the staff room for the formal welcome party for Mike Nelson and two other new members of staff. The other two new teachers have just given a short speech of self-introduction (*jiko shookai*), and now it's Mike's turn.

Nelson	**Mina san, hajimemashite. Watashi wa Maiku Neruson to mooshimasu. Amerika no Ohaio-shuu kara kimashita. Watashi wa san-shuukan mae ni Nihon e kimashita. Gakkoo no shigoto wa omoshiroi to omoimasu. Ganbarimasu. Yoroshiku onegai shimasu.** How do you do, everyone. I'm Mike Nelson. I'm from Ohio. I came to Japan three weeks ago. I think the work in this school is going to be very interesting. I intend to do my best. Thank you.
Takahashi	**Totemo yokatta desu yo. Nihongo ga joozu desu ne.** It was very good. Your Japanese is (very) good, isn't it?

Nelson
Iie, mada mada dame desu. Hazukashikute, taihen deshita!
No, it's still poor. It was terrible, because I was so embarrassed!

Takahashi
Daijoobu deshita yo. A, Katoo sensei desu. Neruson san wa mada atte inai deshoo. Atama ga yokute, omoshiroi hito desu yo. Shookai shimashoo.
It was fine. Ah, there's Mr. Kato [Lit: teacher Katoo]. You probably haven't met him yet, have you? He's smart, and a very interesting person. I'll introduce you.

Keiko Takahashi introduces Mike to Mr. Kato, and they chat.

Kato
Neruson sensei, Nihon wa mada san-shuukan desu ne. Nihon o doo omoimasu ka.
Mr. Nelson, you've been in Japan for only three weeks, right? What do you think of Japan?

Nelson
Nihon wa totemo omoshirokute iikuni da to omoimasu. Dai-suki desu yo.
Japan is a very interesting and great country. I like it very much.

Kato
Soo desu ka. Ii kotae desu ne. Tabemono mo daijoobu desu ka.
I see. That's a good answer! Are you okay with the food?

Nelson
Hai, Nihon ryoori wa totemo oishii to omoimasu. Sashimi ya sushi ya soba wa zenbu taberu koto ga dekimasu.
Yes, I like Japanese cooking very much. Sashimi, sushi, soba [noodles], I can eat all of it.

Kato
Soo desu ka. Ja, Nihon no seikatsu wa, mondai nai deshoo! Anoo, shumi wa nan desu ka. Supootsu wa suki desu ka.
I see. Well, you shouldn't have any problems with life in Japan! Uh, what are your interests? Do you like sports?

Takahashi
(laughing) Neruson sensei, ki o tsukete kudasai yo. Kore kara gakkoo no sensei no yakyuu chiimu no hanashi ga hajimaru to omoimasu. Katoo sensei wa yakyuu chiimu no maneejaa de, itsumo chiimu no koto dake o kangaete imasu.
Mr. Nelson, please be careful! I think he's going to talk about the school's staff baseball team. Mr. Kato is the team's manager, and he only ever thinks about the team!

> *Kato*   Sore wa uso desu yo! Neruson sensei, sensei no
>   yakyuu chiimu de issho ni yakyuu o shimasen ka.
>   That's not true! Mr. Nelson, would like to play with us in
>   the teacher's baseball team?
>
> *Nelson*   (hesitating) Watashi wa yakyuu wa suki desu kedo,
>   hayaku hashiru koto ga dekimasen.
>   I like baseball, but I can't run fast.
>
> *Kato*   Daijoobu desu yo. Tsugi no geemu wa nichiyoobi
>   no asa desu ga.
>   That's fine. The next game is on Sunday morning...
>
> *Nelson*   Nichiyoobi no asa.
>   Sunday morning?!
>
> *Takahashi* Ja, Neruson sensei, ganbatte kudasai!
>   Well, Mr. Nelson, do your best!

STRUCTURE AND USAGE NOTES

1. JIKO SHOOKAI – INTRODUCING YOURSELF

If you find yourself at any kind of gathering in Japan where some of the
people are meeting for the first time, then the newcomers will probably
be asked to do a jiko shookai, or short speech of self-introduction.
The information you give may differ depending on the kind of occasion,
but usually you would include your name and nationality, your job and
company, or university and major subject of study if you are a student.
As a foreigner, you can also mention how long you have been studying
Japanese, when you came to Japan, and what you like about Japan.
The speech usually finishes with a standard phrase of courtesy such as
yoroshiku onegai shimasu (Very nice meet you/please take good care
of me).

Here are some sentences which you might like to include in a
self-introduction.

[your name] to mooshimasu.
My name is [name].

[company or university name] no **[your name]** desu.
I'm [name] from [company or university].

[country or city name] kara kimashita.
I'm from [country or city].

Ima **[place-name]** ni sunde imasu.
I now live in [place name].

[name] daigaku de **[subject]** o benkyoo shite imasu.
I'm studying [subject] at [name] university.

[company name] ni tsutomete imasu.
I work at [company name].

---

2. ...GA JOOZU DESU – IS GOOD AT...

With the words joozu ("good at") and heta ("poor at"), the thing that
someone is good or bad at is marked by the particle ga. The person who is
good or bad at it is shown by wa.

Ogawa san wa Eigo ga joozu desu ne.
Ms. Ogawa is good at English, isn't she?

Watashi wa ryoori ga amari joozu ja arimasen.
I'm not very good at cooking.

Ane mo imooto mo piano ga joozu desu ga, watashi wa heta desu.
Both my older sister and my younger sister are good at the piano, but I'm
hopeless.

---

3. HAZUKASHIKUTE – CONNECTING -I ADJECTIVES WITH -KUTE

In the last lesson we saw how some sentences can be linked with the -te
form of verbs (Pari ni itte, tanoshikatta desu). It is similar when joining
sentences which end in -i adjectives: drop the final -i and then add -kute.

Omoshiroi eiga deshita. **+** Ii eiga deshita. **=**
Omoshirokute, ii eiga deshita.
It was a good, interesting movie.

Suugaku wa muzukashii desu. **+** Suugaku wa suki ja arimasen. **=**
Suugaku wa muzukashikute, suki ja arimasen.
Mathematics is difficult, and I don't like it.

Here are some more examples of sentences joined with -kute. Note that
in some cases, the first part of the sentence is giving a reason for what is
stated in the second part.

Atama ga itakute, ku-ji han ni nemashita.
I had a headache, and (so) I went to bed at 9:30.

Hazukashikute, dame deshita.
It was no good because I was embarrassed.

Tenki ga warukute, zannen deshita.
It's a pity the weather was bad.

Sensei no kotae wa nagakute, wakarimasen deshita.
The teacher's answer was long, and I didn't understand it.

Suugaku no jugyoo wa nagakute, omoshiroku arimasen deshita.
The math lesson was long and uninteresting.

Sono guree no suutsu wa takakute, kaimasen deshita.
That gray suit was expensive, and (so) I didn't buy it.

Mae no kaisha wa chiisakatta kedo, ima ookikute, yuumei-na kaisha
ni tsutomete imasu.
My previous company was small, but now I'm working at a large,
well-known company.

---

4. THE PLAIN FORMS OF VERBS

As mentioned before, the plain form is used for casual speech at the end of
the sentence. At the same time, there are some grammar patterns such as
deshoo that require the plain form. Remember that as long as the final verb
at the end of a sentence is in the polite form (-masu, -masen, -mashita,
etc.), the use of the plain form in the middle of the sentence does not
affect the overall tone. Some grammar patterns such as kedo can take
both the plain and polite forms. The use of the former sounds slightly more
casual than the latter.

Piano ga dekiru/dekimasu kedo, amari joozu ja arimasen.
I can (play) the piano, but I'm not very good.

Takahashi san wa Eigo ga wakaru deshoo ka.
I wonder if Ms. Takahashi understands English.

Juugyoo wa sugu hajimaru/hajimarimasu kedo, minna wa doko ni
imasu ka.
The lesson is going to begin soon – where is everyone?

Geemu wa sugu owaru deshoo.
The game will probably finish soon.

Basu wa moo sugu kuru deshoo.
The bus should come soon.

The negative of the plain form ends in -nai. With -iru/-eru verbs (see
Lesson 5, Structure and Usage Note 4), drop the final -ru and then add
-nai. Here are some examples.

Negative	Plain negative		Meaning
tabe-ru	tabe-masen	tabe-nai	doesn't eat
kangae-ru	kangae-masen	kangae-nai	doesn't think of
mi-ru	mi-masen	mi-nai	doesn't see
tsukare-ru	tsukare-masen	tsukare-nai	doesn't tire
wasure-ru	wasure-masen	wasure-nai	doesn't forget
oshie-ru	oshie-masen	oshie-nai	doesn't teach
i-ru	i-masen	i-nai	isn't in

Saitoo san wa sakana o tabenai deshoo.
Ms. Saitoo doesn't eat fish, am I right?

Watashi wa ashita kaisha ni inai/imasen kedo, asatte hachi-ji han ni wa kaisha ni imasu.
I won't be in the office tomorrow, but I'll be in at 8:30 the day after tomorrow.

Terebi wa amari minai deshoo.
You don't usually watch TV, do you?

Kao wa wasurenai/wasuremasen kedo, namae wa sugu wasuremasu.
I don't forget faces, but I quickly forget names.

With the other group of verbs – those that drop -u to make other forms – you need to add -anai to make the plain negative. (In cases where the stem ends with a vowel, -wanai is added.)

Negative	Plain negative		Meaning
nom-u	nom-imasen	nom-anai	doesn't drink
hanas-u	hanash-imasen	hanas-anai	doesn't speak
omo-u	omo-imasen	omo-wanai	doesn't think
hashir-u	hashir-imasen	hashir-anai	doesn't run
ka-u	ka-imasen	ka-wanai	doesn't buy
mats-u	mach-imasen	mat-anai	doesn't wait

ik-u	ik-imasen	ik-anai	doesn't go
kak-u	kak-imasen	kak-anai	doesn't write
wakar-u	wakar-imasen	wakar-anai	doesn't understand

Takahashi san wa Eigo ga amari wakaranai/wakarimasen kedo, Eigo no juugyoo de yoku ganbarimasu.
Ms. Takahashi doesn't really understand English, but she tries hard in English class.

Ani wa ikanai/ikimasen kedo, watashi wa ikimasu.
My older brother isn't going, but I am.

Itoo san wa koohii o nomanai deshoo.
Mr. Itoo doesn't drink coffee, does he?

Kaigi wa mada mada owaranai deshoo.
The meeting probably isn't going to finish yet.

The irregular verbs are:

kuru	kimasen	konai	doesn't come
suru	shimasen	shinai	doesn't do
aru	arimasen	nai	there isn't

Kotae wa nai deshoo.
There isn't an answer, is there?

Ogawa sensei wa kyoo konai deshoo. Doo shimashoo ka.
Mr. Ogawa probably isn't coming today. What shall we do?

Supootsu wa amari shinai/shimasen kedo, terebi de yoku mimasu.
I don't do many sports, but I often watch it on TV.

The plain forms of desu are da (positive) and dewa nai or ja nai (negative).

Taiiku no sensei wa ii hito da/desu kedo, chotto hen desu ne!
The physical education teacher is nice, but he's a bit strange, isn't he!

Soo ja nai deshoo.
That's probably not so.

Muzukashii mondai ja nai/arimasen kedo, chotto jikan ga kakarimasu.
It's not a difficult problem, but it will take a little time.

We will look at the plain form of past tenses in the next lesson.

5. MADA ATTE INAI – NOT YET

When something hasn't yet happened, it is often described using the -te imasen/-te inai form.

Hiru-gohan o mada tabete imasen.
I haven't eaten lunch yet.

Rekishi no shukudai wa mada owatte inai deshoo.
You haven't finished your history homework yet, right?

Neruson san wa, sensei no yakyuu chiimu ni mada haitte imasen ne.
You haven't joined the staff baseball team yet, have you Mr. Nelson?

Taiiku no sensei wa mada kite imasen.
The physical education teacher isn't here yet.

Takashi san ni mada denwa shite imasen. Kore kara denwa shimasu.
I haven't called Takashi yet. I'll call him now.

---

6. ...TO OMOIMASU – I THINK THAT...

Unlike English, the phrase for "I think" – to omoimasu – is often added to the end of a sentence when giving an opinion. You'll see by comparing the pairs of sentences below that there's no need to make any changes to the sentence which is expressed as the thought, except that the predicate of the sentence is put into the plain form. The word to before omoimasu is used to mark a quotation, so it is also used before verbs with meanings such as "say", "think", "ask", "shout", etc.

Sore wa zannen desu.
That's a pity.

Sore wa zannen da to omoimasu.
I think that's a pity.

Takahashi san wa kimasen.
Ms. Takahashi isn't coming.

Takahashi san wa konai to omoimasu.
I don't think Ms. Takahashi is coming. [Lit: I think...isn't coming.]

Neruson san wa ima Eigo no kurasu o oshiete imasu.
Mr. Nelson is teaching an English class at the moment.

Neruson san wa ima Eigo no kurasu o oshiete iru to omoimasu.
I think Mr. Nelson is teaching an English class at the moment.

Mondai wa arimasen.
There aren't any problems.

Mondai wa nai to omoimasu.
I don't think there are any problems.

Here are some other examples using to omoimasu.

Are wa uso da to omoimasu.
I don't think that's true.

Ano Furansu ryoori no resutoran wa zenzen oishiku nai to omoimasu.
I don't think that French restaurant is good at all.

Sono hito wa Nihon no koto ga zenzen wakaranai to omoimasu.
I don't think he understands anything about Japan.

Nihon de no seikatsu wa muzukashii to omoimasu ka.
Do you think living in Japan is difficult?

If you want to talk about what someone else is thinking, then it's common to use omotte imasu.

Maiku san wa, Nihon wa ii kuni da to omotte imasu.
Mike thinks that Japan is a great country.

Takahashi san mo soo omotte imasu.
Ms. Takahashi thinks so too.

Maiku san wa Nihon no terebi wa amari omoshiroku nai to omotte imasu.
Mike thinks that Japanese television isn't very interesting.

As the question in the dialogue, doo is the question word to go with to omoimasu.

Nihon o doo omoimasu ka.
What do you think of Japan?

Often times, no koto is added like in the following example, especially when talking about people.

Watanabe san no koto o doo omoimasu ka.
What do you think about Mr. Watanabe?

Both kangaeru and omou may be translated into English as "think", but there is a difference between them. Omou is used when you are talking about an opinion or feeling, whereas kangaeru means "to consider/think about".

Nani o kangaete imasu ka.
What are you thinking about?

Chiimu no koto o kangaete imashita.
I was thinking about the team.

7. SASHIMI YA SUSHI YA – SASHIMI AND SUSHI, ETC.

The word ya, like to, means "and" when used to join a list of items, but when ya is used, it implies that the items you have mentioned are just a sample, and that there are others on the list that you haven't mentioned. (To make this meaning more obvious, you can also add nado, "*et cetera*", if you wish.)

Sono gakkoo dewa Eigo ya Furansugo ya Doitsugo (nado) no jugyoo ga arimasu.
At that school there are classes such as English, French, German and the like.

Kyooto ya Nara (nado) e ikimashita.
I went to Kyoto, Nara, etc.

Kaisha ni yakyuu chiimu ya basukettobooru chiimu ga arimasu.
At work we have a baseball team, a basketball team, etc.

---

8. ...KOTO GA DEKIMASU – CAN/BE ABLE TO

There are several ways of saying "can/am able to" in Japanese, but the easiest way is to add koto ga dekimasu to the plain form of the verb. It literally means "—ing is possible".

Maiku san wa kanji o kaku koto ga dekimasu ka.
Mike, can you write kanji characters?

Soko e wa, basu de iku koto ga dekimasen.
You can't get there by bus.

Sumimasen ga, ashita made ni kagaku no shukudai o dasu koto ga dekimasen.
I'm sorry, but I won't be able to turn in my science homework by tomorrow.

Kore o zenbu taberu koto ga dekinai to omoimasu.
I don't think I can eat all this. [Lit: I can't eat all this, I think.]

Sumimasen ga, shigoto ga mada takusan atte, konban au koto ga dekinai to omoimasu.
I'm sorry, but I still have a lot of work to do, and (so) I don't think we'll be able to meet this evening.

In cases where it is obvious what the verb is going to be, it isn't necessary to mention it.

Nihongo ga dekimasu ka.
Can you (speak) Japanese?

Tenisu ga dekimasu ka.
Can you (play) tennis?

Piano ga dekimasu ka.
Can you (play) the piano?

VOCABULARY

aru: there is/are [plain form of arimasu]
atama ga yokute: is clever and…
atte inai: haven't met [from au]
basu: bus
basukettobooru: basketball
booifurendo: boyfriend
chiimu: team
da: is/are [plain form of desu]
dasu: submit
dekimashita: were able to [from dekiru]
Doo omoimasu ka.: What do you think?
Doitsugo: German language
Furansu: France
Furansugo: French language
Ganbarimasu.: I'll do my best. [from ganbaru]
geemu: game
hashiru: run
hayaku: quickly
hazukashikute: embarrassed and…[from hazukashii]
jiko shookai: self-introduction
jugyoo: lesson, class
kagaku: science
kangaete imasu: think about [from kangaeru]
kao: face
kotae: answer, response
koto ga dekimasu: can, be possible [from dekiru]
koto: thing, event, fact
kuni: country
Mada mada dame desu.: I'm still no good (at…)
made ni: by, by the time
mae ni: before, previously
maneejaa: manager
nado: and so on, *et cetera*
nagai: long
nai: there isn't/aren't [from aru]
Ohaio-shuu: the state of Ohio
omoshirokute: interesting and…
owaru: finish, end [verb]

piano: piano
rekishi: history
ryoori: cooking, cuisine
soba: noodles
san-shuukan: three weeks
seikatsu: life, living
Shookai shimashoo.: Let me introduce you.
...shuukan: ...weeks [e.g. two weeks: ni-shuukan]
shumi: interest, hobby
suugaku: mathematics
supootsu: sport
sushi: raw fish with rice
tabemono: food
taiiku: physical education, training
to mooshimasu: am called [from moosu]
to omoimasu: I think [from omou]
tsutomete imasu: be employed [from tsutomeru]
uso: untruth, story, lie
Watanabe san no koto: about Mr. Watanabe
ya: and [so on]
zenzen: not at all [with negative ending]

TEST YOURSELF

Read through the dialogue at the beginning of the lesson again, and then say if the following statements are true or false.

1. Maiku san wa ni-shuukan mae ni Nihon ni imashita. T/F

2. Katoo san wa Maiku san no gakkoo de oshiete imasen. T/F

3. Watanabe san wa, Katoo san ga omoshiroi hito da to omotte imasu. T/F

4. Maiku san wa Nihon ryoori ga zenzen suki ja arimasen. T/F

5. Katoo san wa sensei no yakyuu chiimu no koto o hanashimasu. T/F

6. Maiku san wa yakyuu ga dekimasu. T/F

Exercise A

Exercise B

The other new teachers at the welcome party also had to introduce themselves. Here is some information about one of them. How do you think she introduced herself?

Name: Yoko Fukuda
From: Kyoto
Teaches: French
Background: Studied French at Osaka University, then went to France, and studied French again at a university in Paris.
Interests: movies, sports

"Watashi wa Fukuda Yooko to _____. Hajimemashite. Kyooto _____. Furansugo _____ _____. Oosaka Daigaku de _____. Sore kara Furansu e _____, Pari _____ mata _____. Shumi wa _____ to _____. Doozo yoroshiku onegai shimasu."

Exercise C

It's already late on Friday afternoon, but the teachers at Mike's school have to stay behind for a teachers' meeting. Everyone around the table is finding it hard to concentrate, as the principal makes a long and boring speech. Make sentences about what each person is thinking, as in the example.

Example: Takahashi: "It'll soon be 5:30".
           Takahashi san wa, moo sugu go-ji han da to omotte imasu.

1. Ms. Wada: "My friend's waiting in front of the station".

   _____

2. Ms. Fukuda: "This school is strange!"

   _____

3. Mr. Itoo: "The coffee isn't very tasty".

   _____

4. Mike: "I don't understand Mr. Ogawa's Japanese very well".

   _____

5. Mr. Katoo: "Mr. Watanabe is sleeping!"

   _____

6. Ms. Nakayama: "I can't meet Ms. Tanaka tonight".

   _____

Respond to the following comments by adding comments of your own, as in the example.

Example: Kono akai seetaa wa takai desu ne. (kirei ja nai)
Soo desu ne. Takakute, kirei ja arimasen ne.

1. Kagaku no jugyoo wa nagai desu ne. (omoshiroku nai)

2. Kono resutoran wa yasui desu ne. (oishii)

3. Doitsugo wa muzukashii desu ne. (suki ja nai)

4. Nakayama san wa atama ga ii desu ne. (kirei)

5. Kyoo wa atsui desu ne. (ii tenki)

6. Kono basu wa hayai desu ne. (yasui)

How would you say the following sentences in Japanese?

1. Mr. Tanaka is always thinking about work.

2. The next lesson begins at 2:30, and finishes at 3:20, I think.

3. The fish was good, and I ate lots.

4. I don't like math, but I like science.

5. The train will probably come soon.

6. Can you read a Japanese newspaper?

Exercise D

Exercise E

学校   **Gakkoo,** the word for "school", uses a combination of the kanji characters for "learning/study" and "school/correction".

 Visit www.berlitzpublishing.com for a bonus internet activity—go to the downloads section and connect to the world in Japanese!

MADA O-HITORI DESU KA.
ARE YOU STILL SINGLE?

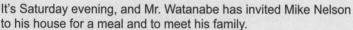

It's Saturday evening, and Mr. Watanabe has invited Mike Nelson to his house for a meal and to meet his family.

Nelson   **Oishi-soo desu ne.**
This looks good.

Miho   **Doozo, enryo shinaide tabete kudasai.**
Please help yourself. [Lit: Please eat, don't be shy.]

Nelson   **Ja, itadakimasu.**
Thank you.

Miho   **O-hashi ga o-joozu desu ne.**
You're very good with chopsticks, aren't you?

Nelson   **Arigatoo gozaimasu. Demo hashi wa Amerika de mo tokidoki tsukaimasu yo.**
Thank you. But we use chopsticks sometimes in America too, you know.

Miho   **Ee? Amerikajin mo o-hashi o tsukau n desu ka.**
What? Americans use chopsticks too?

Nelson	Ee, Nihon ryoori ya Chuuka ryoori no resutoran ga takusan arimasu kara, tokidoki tsukaimasu. Yes, there are lots of Japanese and Chinese restaurants, so we sometimes use them.
Hiro	Neruson san, Nihon ryoori no naka de, nani ga ichiban suki desu ka. Mr. Nelson, What is your favorite dish [what Japanese dish do you like the best]?
Nelson	Muzukashii shitsumon desu ne. Iroiro suki da kara. Hmmmm. Ichiban suki-na no wa tenpura desu. Sushi mo dai-suki desu. That's a difficult question. I like all kinds, so… Hmmm. The (food) I like best is tempura. I also really like sushi.
Miho	Kyoo wa o-sushi ga takusan arimasu kara, doozo tabete kudasai! We have lots of sushi today, so please eat up!
Hiro	Neruson san wa yon-shuukan mae ni Nihon e kita n desu ne. You came to Japan four weeks ago, didn't you, Mr. Nelson?
Nelson	Hai, soo desu. Choodo yon-shuukan mae desu. Yes, that's right. Exactly four weeks ago.
Hiro	Nihongo ga yoku dekiru ne! Boku wa ni-nen-kan Eigo o benkyoo shite iru kedo, mada zenzen joozu ja nai yo. You can speak Japanese well, can't you! My older brother has been studying English for two years, but he's still no good at it.
Miho	Sonna koto arimasen yo. O-niisan wa kurasu no naka de ichiban na n desu yo. That's not true! He's number one in the class!
Nelson	(laughing) Nihongo no benkyoo wa kono yon-shuukan dake ja nai n desu yo. Amerika no daigaku de mo, ni-nen-kan benkyoo shita kara, ima sukoshi dekiru n desu. My study of Japanese hasn't been just these four weeks. I also studied for two years at a university in the USA, so I can speak a little.
Miho	Soo desu ka. Ne, Neruson san, shitsurei desu ga, o-ikutsu desu ka. I see. Uh, Mr. Nelson, excuse me, but how old are you?

Nelson	Yoku aru shitsumon desu ne. Watashi wa san-juu roku desu.
	That's a common question, isn't it? I'm thirty-six.
Miho	San-juu-roku-sai desu ka. Mada o-hitori desu ka.
	Thirty-six years old? Are you still single?
Nelson	Ima hitori desu. Mae ni kekkon shite ita n desu kedo, ni-nen mae ni rikon shita n desu.
	I am now. I was married before, but I got divorced two years ago.
Miho	Soo desu ka. Hen-na shitsumon o shite, gomen nasai. Sa, Neruson san, biiru moo sukoshi doo desu ka.
	Oh, I see. I'm sorry for asking a strange question. Well, Mr. Nelson, how about some more beer?

STRUCTURE AND USAGE NOTES

1. QUESTIONS FOREIGNERS ARE OFTEN ASKED

There are certain questions that you are likely to be asked over and over again in Japan, so you should be able to answer them smoothly. Here are some of them, with possible responses.

Q. Nan-sai desu ka./O-ikutsu desu ka.
How old are you?

A. Juu-nana-sai desu./Ni-juu-kyuu-sai desu./Go-jus-sai desu.
I'm seventeen./I'm twenty-nine./I'm fifty.

Q. O-kuni wa dochira desu ka.
What country are you from?

A. Amerika desu./Amerikajin desu.
I'm from the USA./I'm American.

Q. Amerikajin desu ka.
Are you American?

A. Hai, soo desu./Iie, Igirisujin desu./Iie, Kanadajin desu.
Yes, I am./No, I'm British./No, I'm Canadian.

Q. Nihon o doo omoimasu ka.
What do you think of Japan?

A. Dai-suki desu./Hito ga ooi desu ne./Ii kuni da to omoimasu.
I like it very much./It's very crowded, isn't it?/I think it's a great country.

Q. Itsu Nihon e kimashita ka.
When did you come to Japan?
A. Senshuu no kayoobi ni kimashita./Ichi-nen mae ni kimashita.
Last Tuesday. [Lit: Last week's Tuesday.]/A year ago.

Q. Itsu made Nihon ni imasu ka.
When are you in Japan until?
A. Raishuu no mokuyoobi made desu.
Until next Thursday. [Lit: Until next week's Thursday.]

Q. O-hashi wa daijoobu desu ka.
Are you okay with chopsticks?
A. Hai, daijoobu desu.
Yes, I'm fine.

Q. O-hashi ga joozu desu ne.
You're good at (using) chopsticks.
A. Arigatoo gozaimasu.
Thank you.

Q. Sashimi o taberu koto ga dekimasu ka.
Can you eat raw fish?
A. Hai, dai-suki desu.
Yes, I like it very much.

Q. Kekkon shite imasu ka./O-hitori desu ka.
Are you married?/Are you single?
A. Hai, soo desu./Iie, mada desu./Iie, kekkon shite imasu./Rikkon shite imasu.
Yes, I am./No, not yet./No, I'm married./I'm divorced.

---

2. DESCRIBING HOW SOMETHING LOOKS

To describe how something looks or appears to be, add -soo to the appropriate adjective. With -i adjectives, you need to drop the final -i first. With -na adjectives, simply add -soo after them. This is the equivalent of saying "it looks/seems…"

Hashi wa muzukashi-soo da kedo, jitsu wa muzukashiku arimasen.
Chopsticks look difficult (to use), but in fact they're not (difficult).

Wada san no atarashii suutsu o mite kudasai yo. Taka-soo desu ne.
Hey, look at Mr. Wada's new suit. It looks expensive, doesn't it?

Watanabe san no kodomotachi wa genki-soo desu ne.
Mr. Watanabe's children seem lively, don't they?

Maiku san wa yakyuu ga joozu-soo desu ne!
Mike seems good at baseball, doesn't he?

The -soo form of ii/yoi is irregular: yosa-soo ("looks good").

Kono kissaten wa yosa-soo desu yo. Hairimashoo.
This coffee shop looks good. Let's go in.

Katoo sensei wa atama ga yosa-soo desu ne.
Mr. Katoo looks clever, doesn't he?

This pattern is also used to describe how you think someone else is feeling, as it is generally considered that you can't really *know* how they're feeling, only how they *appear* to be feeling.

Takashi san wa tomodachi ga takusan iru kedo, itsumo sabishi-soo ne.
Takashi has lots of friends, but he always looks lonely, doesn't he?

Watanabe san wa atama ga ita-soo desu ne. Daijoobu deshoo ka.
Mr. Watanabe looks as if he has a headache. I wonder if he's all right.

Maiku san wa kyoo ureshi-soo desu ne.
Mike looks happy today, doesn't he?

---

3. PLAIN FORM + NO DESU

When a sentence ends in no desu, or more colloquially n desu, it often indicates that the speaker is explaining something, or asking for an explanation of something. It is also used to indicate emphasis, where a speaker shares a particular situation with his/her listener. In English, it can be translated as "it's that...." N desu can follow the plain form of a verb, an -i adjective, or a -na adjective (with -na). Pronounce it as if the n ends the previous word (e.g. takai n desu = takain desu).

Iroiro-na mondai ga arimasu kedo, doo suru n desu ka.
There are all sort of problems, but what are you going to do?

Nani o shite iru n desu ka.
What are you doing?

Kono terebi wa moo dame-na n desu yo. Atarashii no o kaimashoo.
This TV is no good any more! Let's buy a new one.

Doo shite atarashii konpyuutaa o tsukawanai n desu ka.
Why don't you use the new computer?

Q: Doo shite kawanai n desu ka.
  Why aren't you going to buy (that)?

A: Totemo takai n desu yo. Dakara kawanai n desu.
  It's really expensive! That's why I'm not buying it.

4. ICHIBAN – SUPERLATIVES

If you want to say that something is biggest, best, fastest, most beautiful, then all you need do is add ichiban before the relevant adjective. Think of it as meaning "most", or more literally "number one".

Nihon de ichiban takai yama wa Fuji-san desu.
The highest mountain in Japan is Mount Fuji.

Tenpura ga ichiban oishii to omoimasu.
I think tempura tastes the best.

Kurasu no naka de, dare ga ichiban wakai desu ka.
Who's the youngest in the class?

Nihonjin no namae no naka de, nani ga ichiban ooi desu ka.
Which Japanese name is most common?

Ichiban suki-na tokoro wa doko desu ka.
What is your favorite place?

5. PLAIN FORM OF PAST TENSE VERBS

In the previous lesson we looked at the plain form of present tense verbs (taberu, nomu, ikanai). There are also plain forms of the past tenses. In the positive ("went", "did", "ate", "drank", etc.), it is formed like the -te form, but ends in -ta instead.

Present plain	-te form	Past plain	Meaning
iku	itte	itta	went
kuru	kite	kita	came
suru	shite	shita	did
tsukau	tsukatte	tsukatta	used
aru	atte	atta	there was/were
iru	ite	ita	was/were
omou	omotte	omotta	thought
wakaru	wakatte	wakatta	understood
au	atte	atta	met

Doo shita n deshoo.
I wonder what happened.

Sensei wa doko ni itta n desu ka.
Where's the teacher gone?

Kyoo wa kin'yoobi da to omotta kedo, chigaimasu ne!
I thought it was Friday today, but it isn't, is it!

Choodo ichi-nen mae ni Nihon e kita n desu kedo, Nihongo wa mada mada joozu ja nai n desu.
I came to Japan exactly a year ago, but my Japanese still isn't very good.

Kaigi de wa, iroiro-na shitsumon ga atta n desu kedo, ii setsumei ga amari arimasen deshita.
There were all kinds of questions at the meeting, but there weren't really any answers.

Doko de ano hito ni atta n desu ka.
Where did you meet her/him (that person)?

Ano hito no kao wa oboete imasu kedo, namae o wasurete imashita.
I remember her/his face, but I didn't remember her/his name.

With the negative past ("didn't go", "didn't do", "didn't eat", etc.), change the present negative -nai ending to -nakatta.

Present plain	Negative plain	Negative past plain	Meaning
iku	ikanai	ikanakatta	didn't go
kuru	konai	konakatta	didn't come
wakaru	wakaranai	wakaranakatta	didn't understand
tsukau	tsukawanai	tsukawanakatta	didn't use
suru	shinai	shinakatta	didn't do
aru	nai	nakatta	there wasn't
iru	inai	inakatta	wasn't in
yomu	yomanai	yomanakatta	didn't read
kaku	kakanai	kakanakatta	didn't write
taberu	tabenai	tabenakatta	didn't eat

Takahashi san wa doo shite kinoo no ban konakatta n deshoo ka.
I wonder why Ms. Takahashi didn't come yesterday evening.

Sono kotae wa yoku wakaranakatta n desu kedo, moo ichido
setsumei shite kudasai.
I didn't understand that answer very well. Could you explain it once more,
please?

Kinoo no asa Wada san ni denwa shita kedo, kaisha ni inakatta n
desu.
I called Ms. Wada yesterday morning, but she wasn't in the office.

Doo shite Shinkansen de ikanakatta n desu ka.
Why didn't you go by Shinkansen (Bullet Train)?

The comparable forms for desu are datta ("was/were") and ja nakatta
("wasn't/weren't").

Senshuu no tesuto de watashi wa ichiban datta n desu ga, konshuu
wa moo dame da to omoimasu.
In last week's test, I was first, but this week I don't think I'll be any good.

San-nen-kan Nyuu Yooku ni sunde ita n desu kedo, amari suki ja
arimasen deshita.
I lived in New York for three years, but I didn't like it much.

---

6. PLAIN FORM + KARA – BECAUSE

When you want to explain the reason for something (in other words, where
you might say "because" or "so" in English), the word you need is kara.
Note that unlike "because" in English, kara always comes after a reason. In
other words, the order in a sentence has to be "reason", kara and "result".
Both polite and plain forms are used before kara.

Shinkansen de itta kara, jikan ga amari kakarimasen deshita.
We went by Shinkansen, so it didn't take very long. [Lit: Because we went
by Shinkansen, ...]

Shitsumon ga mada ooi desu kara, moo ichido setsumei shimashoo.
There are still a lot of questions, so let me explain it again. [Lit: Because
there are still a lot of questions, ...]

Katoo san wa omoshirokute ii hito da kara, tomodachi ga ooi deshoo.
Mr. Kato is an interesting and nice man, so I'm sure he has many friends.

Maiku san wa Nihon no koto ga yoku wakaru kara, Nihon no seikatsu
wa mondai nai to omoimasu.
Mike understands well about Japan, so I don't think he'll have any
problems with Japanese life.

Kono purintaa wa amari yokunai kara, are o tsukatte kudasai.
Because this printer is not very good, please use that one.

Like English, it is possible to state a reason.

A. Saitoo san wa isogashi-soo desu ne.
Ms. Saito looks busy, doesn't she?

B. Ee, shigoto ga takusan arimasu kara.
Yes, because she has a lot of work.

When you put kara at the end of the sentence, what's before it has to be in a polite form. Another way is to end with kara desu, with which a plain form is required before kara. The last option is to use no desu (n desu). Look at the following examples.

A. Doo shite kyoo yakyuu o shinai n desu ka.
Why don't you play baseball today?

B. Kyoo wa kaimono ni ikimasu kara.
Kyoo wa kaimono ni iku kara desu.
Kyoo wa kaimono ni iku n desu.
Because I'm going shopping today.

---

7. TALKING ABOUT PERIODS OF TIME

To talk about something which has been going on for some time simply use the -te imasu form. This corresponds to the "have/has been -ing" form in English.

Ni-nen-kan Nihongo o benkyoo shite imasu.
I've been studying Japanese for two years.

Choodo ichi-nen-kan kono uchi ni sunde imasu.
I've been living in this house for just a year.

San-ji han kara denwa de hanashite imasu yo.
She's been talking on the phone since 3:30!

Chichi wa juu-nen mae kara sono kaisha ni tsutomete imasu.
My father has been working at that company for ten years. [Lit: since ten years ago]

Moo ichi-jikan-han matte imasu ga, mada kite imasen.
I've been waiting an hour and a half already, but he hasn't come yet.

VOCABULARY

Amerika de mo: in the U.S. too
ban: evening
boku: I [informal, used by men and young boys]
choodo: exactly, precisely
Chuuka ryoori: Chinese cuisine
dansei: males, men

dochira: where? [formal]
enryo sezuni: without any hesitation
Fuji san: Mount Fuji
gaarufurendo: girlfriend
ichiban suki (desu): like the most
ichiban: the first, number one, most
iroiro: all kinds of, various
jitsu wa: in fact
josei: females, women
kara: because
kekkon shite ita: was married [from kekkon suru]
kinoo no ban: yesterday evening
kita: came [from kuru]
kodomotachi: children
moo ichido: once more
ni-nen mae ni: two years ago
ni-nen-kan: a two-year period
no naka de: among, within
o-hitori: single, unmarried
o-ikutsu: how old?
ooi: many, abundant, a lot of
oishi-soo: looks tasty
rikon shita: got divorced [from rikon suru]
sabishii: lonely
...-sai: ...years old
san-juu-roku-sai: thirty-six years old
setsumei: explanation
Shinkansen: (name of Japan's high-speed train) Bullet Train
shita: did [from suru]
shitsumon: question
tenpura: tempura (deep fried food)
tsukaimasu: use [from tsukau]
...tsukau n desu ka.: Do you use...?
ureshii: happy
yoku aru: frequently occurring

TEST YOURSELF

Read through the dialogue at the beginning of the lesson again, and then say if the following statements are true or false.

1. Nelson san wa hashi o tsukau koto ga dekimasu. T/F

2. Nelson san wa tenpura mo sushi mo dai-suki desu. T/F

3. Takashi san no o-niisan wa gakkoo de Eigo o benkyoo shite imasu. T/F

4. Nelson san wa Nihon de dake Nihongo o benkyoo shite imasu. T/F

5. Nelson san wa biiru o nonde imasu. T/F

6. Nelson san wa kekkon shite imasu. T/F

Exercise B

Complete the crossword by filling in the answers to the clues, and find out who is coming to visit Mike in Japan next month.

1. once more
2. used (informal)
3. marriage
4. most, number one
5. drank (informal)
6. various

7. expensive looking
8. question
9. explanation
10. bought (informal)
11. last week

Exercise C

Make up questions and give answers about which of the choices given is the longest, shortest, biggest, etc., as in the example.

Example: kuruma, densha, Shinkansen - hayai
       Q. Kuruma to densha to Shinkansen no naka de, dore ga ichiban hayai desu ka.
       A. Shinkansen ga ichiban hayai to omoimasu.

1. Fuji san, Eberesuto, Makkinrii - takai

_____

_____

2. Tookyoo, Rondon, Manira - atsui

3. Eigo, Nihongo, Doitsugo - muzukashii

4. sake, biiru, wain - suki

5. eiga, supootsu, kaimono - tanoshii

6. aka, shiro, kuro - suki

Exercise D

You've just come out of a long meeting, and your friend, who's been waiting for you, questions you too closely for comfort about it. Answer his questions, in each case predicting what his next question is going to be based on your answer, as in the example.

Example: Q. Doo shite issho ni tenisu o shinakatta n desu ka.
A. (have a lot of studying) Benkyoo ga takusan atta kara.
Q. Doo shite benkyoo ga takusan atta n desu ka.
A. (had a test)Tesuto ga atta kara.
Q. Doo shite etc.

1. Doo shite kaigi ga san-ji ni owaranakatta n desu ka.
(there were lots of questions)

2. Why were there lots of questions?
(because the explanation wasn't very good)

3. Why wasn't the ...?
(because I hadn't studied the report much)

4. Why hadn't you ...?
(because I had a headache)

5. Why…?
(because last night [kinoo no ban] I drank a lot)

_____

6. Why…?
(because it was my friend's birthday)

_____

How would you say the following sentences in Japanese?

1. Mr. Fukuda got married three years ago.

_____

2. Ms. Takahashi's boyfriend is handsome and kind-looking, isn't he?

_____

3. What sport do you like best?

_____

4. I think that he phoned at 2:30.

_____

5. Ms. Tanaka has a headache this morning, so I don't think she'll go to work.

_____

6. I bought my car three years ago, but it still looks new.

_____

The word joozu, meaning "skillful/good at", is made up of the characters for "top/above" and "hand".

Visit www.berlitzpublishing.com for a bonus internet activity—go to the downloads section and connect to the world in Japanese!

DAI NANA-KA KARA DAI JUU-IK-KA MADE NO FUKUSHUU.
REVIEW OF LESSONS 7 TO 11.

Read Dialogues 7 to 11 aloud, and try to understand the meaning without referring back to the English translations in previous lessons.

Dialogue 7: Aa atama ga itai!

Ikuo Watanabe had a late night out last night, and he has just woken up, feeling somewhat the worse for wear. He goes downstairs and greets his wife, Miho.

> Miho   A, ohayoo. Chooshi wa doo.
>
> Ikuo   Itai! Atama ga itai! Ima nan-ji.
>
> Miho   Osoi wa yo. Moo juu-ni-ji jup-pun mae yo. Koohii wa.
>
> Ikuo   A, ii ne. Tomoko to Takashi to Hiro wa doko ni iru.

Miho	Tomoko wa tonari no uchi de, tomodachi to issho ni terebi o miteru. Takashi wa ni-kai de gakkoo no Eigo no shukudai o shiteru.
Ikuo	Hiro wa.
Miho	Hiro wa gakkoo de yakyuu no renshuu. Moo sugu kaettekuru. Hai, koohii. Atsui yo. Ki o tsukete.
Takashi	(running downstairs) O-toosan, ohayoo!
Miho	Takashi, ki o tsukete. O-toosan wa koohii o nonde iru no yo.
Ikuo	Takashi, Eigo no shukudai wa doo. Muzukashii.
Takashi	Unn, muzukashiku nai yo. Eigo wa suki dakara.
Miho	A, moo hiru-gohan no jikan ne. Takashi, Tomoko o yonde kite. Mada tonari ni iru no yo.
Takashi	Hai.
Miho	(to her husband) Ne, kyoo no gogo wa minna de Kawasaki ni ittekuru ne.
Ikuo	Ee. Kawasaki. Doo shite.
Miho	Oboete nai no. Kyoo wa okaasan no tanjoobi deshoo.
Ikuo	O-kaasan no tanjoobi. Itte (i)rasshai. A, atama ga itai! Mata neru yo.

1. QUESTIONS:

1. Watanabe san wa kesa genki desu ka.
2. Moo juu-ni-ji desu ka.
3. Kodomotachi no naka de, dare ga uchi ni imasu ka.
4. Watanabe san no okusan wa doo shite kyoo no gogo Kawasaki ni ikimasu ka.

Dialogue 8: Iya desu ne.

Ikuo Watanabe has reluctantly agreed to go shopping with his wife, Miho, as she has persuaded him that he needs a new suit. They are now in the menswear section of a large department store in Ginza, Tokyo's central shopping area.

Miho	Suutsu wa doko kashira. (to sales assistant) Anoo, sumimasen, suutsu wa doko deshoo ka.
Clerk	Suutsu desu ka. Koko o moo sukoshi massugu itte kudasai. Migi-gawa ni gozaimasu.

143

Miho	Doomo. A, koko da. Kono guree no suutsu wa ii ne.
Ikuo	Guree wa dame. Suki ja nai yo.
Miho	Soo. Ja, kono buruu no wa doo. (looking inside at the label) A, kono dezainaa wa yuumei yo. Ii ne.
Ikuo	Yuumei-na dezainaa. Takai daro. Motto yasui suutsu ga ii na. A, kore ga ii.
Miho	Sore wa ii kedo, saizu wa chotto chiisai ne. (to sales assistant) Sumimasen, motto ookii saizu wa arimasu ka.
Clerk	Gozaimasu. Kochira e doozo.

Mr. Watanabe goes off to try on the suit, and while the rest of the family is waiting for him, Mrs. Watanabe suddenly sees one of her acquaintances.

Miho	A, Kawada san, konnichiwa! O-hisashiburi desu ne.
Kawada	A, Watanabe san, konnichiwa. O-genki desu ka.
Miho	Hai, genki desu. O-kage sama de. Kawada san wa.
Kawada	Hai, o-kage sama de. Watashi mo genki desu.
Miho	Kyoo wa konde imasu ne.
Kawada	Soo desu ne. Iya desu ne. Kaimono wa kirai ja nai desu ga, Ginza no depaato wa itsumo konde iru deshoo. Watanabe san wa yoku Ginza e kimasu ka.
Miho	Tokidoki kimasu. Watashi mo kaimono wa suki desu ga, kyoo wa shujin no atarashii suutsu o mite imasu…
Kawada	A, soo desu ka. Go-shujin to issho desu ka.
Miho	Soo desu! (Mr. Watanabe comes out of the room where he changed suits) A, shujin desu. Doo. Saizu wa daijoobu.
Ikuo	Saizu wa daijoobu da kedo, dezain ga chotto…

1. QUESTIONS:

1. Watanabe san to okusan wa, doko de kaimono o shite imasu ka.
2. Ima nani o mite imasu ka.
3. Watanabe san wa doo shite buruu no suutsu wa dame da to omotte imasu ka.
4. Watanabe san wa kaimono ga suki da to omoimasu ka.

Dialogue 9: Shuumatsu wa doo deshita ka.

It's Monday morning, and as Ikuo Watanabe waits on the station platform for the train to work, he bumps into Mike Nelson.

Watanabe   Ohayoo gozaimasu.

Nelson   Ohayoo gozaimasu. Kyoo wa, densha wa konde imasu ne.

Watanabe   Soo desu ne. Getsuyoobi wa itsumo soo desu ne. Tokorode, shuumatsu wa doo deshita ka. Dokoka e ikimashita ka.

Nelson   Ee, totemo tanoshikatta desu. Tomodachi futari to issho ni, yama e ikimashita. Doyoobi no asa itte, kinoo no yoru kaette kimashita. Dakara kesa chotto tsukarete imasu.

Watanabe   Ii desu ne. Doko ni ikimashita ka.

Nelson   Nihon Arupusu no onsen ni ikimashita. Machi no namae wa wasuremashita kedo, totemo kirei-na tokoro deshita.

Watanabe   Onsen! Ii desune. Soto no onsen mo arimashita ka.

Nelson   Arimashita. Doyoobi no yoru mo, nichiyoobi no asa mo hairimashita. Chotto samukatta kedo, onsen no yu wa taihen atsukatta desu.

Watanabe   Ryokan ni tomarimashita ka.

Nelson   Hai, tomarimashita. Konde imashita yo. Wakai hito-tachi ga takusan tomatte imashita yo. Amerikajin mo imashita.

Watanabe   Soo desu ka. Hanashi o shimashita ka.

Nelson   Iie, chansu ga arimasen deshita.

Watanabe   Sore wa zannen deshita ne.

Nelson   Ee, soo desu ne. Tokorode, Watanabe san wa nani o shimashita ka. Dokoka e ikimashita ka.

Watanabe   Taihen deshita yo. Zenzen omoshiroku arimasen deshita. Kazoku to issho ni Tookyoo e itte, kaimono o shimashita ga, nichiyoobi no depaato wa, moo iya desu yo.

Nelson   Nanika kaimashita ka.

Watanabe   Ee, atarashii suutsu o kaimashita kedo, hontoo ni jikan ga kakarimashita. Kyoo wa, watashi mo taihen tsukarete imasu yo.

1. QUESTIONS:

1. Kyoo wa nanyoobi desu ka.
2. Maiku san wa hitori de onsen e ikimashita ka.
3. Maiku san wa Amerikajin to hanashimashita ka. Dooshite desu
   ka.
4. Maiku san wa onsen ga suki da to omoimasu ka.

Dialogue 10: Nihon o doo omoimasu ka.

It's Friday evening, and everyone has gathered in the staff room for
the formal welcome party for Mike Nelson and two other new members
of staff. The other two new teachers have just given a short speech of
self-introduction (jiko shookai), and now it's Mike's turn.

Nelson	Mina san, hajimemashite. Watashi wa Maiku Neruson to mooshimasu. Amerika no Ohaio-shuu kara kimashita. Watashi wa san-shuukan mae ni Nihon e kimashita. Gakkoo no shigoto wa omoshiroi to omoimasu. Ganbarimasu. Yoroshiku onegai shimasu.
Takahashi	Totemo yokatta desu yo. Nihongo ga joozu desu ne.
Nelson	Iie, mada mada dame desu. Hazukashikute, taihen deshita!
Takahashi	Daijoobu deshita yo. A, Katoo sensei desu. Neruson san wa mada atte inai deshoo. Atama ga yokute, omoshiroi hito desu yo. Shookai shimashoo.

Keiko Takahashi introduces Mike to Mr. Kato, and they chat.

Kato	Neruson sensei, Nihon wa mada san-shuukan desu ne. Nihon o doo omoimasu ka.
Nelson	Nihon wa totemo omoshirokute iikuni da to omoimasu. Dai-suki desu yo.
Kato	Soo desu ka. Ii kotae desu ne. Tabemono mo daijoobu desu ka.
Nelson	Hai, Nihon ryoori wa totemo oishii to omoimasu. Sashimi ya sushi ya soba wa zenbu taberu koto ga dekimasu.
Kato	Soo desu ka. Ja, Nihon no seikatsu wa, mondai nai deshoo! Anoo, shumi wa nan desu ka. Supootsu wa suki desu ka.
Takahashi	(laughing) Neruson sensei, ki o tsukete kudasai yo. Kore kara gakkoo no sensei no yakyuu chiimu no

hanashi ga hajimaru to omoimasu. Katoo sensei wa yakyuu chiimu no maneejaa de, itsumo chiimu no koto dake o kangaete imasu.

Kato   Sore wa uso desu yo! Neruson sensei, sensei no yakyuu chiimu de issho ni yakyuu o shimasen ka.

Nelson   (hesitating) Watashi wa yakyuu wa suki desu kedo, hayaku hashiru koto ga dekimasen.

Kato   Daijoobu desu yo. Tsugi no geemu wa nichiyoobi no asa desu ga.

Nelson   Nichiyoobi no asa.

Takahashi   Ja, Neruson sensei, ganbatte kudasai.

---

1. QUESTIONS:

1. Maiku san wa itsu kara Nihon ni imasu ka.
2. Maiku san wa sashimi o taberu koto ga dekimasu ka.
3. Katoo sensei wa nani o yoku kangaete imasu ka.
4. Maiku san wa kono tsugi no nichiyoobi no asa ni nani o suru to omoimasu ka.

Dialogue 11: Mada o-hitori desu ka.

It's Saturday evening, and Mr. Watanabe has invited Mike Nelson to his house for a meal and to meet his family.

Nelson   Oishi-soo desu ne.

Miho   Doozo, enryo shinaide tabete kudasai.

Nelson   Ja, itadakimasu.

Miho   O-hashi ga o-joozu desu ne.

Nelson   Arigatoo gozaimasu. Demo hashi wa Amerika de mo tokidoki tsukaimasu yo.

Miho   Ee? Amerikajin mo o-hashi o tsukau n desu ka.

Nelson   Ee, Nihon ryoori ya Chuuka ryoori no resutoran ga takusan arimasu kara, tokidoki tsukaimasu.

Hiro   Neruson san, Nihon ryoori no naka de, nani ga ichiban suki desu ka.

Nelson   Muzukashii shitsumon desu ne. Iroiro suki da kara. Hmmmm. Ichiban suki-na no wa tenpura desu. Sushi mo dai-suki desu.

Miho	Kyoo wa o-sushi ga takusan arimasu kara, doozo tabete kudasai!
Hiro	Neruson san wa yon-shuukan mae ni Nihon e kita n desu ne.
Nelson	Hai, soo desu. Choodo yon-shuukan mae desu.
Hiro	Nihongo ga yoku dekiru ne! Boku wa ni-nen-kan Eigo o benkyoo shite iru kedo, mada zenzen joozu ja nai yo.
Miho	Sonna koto arimasen yo. O-niisan wa kurasu no naka de ichiban na n desu yo.
Nelson	(laughing) Nihongo no benkyoo wa kono yon-shuukan dake ja nai n desu yo. Amerika no daigaku de mo, ni-nen-kan benkyoo shita kara, ima sukoshi dekiru n desu.
Miho	Soo desu ka. Ne, Neruson san, shitsurei desu ga, o-ikutsu desu ka.
Nelson	Yoku aru shitsumon desu ne. Watashi wa san-juu roku desu.
Miho	San-juu-roku-sai desu ka. Mada o-hitori desu ka.
Nelson	Ima hitori desu. Mae ni kekkon shite ita n desu kedo, ni-nen mae ni rikon shita n desu.
Miho	Soo desu ka. Hen-na shitsumon o shite, gomen nasai. Sa, Neruson san, biiru moo sukoshi doo desu ka.

1. **QUESTIONS:**

    1. Amerikajin wa yoku hashi o tsukaimasu ka.
    2. Takashi san wa, o-niisan wa Eigo ga yoku dekiru to omotte imasu ka.
    3. O-niisan wa itsu kara Eigo no benkyoo o shite imasu ka.
    4. Maiku san wa kekkon shite imasu ka.

TEST YOURSELF

Pair each of the words or phrases in the left-hand column with a word or phrase of similar (though perhaps not exactly the same) meaning from the right-hand column. Be careful! There is one word too many in each column, so you should be left with two words that don't make a pair.

ban	tsutomeru
buraun	omou
chotto	kurasu
dame	ooi
hataraku	yoru
heta	ikutsu
jugyoo	uso ja nai
kangaeru	hen
minna de	chairo
nan-sai	o-kaasan
haha	sukoshi
takusan	joozu ja nai
zenzen	warui
hontoo	issho ni

Mr. Watanabe has been asking Mike about the baseball game yesterday. Their conversation is below, but the lines are mixed up. Unscramble the lines and label them A, B, C, etc., in the correct order.

1. _____ Aa, dakara yakyuu ga dekinakatta n desu ka.

2. _____ Aa soo desu ka. Doo shite desu ka. Hayaku hashiru koto ga dekinakatta n desu ka.

3. _____ Daijoobu desu yo. Sono chiimu wa minna heta deshoo.

4. _____ Sore dake ja nai n desu. Sono mae no ban, tomodachi no uchi ni itte, takusan nonda kara, nichiyoobi no asa atama ga taihen itakatta desu yo.

5. _____ Hai, shimashita ga, watashi wa zenzen dame deshita yo.

6. _____ Kinoo, yakyuu o shimashita ka.

7. _____ Ee, soo desu. Watashi wa chiimu no naka de ichiban heta datta kara, totemo hazukashikatta desu.

149

Exercise C

Look at the clues below, and see if you can find the Japanese equivalents in the word search.

1. hobby
2. lie
3. finish
4. face
5. meet
6. met
7. this morning
8. sleep
9. because, and so
10. morning
11. was able to
12. not at all, never
13. painful
14. when?
15. blue-green
16. red
17. older brother
18. but
19. well, healthy
20. think about
21. buy
22. only
23. expensive

P	A	K	E	S	A	O	I	T
I	T	S	U	K	I	W	R	D
I	T	A	I	K	P	A	T	E
K	A	N	G	A	E	R	U	K
N	E	R	U	S	H	U	M	I
E	S	D	A	A	A	S	B	T
G	S	A	O	K	A	O	S	A
A	I	K	N	E	Z	N	E	Z
I	O	E	T	A	K	A	I	N

Exercise D

Imagine you are in Japan on a short business trip – you arrived in the country last Tuesday, and you're leaving tomorrow – and now you're traveling down to Osaka on the Shinkansen. As often happens in Japan, the person sitting next to you starts up a conversation. Fill in your part with appropriate responses.

Stranger **Shitsurei desu ga, kuni wa dochira desu ka.**

You _____

Stranger **Soo desu ka. Itsu Nihon e kita n desu ka.**

You _____

Stranger **Itsu made desu ka.**

You _____

Stranger	Mijikai desu ne! Nihon o doo omoimasu ka.
You	(in Tokyo, a lot of people!)
Stranger	Soo desu ne. Konde imasu ne. Shitsurei desu ga, o-ikutsu desu ka.
You	_____
Stranger	Soo desu ka. O-hitori desu ka.
You	_____
Stranger	Ii desu ne. Tokorode, Nihongo wa o-joozu desu ne. Muzukashii desu ka.
You	_____
Stranger	Kanji o yomu koto mo dekimasu ka.
You	_____
Stranger	Kanji wa muzukashii deshoo.

Answer the following questions about yourself.

1. Kyoo wa nan-yoobi desu ka.

   _____

2. Tokidoki hashi o tsukaimasu ka.

   _____

3. Ichiban suki-na tabemono wa nan desu ka.

   _____

4. Kekkon shite imasu ka.

   _____

5. Doko ni sunde imasu ka.

   _____

6. Nihongo wa muzukashii to omoimasu ka.

   _____

7. Mainichi Nihongo no benkyoo o shimasu ka.

   _____

8. Shumi wa nan desu ka.

   _____

9. Tenisu ga dekimasu ka.

   _____

10. Nihon no koto ga yoku wakarimasu ka.

   _____

Exercise E

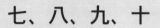 These are the kanji characters for the numbers seven to ten, pronounced shichi or nana, hachi, kyuu or ku, juu.

 Visit www.berlitzpublishing.com for a bonus internet activity—go to the downloads section and connect to the world in Japanese!

NI-JUU-ICHI-NICHI WA YASUMI DESU.
THE TWENTY-FIRST IS A HOLIDAY.

Mike Nelson is still at the Watanabe's house, and Mrs. Watanabe is doing most of the talking now.

Mrs. Watanabe	**Neruson san wa sukii ga dekimasu ka.** Can you ski, Mr. Nelson?
Nelson	**Hai, sukoshi dekimasu. Amari joozu ja nai desu kedo.** Yes, a little. I'm not very good, though.
Mrs. Watanabe	**Soo desu ka. Jitsu wa, watashitachi wa sangatsu ni sukii ni ikimasu ga, moshi yokattara, Neruson san mo issho ni ikimasen ka.** I see. Actually, we're going skiing in March, but would you like to join us?
Nelson	**Doomo arigatoo gozaimasu, sore wa ii desu ne. Nan-nichi ni ikimasu ka.** Thank you, that would be nice. What date are you going?

Mrs. Watanabe	Juu-hachi-nichi no yoru ni itte, ni-juu-ichi-nichi no gogo kaerimasu. Kin'yoobi kara getsuyoobi made desu. Ni-juu-ichi-nichi wa yasumi da kara, sukii-joo wa konde iru to omoimasu ga. We're going on the evening of the 18th, and coming back on the afternoon of the 21st. That's from Friday to Monday. The 21st is a holiday, so I think the ski resort will be crowded.
Nelson	Yasumi desu ka. Donna yasumi. A holiday? What kind of holiday?
Mrs. Watanabe	San-gatsu ni-juu-ichi-nichi wa shunbun no hi desu. March 21st is "shunbun no hi".
Nelson	Shunbun no hi. "Shunbun" wa Eigo de nan to iimasu ka. "Shunbun no hi". How do you say "shunbun" in English?
Mrs. Watanabe	Sa, eigo no kotoba ga wakarimasen ga, sono hi ni wa, yoru no jikan to hiruma no jikan ga onaji desu. Well, I don't know the English word, but on that day the hours of night and day are the same.
Nelson	Aa, hai, wakarimashita. Ah, yes, I understand.
Mrs. Watanabe	Neruson san, biiru ga arimasen ne. Gomen nasai. Doozo. A, Hiro, sorosoro neru jikan desu yo. Mr. Nelson, you don't have any beer! Please excuse me – here you are. Oh, well, Hiro, it's getting close to bedtime.
Hiro	Moo sukoshi Neruson san to hanashitemo ii deshoo. It's okay to talk with Mr. Nelson a little more, right?
Mrs. Watanabe	Hiro, dame desu yo. Sonna koto ittewa ikemasen yo. Hiro, no you can't! You should not say such a thing.
Hiro	O-kaasan. Neruson san ga kuru kara, osoku made okite ite mo ii, to kinoo itta deshoo. Mom! Yesterday you said that because Mr. Nelson was coming it would be all right to stay up late, didn't you?
Mrs. Watanabe	Hai hai, soo itta kedo, moo osoi deshoo. Yes, I said that, but it's already late.

Nelson	Sa, watashi mo sorosoro shiturei shimasu. Well, I must be going shortly.
Mrs. Watanabe	E? Moo? Mada ii deshoo. What? Already? You don't need to go yet, do you?
Nelson	Sumimasen ne. Demo, ashita no asa mata yakyuu da kara. Thank you. But tomorrow morning it's baseball again, so...
Mrs. Watanabe	Soo desu ka. Yakyuu no geemu desu ka. Ja, ganbatte kudasai ne. Ah, a baseball game. Well, have a good game.
Nelson	Hai, ganbarimasu. Dewa, kore de shitsurei shimasu. Iroiro arigatoo gozaimashita. Konban wa taihen tanoshikatta desu. Yes, I will. Well, please excuse me. Thank you for everything. This evening has been extremely enjoyable.
Mrs. Watanabe	Iie, kochira koso. Mata doozo. The pleasure's ours. Please come again.

STRUCTURE AND USAGE NOTES

1. THE MONTHS

The names of the months are very straightforward in Japanese, as they are simply the equivalents of "month one, month two, month three", etc.

nan-gatsu	what month?		
ichi-gatsu	January	shichi-gatsu	July
ni-gatsu	February	hachi-gatsu	August
san-gatsu	March	ku-gatsu	September
shi-gatsu	April	juu-gatsu	October
go-gatsu	May	juu-ichi-gatsu	November
roku-gatsu	June	juu-ni-gatsu	December

Kodomo no hi wa nan-gatsu desu ka. Go-gatsu desu ka.
What month is Children's Day? Is it May?

Nihon de wa, shichi-gatsu to hachi-gatsu ga ichiban atsui desu.
In Japan, July and August are the hottest.

Shi-gatsu ni Amerika e kaerimasu.
I'm returning to the USA in April.

Shujin no tanjoobi mo watashi no tanjoobi mo juu-ichi-gatsu desu.
My husband's birthday and my birthday are both in November.

Other associated words are sengetsu ("last month"), kongetsu ("this month"), and raigetsu ("next month").

Sengetsu wa shutchoo ga ookatta n desu kedo, kongetsu wa amari arimasen.
I had a lot of business trips last month, but I don't have many this month.

Jitsu wa, raigetsu kekkon suru n desu.
The truth is, I'm getting married next month.

---

2. THE DATES

The words for the dates are irregular up to the 10th, so it's probably best to learn them by heart.

nan-nichi	what date?		
tsuitachi	1st	muika	6th
futsuka	2nd	nanoka	7th
mikka	3rd	yooka	8th
yokka	4th	kokonoka	9th
itsuka	5th	tooka	10th

After the tenth, the numbers revert back to ones you are already familiar with, followed by -nichi, the word for "day". Note that there are three exceptions: the 14th, 20th and 24th.

juu-ichi-nichi	11th	ni-juu-ichi-nichi	21st
juu-ni-nichi	12th	ni-juu-ni-nichi	22nd
juu-san-nichi	13th	ni-juu-san-nichi	23rd
juu-yokka	14th	ni-juu-yokka	24th
juu-go-nichi	15th	ni-juu-go-nichi	25th
juu-roku-nichi	16th	ni-juu-roku-nichi	26th
juu-shichi-nichi	17th	ni-juu-shichi-nichi	27th
juu-hachi-nichi	18th	ni-juu-hachi-nichi	28th
juu-ku-nichi	19th	ni-juu-ku-nichi	29th
hatsuka	20th	san-juu-nichi	30th
		san-juu-ichi-nichi	31st

Watashi no tanjoobi wa hachi-gatsu tooka desu.
My birthday is August (the) 10th.

A. Saitoo san no natsu-yasumi wa nan-nichi kara nan-nichi made
desu ka.
When is your summer vacation, Ms. Saitoo? [Lit: From what date to
what date…?]
B. Mikka kara tooka made desu.
From the 3rd to the 10th.

Juu-go-nichi ni Yooroppa no shutchoo kara kaette kimasu.
I return from my European business trip on the 15th.

Tsugi no geemu wa kongetsu no juu-san-nichi desu.
The next game is on the 13th of this month.

Shi-gatsu tsuitachi ni atarashii konpyuutaa koosu ga hajimarimasu.
On April 1st the new computer course begins.

---

3. DONNA – "WHAT KIND OF…?"

This word belongs to another group of ko-, so-, a- and do- words. They
are konna ("this kind of"), sonna ("that kind of"), anna ("that kind of", – not
connected to either of us), and donna ("what kind of?").

Nihon no fuyu wa donna tenki desu ka.
What kind of weather do you have in Japan during the winter?

Sonna shitsumon ni kotaeru koto ga dekimasen.
I can't answer that kind of question.

Donna supootsu ga suki desu ka.
What kind of sports do you like?

Konna resutoran wa iya desu ne.
This kind of restaurant is horrible, isn't it?

Anna uchi ga ii desu ne.
That kind of house is good, isn't it?

These words can also be used in front of adjectives to mean "this much, to this extent", etc., in which case they need to be followed by ni.

Kongetsu, sonna ni isogashiku arimasen.
This month, we're not that busy.

Konna ni atsui hi wa amari nai n desu ne.
We don't have many days this hot, do we!

Sono Chuuka ryoori no resutoran wa sonna ni takaku nai to omoimasu.
I don't think that Chinese restaurant is very expensive.

Konna ni muzukashii to omoimasen deshita.
I didn't think it would be this difficult.

---

4. ...TO IIMASHITA – REPORTED SPEECH

The verb iimasu (plain form: iu) means "say", "speak", "report", so it is often used to relate what someone else has said. In such a case, it is preceded by the particle to, which signals a quotation.

Maiku san wa, "Hayaku hashiru koto ga dekimasen," to iimashita ga, jitsu wa totemo hayai desu.
Mike said, "I can't run fast", but in fact he's very fast.

Wada san wa, "Kore de shitsurei shimasu," to itte, kaerimashita.
Mr. Wada said, "Excuse me", and went home.

In reported speech, when you're talking about what someone else said rather than quoting their actual words, simply put everything that was said into the plain form.

Maiku san wa, ashita yakyuu o suru to iimashita. [= Maiku san wa, "Ashita yakyuu o shimasu," to iimashita.]
Mike said he's playing baseball tomorrow.

Watanabe san wa chotto isogashii kara, kaigi ni denai to iimashita.
[= Watanabe san wa, "Chotto isogashii kara, kaigi ni demasen," to iimashita.]
Mr. Watanabe said he's busy, so he won't attend the meeting.

Fukuda san wa san-ji han ni kuru to iimashita ka. [= Fukuda san wa, "San-ji han ni kimasu," to iimashita ka.]
Did Ms. Fukuda say she would come at 3:30?

Takahashi san wa shi-gatsu tsuitachi ni kekkon suru to iimashita ga, hontoo desu ka.
Ms. Takahashi said she's getting married on April 1st – is it true?

Saitoo san wa nan to iimashita ka.
What did Ms. Saitoo say?

Keiko chan wa kinoo atama ga itakatta kara konakatta to iimashita.
Keiko said she didn't come yesterday because she had a headache.

The particle to is also used with other verbs which show some sort of quotation, such as kiku ("ask", "hear"), omou ("think"), kaku ("write"), and kotaeru ("reply").

Haha wa, Ohaio wa ima totemo atsui to tegami ni kakimashita.
My mother wrote in her letter that it's very hot in Ohio now.

Watanabe san ni, itsu sukii ni iku ka to kikimashita. Demo, mada wakaranai to kotaemashita.
I asked Mr. Watanabe when he was going skiing, but he replied that he didn't know yet.

Wada san to Ogawa san wa onaji kaisha ni tsutomete iru ka to kikimashita.
He asked if Mr. Wada and Mr. Ogawa were working in the same company.

It's common to leave out da when reporting on questions.

Watashi wa Amerikajin ka to kikimashita.
He asked if I was American.

Kyoo wa juu-san-nichi ka to kikimashita.
He asked if it was the 13th today.

When you are talking about what someone else says in the present tense, then it's usual to use the -te iru form.

Takahashi san wa tsukareta to itte imasu.
Ms. Takahashi says she's tired.

Suuzan san wa itsumo wakaranai to itte imasu.
Susan is always saying she doesn't understand.

Tomodachi wa haru ni Nihon e kuru to itte imasu
My friend says she'll come to Japan in the spring.

5. EIGO DE NAN TO IIMASU KA – "WHAT DO YOU SAY IN ENGLISH?"

The verb iimasu is also useful for when you want to ask how to say something in English or Japanese.

A. Sensei, sumimasen ga, "the fall" wa Nihongo de nan to iimasu ka.
Teacher, excuse me, but how do you say "the fall" in Japanese?
B. "Aki" to iimasu.
It's "aki".

"Tegami" o Eigo de "letter" to iimasu ka.
For "tegami," do you say "letter" in English?

"Itadakimasu" wa Eigo de nan to iu deshoo ka.
I wonder what you say for "Itadakimasu" in English.

---

6. ASKING PERMISSION

When you want to ask permission to do something, add mo ii desu ka to the -te form, which is like saying "-ing, is it alright?" A positive answer to such a request can simply be "Hai, ii desu," "Hai, -te mo ii desu" or "Doozo".

A. Sumimasen ga, koko ni suwatte mo ii desu ka.
Excuse me, but is it all right if I sit here?
B. Ii desu. Doozo.
Yes, please go ahead.

A. Denwa o tsukatte mo ii desu ka.
Is it all right if I use the phone?
B. Hai, tsukatte mo ii desu yo. Doozo.
Yes, it's all right to use it. Go ahead.

Nihongo de setsumei shite mo ii desu ka.
Is it okay to explain it in Japanese?

Kyoo hayaku kaette mo ii desu ka.
Is it all right to go home early today?

Shitsumon o shite mo ii desu ka.
May I ask a question?

Haha wa, itte mo ii to iimashita ga, chichi wa dame da to iimashita.
My mother said I could go, but my father said I couldn't. [Lit: ...said it was no good.]

When you want to ask if it's all right *not* to do something, then find the negative -nai form (e.g. ikanai, "don't go" or tabenai, "don't eat"), and change it to -nakute. Then add the ending -mo ii desu. This is the equivalent of "It's all right not to...", or "You don't need to...".

A. Kore o zenbu tabenakute mo ii desu ka.
   Is it all right if I don't eat all of this?
B. Hai, (tabenakute mo) ii desu yo.
   Yes, it's all right (if you don't eat it).

Chotto isogashii kara, kyoo no kaigi ni denakute mo ii desu ka.
I'm a bit busy, so is it okay if I don't attend today's meeting?

Hazukashii kara, Nihongo de no jiko shookai o shinakute mo ii desu ka.
I'm embarrassed, so is it all right if I don't introduce myself in Japanese?

Issho ni ikanakute mo ii desu ka.
Is it all right if I don't go with you?

You can also use this pattern to give permission, as well as ask for it.

Namae to juusho o kakanakute mo ii desu.
It's all right not to write your name and address.

Kongetsu wa taihen atsui kara, kaisha no naka de nekutai o shinakute mo ii desu.
As it's extremely hot this month, you don't need to wear neckties in the office.

---

7. PROHIBITION

To say "cannot do something", again find the -te form of the verb, and then add wa ikemasen. The word ikemasen means "must not", "forbidden", "bad", so this is a very strong refusal. (In the next lesson we will be learning a more indirect way of suggesting you shouldn't do something.)

Sono heya ni haitte wa ikemasen yo.
Hey, you cannot go into that room.

Nihongo no jugyoo de wa, Eigo de hanashite wa ikemasen.
In the Japanese class, you cannot speak in English.

Sonna shitsumon o shite wa ikemasen yo.
You cannot ask that kind of question.

Sono tegami o yonde wa ikemasen.
You cannot read that letter.

Kono koto o denwa de hanashite wa ikemasen.
You cannot talk about this matter on the phone.

8. SHUNBUN NO HI – AND OTHER NATIONAL HOLIDAYS

The national holidays in Japan (when banks, government offices and business are closed) are as follows:

Ganjitsu	New Year's Day	January 1
Seijin-no-hi	Coming-of-Age Day	2nd Monday of January
Kenkoku Kinen-no-hi	National Founding Day	February 11
Shunbun-no-hi	Vernal Equinox Day	March 20 or 21
Showa-no-hi	Day of Showa	April 29
Kenpoo Kinenbi	Constitution Memorial Day	May 3
Midori-no-hi	Greenery Day	May 4
Kodomo-no-hi	Children's Day	May 5
Umi-no-hi	Marine Day	3rd Monday of July
Keiroo-no-hi	Respect for the Aged Day	3rd Monday of September
Shuubun-no-hi	Autumnal Equinox Day	September 22 or 23
Taiiku-no-hi	Health-Sports Day	2nd Monday of October
Bunka-no-hi	Culture Day	November 3
Kinroo Kansha-no-hi	Labor Thanksgiving Day	November 23
Tennoo Tanjoobi	Emperor's Birthday	December 23

If a national holiday falls on a Sunday, the next day (Monday) becomes a holiday. The period from the end of April to the beginning of May, when there are a number of holidays in a short period of time, is generally known as Golden Week, and is a popular time for taking a short vacation.

VOCABULARY

aki: fall/autumn
anna: that kind of
bunka no hi: Culture Day
denai: doesn't attend [from deru]
deru: go out, appear, attend
donna: what kind of...?
fuyu: winter
ganjitsu: New Year's Day
go-gatsu: May
gomen nasai: excuse me, I beg your pardon
hachi-gatsu: August
haru: spring
heya: room
hi: day
hiruma: daytime
ichi-gatsu: January
iimasu: say [from iu]
Iroiro arigatoo gozaimashita.: Thank you for everything.
isogashii: busy
juu-gatsu: October
juu-hachi-nichi: 18th (of the month)
juu-ichi-gatsu: November
juu-ni-gatsu: December
kaigi ni deru: attend a meeting
keiroo no hi: Respect for the Aged Day
kenkoku kinenbi: National Foundation Day
kenpoo kinenbi: Constitution Day
kinroo kansha no hi: Labor Thanksgiving Day
Kochira koso.: The pleasure's mine.
kodomo no hi: Children's Day
kongetsu: this month
konna: this kind of
koosu: course (of study)
kotaeru: answer, respond
kotoba: word
ku-gatsu: September
Mata doozo.: Please come again.
midori no hi: Greenery Day
Moshi yokattara,...: If it's all right,...
nan-gatsu: which month?
nan-nichi: what date?
natsu-yasumi: summer vacation/holiday
natsu: summer
neru jikan: time to sleep

-nichi: [added to numbers to give the date]
ni-gatsu: February
ni-juu-ichi-nichi: 21st (of the month)
Nonde mo ii.: It's all right to drink.
Nonde wa ikemasen.: You must not drink.
okite mo ii: all right to stay up [from okiru, to get up]
onaji: same
osoku made: until late
raigetsu: next month
roku-gatsu: June
san-gatsu: March
seijin no hi: Coming-of-Age Day
sengetsu: last month
shi-gatsu: April
shichi-gatsu: July
shuubun no hi: Autumnal Equinox Day
shunbun no hi: Spring Equinox Day
shutchoo: business trip
soo iimashita: said so [from iu]
sonna: that kind of
sorosoro: slowly, gradually, soon
sukii ni ikimasu: go skiing
sukii-joo: ski resort
sukii: skiing
taiiku no hi: Sports Health Day
tegami: letter
tennoo tanjoobi: Emperor's Birthday
toki: time, period
yasumi no hi: vacation, holiday
yasumi: vacation, rest, pause
Yooroppa: Europe

TEST YOURSELF

Exercise A

Read through the dialogue at the beginning of the lesson again, and then say if the following statements are true or false.

1. Sangatsu ni-juu-ichi-nichi wa shunbun no hi desu. T/F

2. Neruson san wa sukii ga joozu ja nai kedo, sukoshi dekimasu. T/F

3. Watanabe wa, "shunbun" no koto o Nihongo de setsumei dekimasen deshita. T/F

4. Okaasan wa Hiro san ni mada nenakutemo ii to iimashita. T/F

5. Neruson san ga kite iru kara Hiro san wa mada okite imasu. T/F

6. Maiku san wa ashita mata yakyuu geemu o mimasu. T/F

Here are some of the events Mike has marked on his calendar over the next couple of months. Make sentences about what will be happening on the various days, as in the example.

Exercise B

Example:

March
18
go skiing

San-gatsu juu-hachi-nichi ni sukii ni ikimasu.

1.

March
28
tennis in Kawasaki

_____

2.

March
31
Ms. Takahashi's party

_____

3.

April
4
Sue coming to Japan!

_____

4.

April
14
Japanese course finishes

_____

5.

April
29
Golden Week begins

_____

Exercise C

A new secretary, Ms. Obata, has joined the staff at Yokohama High School, and Mr. Watanabe is explaining some of the things it's all right for her to do and not do. How does he tell her that it's all right:

1. to use both the red phone and the black phone?

   _____

2. not to attend the 2:00 meeting?

   _____

3. to go home at 4:30?

   _____

4. to drink coffee in this room?

   _____

5. to talk to Mr. Nelson in Japanese?

   _____

6. not to do a self-introduction in front of everyone?

   _____

Exercise D

On this first morning at the school, Ms. Obata has a short, simple conversation with Mike Nelson in English, and she's so excited about it that she tells her mother all about it when she gets home. How does she relate the conversation? The first three lines have been done for you.

Nelson	Are you Ms. Obata?	**Neruson san wa, Obata san ka to kikimashita.**
Obata	Yes, I am.	**Watashi wa, hai, soo da to kotaemashita**
Nelson	How do you do?	**Neruson san wa, hajimemashite to iimashita.**
Nelson	Excuse me, but what time does today's meeting begin? (**kiku**)	
Obata	At 2:00. (**kotaeru**)	
Nelson	Which room is it in? (**kiku**)	
Obata	I'm sorry, but I don't know. (**kotaeru**)	
Nelson	Ah, time for lunch. (**iu**) Are you also going now, Ms. Obata? (**kiku**)	
Obata	No, I'm not going yet. (**iu**)	

How would you say these sentences in Japanese?

1. How do you say "kochira koso" in English?

   _____

2. Mr. Tanaka said he'd be at the office until 6:00.

   _____

3. You cannot use that kind of word.

   _____

4. Next month's business trip is from the 3rd to the 7th.

   _____

5. Is it all right if I use this desk?

   _____

6. Thank you for everything. It's been very enjoyable.

   _____

3月21日

The names of the months use a combination of the number of the month plus the character for "moon/month", which is pronounced gatsu. The dates combine numbers with the character for "day", which is pronounced ka or nichi depending on the number. Arabic numbers are often used instead of kanji numbers.

Visit www.berlitzpublishing.com for a bonus internet activity—go to the downloads section and connect to the world in Japanese!

14

HANASANAI HOO GA II DESU YO.
IT'S BETTER NOT TO TALK TO HIM.

A group of the staff at Yokohama High School are going to see a movie together tonight. Mike Nelson and Ms. Takahashi agree to meet in a coffee shop for something to eat before going to meet the others. Ms. Takahashi is already waiting when Mike goes in.

Nelson   A, Takahashi san, konbanwa. Moo chuumon shita n desu ka.
Ah, Ms. Takahashi, good evening. Have you already ordered?

Takahashi   Iie, mada desu. Menyuu o doozo.
No, not yet. Here's the menu.

Nelson   Arigatoo. Sa, nani ni shimashoo ka. (reading the menu) Hamu sando...tsuna sarada...supagetti... piza...aa, watashi wa piza ni shimasu. Piza to hotto koohii. Takahashi san wa?
Thank you. Let's see, what shall I have? Ham sandwiches...tuna salad...spaghetti...pizza...I'll have pizza...Pizza and a hot coffee. How about you?

Takahashi   O-naka ga suita kara, watashi mo piza desu. Sore kara, remon tii. (to waiter) Sumimasen. Piza futatsu to, hotto hitotsu to remon tii o hitotsu onegai shimasu.
I'm hungry, so I'll have pizza, too. And a lemon tea. Excuse me! Two pizzas, one coffee and one lemon tea, please.

Waiter   Piza futatsu, hotto hitotsu, remon tii o hitotsu desu ne. Kashikomarimashita.
Two pizzas, one coffee and one lemon tea. Certainly.

Takahashi   (looking out of the window) Ara, Kenji san da. Are wa Kenji san desu.
Ah, Kenji! That's Kenji!

Nelson   Booifurendo desu ka. Doko? Dono hito ga Kenji san desu ka.
Your boyfriend? Where? Which one is Kenji?

Takahashi   Yuubinkyoku no mae ni imasu. Kooshuu denwa no tonari desu.
He's in front of the post office. Next to the public telephone.

Nelson   Hai, hai. Aa, ima Takahashi san o mita deshoo. Ee. Doo shite mukoo e aruite iku n desu ka. Hen desu ne.
Yes, yes. Ah, he just saw you, didn't he! Huh? Why is he walking the other way? That's odd, isn't it?

Takahashi   Jitsu wa, kinoo no yoru denwa de kenka shita n desu. Watashi wa konban gakkoo no sutaffu to issho ni, eiga o mi ni iku to itta n desu ne. Sooshitara, Kenji san ga okotta n desu yo. Okashii deshoo. Dakara watashi mo okotte, kore kara moo awanai hoo ga ii, to itta n desu. Sore de, kaiwa ga owarimashita.
The truth is, we had an argument on the phone last night. I said I was going to see a movie with the staff at the school tonight, right? Then, Kenji got angry. That's strange, right? That's why I got angry and said it would be better if we didn't meet any more. And with that, the conversation ended.

Nelson   Soo desu ka. Doo shimasu ka. Ima Kenji san o yonda hoo ga ii deshoo.
I see. What will you do? You'd better call out to him now, shouldn't you?

Takahashi	Iie, kyoo wa Kenji san to hanasanai hoo ga ii to omoimasu.
	No, I think it's better if I don't talk to him today.
Nelson	Soo desu ka. A, piza ga kimashita.
	I see. Ah, here comes the pizza.
Waiter	Hai, hotto no o-kyaku sama wa?
	The customer who ordered coffee?
Nelson	Watashi desu. Doomo.
	That's me. Thank you.
Takahashi	Sa, jikan ga amari nai kara, hayaku tabeta hoo ga ii desu ne. Itadakimasu.
	Well, we don't have much time, so we'd better eat quickly. Enjoy your meal.

STRUCTURE AND USAGE NOTES

1. PIZA – AND OTHER WORDS BORROWED FROM ENGLISH

There are many foreign words which have entered the Japanese language, most of them from English, to describe things not native to Japan, such as Western-style food, clothes (see Lesson 8, Structure and Usage Note 2), and furnishings. Younger people also consider it fashionable to use borrowed foreign words, and you are likely to come across lots of them in the worlds of advertising, fashion and music. These imported words are known as gairaigo, or "words from abroad". Here are a few examples.

In the home	Technology	Food and drink
teeburu table	shii dii CD	piza pizza
kaaten curtain	konpyuutaa computer	hanbaagaa hamburger
ranpu lamp	bideo video	suteeki steak
kaapetto carpet	dii bii dii DVD	sarada salad
beddo bed	fakkusu fax	keeki cake
kusshon cushion	kopii photocopy	koora cola
airon iron	monitaa monitor	chokoreeto chocolate
taoru towel	kiiboodo keyboard	appurupai apple pie

In some cases, the borrowed words are not immediately recognizable because they have been abbreviated.

television =	terebi(jon) =	terebi
sandwich =	sando(itchi) =	sando
air conditioner =	ea kon(dishonaa) =	eakon
apartment =	apaato(mento) =	apaato
department store =	depaato(mento sutoaa) =	depaato
supermarket =	suupaa(maaketto) =	suupaa

2. HITOTSU, FUTATSU – "ONE, TWO" – ANOTHER WAY OF COUNTING

You already know the numbers ichi, ni, san, etc., to which you can add endings such as -nin (to count people), -nichi (to give the date), -ji (to give the time) and -sai (to give your age). As mentioned earlier (Lesson 9, Structure and Usage Note 4) there are also special ways of counting things which are flat, or long and thin, etc., and this too involves attaching special endings to ichi, ni, and san.

However, there is also another set of numbers, for counting *things*. The word ichi by itself simply means the number "one", but hitotsu means "one thing/one object". This counting system which begins with hitotsu is the one you need when shopping, ordering several dishes in a restaurant, or otherwise talking about a number of objects. Note that the number usually comes *after* the item to which it is referring.

ikutsu	how many?		
hitotsu	one	muttsu	six
futatsu	two	nanatsu	seven
mittsu	three	yattsu	eight
yottsu	four	kokonotsu	nine
itsutsu	five	too	ten

Otooto wa, o-naka ga taihen suita kara, chokoreeto keeki o mittsu tabeta to iimashita.
My little brother said he was really hungry, so he ate three chocolate cakes!

Maiku san no atarashii apaato ni wa, heya ga ikutsu arimasu ka.
In Mike's new apartment, how many rooms are there?

Sumimasen, koora o moo futatsu kudasai.
Excuse me, could we have two more colas, please?

Kinoo suupaa de orenji o itsutsu kaimashita.
I bought five oranges at the supermarket yesterday.

Kono yottsu no machi no naka de, dore ga ichiban ookii desu ka.
Which of these four towns is the biggest?

These numbers only go up to ten, and then revert back to the system of ichi, ni, san, etc.

Watashi no kaisha ni, shisha ga juu-san arimasu.
My company has thirteen branch offices.

---

3. YUUBINKYOKU NO MAE NI – "IN FRONT OF THE POST OFFICE" – AND OTHER PREPOSITIONS

When you are talking about the location of something in Japanese, instead of saying, for example, "underneath the table" or "inside the building", you say the equivalent of "the table's underneath" (teeburu no shita) or "the building's inside" (tatemono no naka). Here are some of the most commonly used words for describing the location of something or someone.

ue	on, on top, above	soba	nearby, by the side
shita	below, under	mae	in front of
naka	in, inside	ushiro	behind
tonari	next to	soto	outside
aida	between	chikaku	near

Kissaten wa ginkoo to yuubinkyoku no aida ni arimasu.
The coffee shop is between the bank and the post office.

Eki no mae de aimashoo.
Let's meet in front of the station.

Depaato no naka ni, kissaten ga mittsu to resutoran ga itsutsu arimasu.
Inside the department store, there are three coffee shops and five restaurants.

Maiku san no apaato no naka wa totemo kirei da kedo, tatemono no soto wa kitanai desu.
The inside of Mike's apartment is really nice, but the outside of the building is dirty.

Tanaka san kara no tegami wa teeburu no ue ni atta n desu kedo, ima doko deshoo ka.
The letter from Mr. Tanaka was on top of the table, but where is it now?

Kooshuu denwa wa mukoo no mise no ushiro ni arimasu.
There's a public telephone behind that shop over there.

Saitoo san no apaato wa ichiban ue ni arimasu.
Ms. Saitoo's apartment is right at the top.

---

4. MI NI IKU – "GO TO SEE"

Just as in English we can say "go to see, go to buy, go to eat", etc., so in Japanese it is possible to create phrases with the same kind of meaning. Just remove -masu from the -masu form of the verb, and add ni iku. Here are some examples.

shi ni iku	go to do
tabe ni iku	go to eat
nomi ni iku	go to have a drink
kai ni iku	go to buy
ai ni iku	go to meet
mi ni iku	go to see

Nomi ni ikimashoo.
Let's go for a drink.

Kyoo eiga o mi ni ikimasenka.
Would you like to go see a movie today?

Ashita no asa tomodachi to issho ni kooen e tenisu o shi ni ikimasu.
I'm going to go to the park to play tennis with some friends tomorrow morning.

Kinoo Yokohama e atarashii suutsu o kai ni itta n desu kedo, taihen takakute, kaimasen deshita.
Yesterday I went to Yokohama to buy a new suit, but they were really expensive, so I didn't buy one.

Senshuu no doyoobi wa tanjoobi deshita kara, gaarufurendo to issho ni sono atarashii Indo ryoori no resutoran e tabe ni ikimashita.
Last Saturday it was my birthday, so I went to eat at that new Indian restaurant together with my girlfriend.

5. YONDA HOO GA II – "YOU'D BETTER CALL TO HIM" AND OTHER ADVICE

To make a strong suggestion or recommendation that someone should do something, add hoo ga ii to the plain past form of the verb, that is, the -ta form. This is the equivalent of the English "you'd better…", "you ought to…" or "it would be best if you…".

Kaigi no repooto o rapputoppu de kaita hoo ga ii to omoimasu.
I think it would be best to write up the report of the meeting on the laptop.

Tsukareta n desu ka. Ja, konban hayaku neta hoo ga ii desu ne.
You're tired? Well, you'd better go to bed early tonight.

Jikan ga amari nai kara, moo sugu chuumon shita hoo ga ii desu ne.
We don't have much time, so we should order soon, right?

Osoi kara, takushii de kaetta hoo ga ii to omoimasu yo.
It's late, so I think it would be better if you went home by taxi.

If you want to suggest that someone *shouldn't* do something, then add hoo ga ii to the -nai form of the verb (that is, the plain negative of the present tense).

Sonna ni takusan nomanai hoo ga ii desu yo.
You shouldn't drink so much.

Hidoi tenki da kara, kyoo wa soto e denai hoo ga ii desu yo.
It's best not to go out today because the weather is terrible.

Yoru, hitori de machi o arukanai hoo ga ii desu.
It's best not to walk in the city alone at night.

Sonna ni sugu okoranai hoo ga ii desu yo.
You shouldn't get angry so quickly.

Sore wa Wada san no rapputoppu da kara, tsukawanai hoo ga ii to omoimasu.
That's Mr. Wada's laptop, so I think it would be better not to use it.

VOCABULARY

aida: between
airon: iron
apaato: apartment, flat

appurupai: apple pie
ara: oh! [used mostly by women]
aruite iku: walk away [from aruku]
awanai hoo ga ii: best not to meet [from au]
beddo: bed
chikaku: near, close
chokoreeto: chocolate
chuumon: an order, request
eakon: air conditioner
fakkusu: fax
futatsu: two (objects)
gairaigo: words imported from abroad
hamu: ham
hanasanai hoo ga ii: best not to talk
hanbaagaa: hamburger
hidoi: terrible
hitotsu: one (object)
hotto (koohii): hot (coffee)
ikutsu: how many?
Indo ryoori: Indian cuisine
itsutsu: five (objects)
kaiwa: conversation
kaapetto: carpet
kare: him, he
kashikomarimashita: certainly [formal]
kaaten: curtain
keeki: cake
kiiboodo: keyboard
kitanai: dirty
kokonotsu: nine (objects)
kopii: photocopy
koora: cola
kooshuu denwa: public telephone
kusshon: cushion
menyuu: menu
mi ni iku: go to see
mise: shop
mittsu: three (objects)
monitaa: a monitor
mukoo: the other direction, over there
muttsu: six (objects)
naka: inside
nanatsu: seven (objects)
o-kyaku sama: guest, customer
O-naka ga suita.: I'm hungry. [from suku, become empty]
o-naka: stomach

okotta: got angry [from okoru]
piza: pizza
ranpu: lamp
rapputoppu: laptop
remon tii: lemon tea
sando: sandwich
sarada: salad
shii dii: CD
shisha: branch office
shita: below, under
soba: near, next to
sore de: so, therefore, "and then"
supagetti: spaghetti
sutaffu: staff
suteeki: steak
suupaa: supermarket
tabeta hoo ga ii: had better eat
teeburu: table
too: ten (objects)
toosuto: toast
tsuna: tuna
ue: above, on top
ushiro: behind, in back of
yattsu: eight (objects)
yonda hoo ga ii: best to call [from yobu]
yottsu: four (objects)
yuubinkyoku: post office

TEST YOURSELF

Exercise A

Read through the dialogue at the beginning of the lesson again, and then say if the following statements are true or false.

1. Nelson san mo Takahashi san mo piza o chuumon shimashita. T/F

2. Takahashi san no booifurendo wa kooshuu denwa no mae ni imashita. T/F

3. Takahashi san no booifurendo wa yuubinkyoku no mae kara kissaten made aruite kimashita. T/F

4. Takahashi san no booifurendo wa, Takahashi san ga gakkoo no sutaffu to issho ni eiga o mi ni iku kara, okorimashita. T/F

5. Nelson san wa, Takahashi san ga booifurendo to hanasanai hoo ga ii to omoimashita. T/F

6. Nelson san to Takahashi san wa yukkuri tabete mo ii desu. T/F

Look at the gairaigo words below, and try to guess what English words they come from.

Sports: Countries:

booringu   Airurando

gorufu   Oosutoraria

basukettobooru   Indo

aisu sukeeto   Nyuu Jiirando

haikingu   Burajiru

saafingu   Itaria

uindo saafin   Oosutoria

After the movie, Mike and the other staff from school go for a coffee. In the coffee shop, everyone talks at once, and everyone wants to give advice to the others. What do they say in response to the comments below? Use hoo ga ii in your answers, as in the example.

Example:
A. O-sake o onegai shimasu.
   (best not to drink too much)
B. Takusan nomanai hoo ga ii desu yo.

1. Mina san, shitsurei shimasu. Watashi wa aruite kaerimasu.
   (late, so better to go home by taxi)

   _____

2. Tsukareta.
   (should go home soon)

   _____

3. O-naka ga suita ne.
   (should eat spaghetti or pizza)

   _____

4. **Kono jaketto wa kitanai desu ne.**
   (should buy a new one)

5. **Sono futari wa mainichi mainichi kenka shite imasu ne.**
   (better if they got divorced)

6. **Watashi wa chokoreeto keeki o moo hitotsu chuumon shimasu yo.**
   (shouldn't eat so much chocolate)

Exercise D

Mike has tidied his room a little today. Look at the before and after pictures below, and see if you can spot the differences. Make sentences like the one in the example, using the cues provided.

Example: **(denwa – ue – naka) Kinoo, denwa wa tsukue no shita ni arimashita kedo, ima tsukue no naka ni arimasu.**

1. **shinbun – ue – shita**

2. **ranpu – tonari – shita**

3. rajio – aida – ue

_____

4. suutsukeesu – mae – ushiro

_____

5. tenki – ii – warui

_____

6. kaaten – nai – aru

_____

How would you say these sentences in Japanese?

1. Two hot coffees, one hamburger and one spaghetti, please.

_____

2. I have a headache, so I think it would be best to stay (iru) at home and watch TV.

_____

3. This movie looks interesting, doesn't it? Shall we go to see it tonight?

_____

4. Who lives in that big house next to the post office?

_____

5. Do you think it would be better not to call Mr. Wada?

_____

6. Mr. Watanabe asked how many desks we had altogether in the school.

_____

The word denwa is made up of the kanji characters for "electricity" and "speak", and means "telephone".

Visit www.berlitzpublishing.com for a bonus internet activity—go to the downloads section and connect to the world in Japanese!

15

WATASHI NO KEIYAKU NI TSUITE DESU GA.
IT'S ABOUT MY CONTRACT.

Mike Nelson is talking to Mr. Watanabe in the staff room at school.

Nelson	**Watanabe san, chotto shitsumon ga aru n desu ga, ii desu ka.** Mr. Watanabe, can I ask a question?
Watanabe	**Ii desu yo. Doozo. Nan deshoo ka.** Of course. Go ahead. What is it?
Nelson	**Watashi no keiyaku ni tsuite desu ga.** It's concerning my contract.
Watanabe	**Keiyaku ni tsuite no shitsumon desu ka. Demo watashi wa keiyaku no koto wa yoku wakaranai n desu yo. Koochoo sensei to hanashita hoo ga ii to omoimasu. Nanika, mondai ga dekimashita ka.** A question concerning your contract? But I don't really know about contract matters. I think it would be better to talk to the principal. Has there been some kind of problem?

Nelson	Iie, iie, mondai ja nai n desu. Jitsu wa, raigetsu watashi no tomodachi ga Nihon e kuru yotei na n desu ga, Nihon wa hajimete da kara, kuukoo made mukae ni ikitai to omotte iru n desu ga.
	No, no, it's not a problem. The fact is, my friend plans to come to Japan next month. It's her first time in Japan, so I think I'd like to go to the airport to meet her.
Watanabe	A, wakarimashita. Yasumi no koto desu ka.
	Ah, I see. It's about your day off.
Nelson	Ee, moshi mondai ja nakattara, ichi-nichi yasumi o toritai n desu.
	Yes, if it's not a problem, I'd like to take one day off.
Watanabe	Sore wa mondai nai to omoimasu yo. Tada, sono koto ni tsuite memo o kaite, watashi ni dashite kudasai. Saitoo san ga sono tokubetsu no yooshi o motte imasu kara, kanojo ni kiite kudasai.
	I don't think it's a problem. Just write a memo concerning the details, and submit it to me. Ms. Saitoo has the special forms, so ask her.

Just then, Ms. Takahashi comes into the teachers' room to talk to Mike.

Takahashi	Neruson san, chotto ii desu ka. Koochoo sensei kara no messeeji desu ga, moshi yokattara, kyoo ka ashita Neruson san to uchiawase o shitai to itte imashita ga.
	Mr. Nelson, do you have a moment? There's a message from the principal – he said that, if it's all right with you, he'd like to meet with you today or tomorrow.
Nelson	Koochoo sensei to no uchiawase desu ka. Nanika…
	Meet with the principal? Is there something…?
Takahashi	Shinpai shinaide kudasai. Tada kore kara no keikaku ni tsuite soodan suru tsumori da to omoimasu.
	Don't worry! I think it's just that he intends to consult you about upcoming projects.
Nelson	Soo desu ka. Jikan o ima kimemasu ka.
	I see. Shall we decide the time now?
Takahashi	Hai, onegai shimasu. Koochoo sensei no sukejuuru o motte imasu kara, ima kimemashoo.
	Yes, please do. I have the principal's schedule, so we can decide now.
Nelson	Watashi wa, ashita no asa juu-ji made aite imasu ga.
	I'm free tomorrow morning until 10:00.

> Takahashi Ashita no asa wa chotto. Koochoo sensei wa kyooiku iinkai ni yoru tsumori da to itte imashita kara. Gogo wa?
> Tomorrow morning's not good. It's because I think the principal intends to call in on the education committee. How about the afternoon?
>
> Nelson Gogo wa, san-ji han made jugyoo ga arimasu ga, sono ato wa aite imasu.
> I have classes until 3:30, but I'm free after that.
>
> Takahashi Ja, yo-ji ni shimashoo.
> Right, let's make it 4:00.

STRUCTURE AND USAGE NOTES

1. NI TSUITE – "REGARDING" OR "CONCERNING"

The phrase ni tsuite means "regarding", "concerning", "about", and comes after the thing to which it refers.

Kachoo kara no memo ni tsuite shitsumon ga aru n desu ga.
I have a question concerning the memo from the section chief.

Sumimasen ga, kyuuryoo no koto ni tsuite kiite mo ii desu ka.
Excuse me, but is it all right if I ask about a salary matter?

Moshi moshi, Saitoo san? Ashita no kaigi ni tsuite desu ga.
Hello, Mr. Saitoo? (I'm calling) about tomorrow's meeting.

Kyooiku iinkai no kaigi ni tsuite repooto o kaite kudasai.
Please write a report on the meeting of the education committee.

Kyoo no kaigi wa nan ni tsuite desu ka.
What's today's meeting about?

Buchoo wa, kyonen no keikaku to kotoshi no keikaku ni tsuite iroiro kikimashita.
The department manager asked all sorts of questions concerning last year's projects and this year's projects.

2. YOTEI – MAKING PLANS

The word yotei is very useful for when you are discussing plans and schedules. When it comes after the plain form of a verb, it is the equivalent of "I plan to (do)".

Shachoo no ashita no yotei wa nan desu ka.
What's the president's schedule for tomorrow?

Kotoshi no natsu yasumi ni wa, gaikoku e iku yotei desu.
For my summer vacation this year, my plan is to go abroad.

A. Ashita no asa wa aite imasu ka.
   Are you free tomorrow?
B. Sumimasen ga, ashita wa Yokohama no shisha ni yoru yotei desu
   kara, chotto muzukashii desu.
   I'm sorry, but tomorrow I'm scheduled to drop by at the Yokohama
   branch office, so it's a bit difficult.

Juu-ji ni kachoo to uchiawase o suru yotei deshita ga, mada kite
imasen ne. Doo shita n deshoo ka.
I was supposed to have a consultation with the section manager at 10:00,
but he's not here yet. I wonder what's happened?

Kaigi wa go-ji made ni owaru yotei desu.
The meeting is scheduled to finish at 5:00.

Koochoo sensei wa, sono koto o ashita made ni kimeru yotei da to
iimashita.
The principal said that he plans to decide on that matter by tomorrow.

Keiyaku ni tsuite kanojo to soodan suru yotei desu.
I plan to talk over the contract with her.

---

3. IKITAI – "I WANT TO GO" AND OTHER DESIRES

To express a wish or desire to do something, replace -masu with -tai.

Plain form	-masu form	-tai form	Meaning
iku	iki-masu	iki-tai	want to go
taberu	tabe-masu	tabe-tai	want to eat
hanasu	hanashi-masu	hanashi-tai	want to talk
kimeru	kime-masu	kime-tai	want to decide
toru	tori-masu	tori-tai	want to take
kau	kai-masu	kai-tai	want to buy
uru	uri-masu	uri-tai	want to sell
suru	shi-masu	shi-tai	want to do

The -tai form is generally used to talk about your own wishes and wants, or to ask someone else about their feelings. It is not generally used to describe what someone else wants, because in Japanese it is considered that you can never *really* know what another person wants to do. To get around this, you can use the equivalents of "I think that he wants to …", "He said that he wants to …", "I heard that he wants to …", etc.

Sukoshi yasumitai desu.
I want to rest a little.

Maiku san wa, keiyaku ni tsuite hanashitai to iimashita.
Nelson said he wants to talk about the contract.

Wada san wa kotoshi gaikoku e ikitai to itte imasu.
Mr. Wada says that he wants to go abroad this year.

Piitaa san wa chotto sabishikute, kuni e kaeritai to itte imasu yo.
Peter is a little lonely, and says he wants to go back to his own country.

Shachoo kara no memo ni tsuite kikitai n desu ga.
I'd like to ask you about the memo from the president.

Buchoo wa minna de atarashii keikaku no koto o soodan shitai to iimashita.
The department manager said he wants us all to confer about the new project.

Takahashi san wa, o-kane ga nai kara, kuruma o uritai to iimashita.
Ms. Takahashi said that she doesn't have any money, so she wants to sell her car.

The -tai ending acts in the same way as -i adjectives, so it has a negative form which ends in -taku arimasen, for talking about things you *don't* want to do, and a past form which ends in -takatta desu, for talking about what you wanted to do previously.

Ichi-nichi yasumi o toritakatta kedo, taihen isogashikute, toru koto ga dekimasen deshita.
I wanted to take a day off, but I couldn't because I was extremely busy.

Kyoo wa ii tenki da kara, benkyoo o shitaku nai desu.
It's such nice weather today, I don't want to study.

Tsukarete ita kara, paatii e amari ikitaku nakatta kedo, totemo tanoshikatta desu.
I was tired, so I didn't really want to go to the party, but it was very enjoyable.

The -tai form is attached to a verb meaning that you want to *do* something. If, however, you want a *thing,* then you need the -i adjective hoshii. As with -tai, you need to use phrases like "I think that…", "He said that…", etc., if you are describing what someone else wants. (Note that wa marks the person who wants the object, and ga marks whatever it is they want.)

Watashi wa atarashii konpyuutaa ga hoshii desu ga, o-kane ga nai kara, dame desu.
I want a new computer, but I don't have any money, so it's impossible.

Tanjoobi ni wa, nani ga hoshii desu ka.
For your birthday, what would you like?

Mae wa ii shigoto ga hoshikatta kedo, ima wa himana jikan ga hoshii n desu.
Before I wanted a good job, but now I want free time.

Saitoo san wa motto nagai yasumi ga hoshii to iimashita.
Ms. Saitoo said she wants a longer vacation.

---

4. MARKING ALTERNATIVES

The particle ka is used to mark alternatives, so it is similar to the English "or" when it comes between nouns.

Buchoo ka kachoo ga sore o kimeta hoo ga ii to omoimasu.
I think it's best if the department chief or the section chief decides that.

Doyoobi ka nichiyoobi ni ikimasu.
I'll go on Saturday or Sunday.

Sono koto ni tsuite, Wada san ka Tanaka san to soodan shite kudasai.
With regard to that matter, please consult Mr. Wada or Mr. Tanaka.

Rainen no natsu yasumi ni wa, Yooroppa ka Amerika ni ikitai to omoimasu.
For next (year's) summer vacation, I think I'd like to go to Europe or the USA.

Koora ka koohii ga hoshii desu.
I want some cola or coffee.

---

5. SHINAIDE KUDASAI – "PLEASE DON'T"

You have already come across the -te kudasai form, used when you want to ask someone to do something (e.g. Kore o tsukatte kudasai, "Please use this".). However, you might want to ask them *not* to do something. In this case, start with the negative -nai form, and then add -de kudasai (e.g. Kore o tsukawanaide kudasai, "Please don't use this".).

Sore wa shinaide kudasai.
Please don't do that.

Uchiawase no jikan o mada kimenaide kudasai. Sono mae ni kachoo to soodan shitai desu kara.
Please don't set the time of the meeting yet. Before that, I want to consult the section chief.

Fukuda san ni keiyaku no koto o hanasanaide kudasai.
Please don't talk to Ms. Fukuda about the contract matters.

Sore wa iwanaide kudasai.
Don't say that.

Sono repooto o mada buchoo ni dasanaide kudasai.
Don't give that report to the (department) chief yet, please.

Watashi no koto o wasurenaide kudasai ne.
Please don't forget about me!

---

6. TSUMORI – TALKING ABOUT INTENTIONS

The word tsumori means "intention", so the sentence-ending tsumori desu after the plain form of a verb can usually be translated as "intend to do", or "mean to do".

Sore wa mondai desu ne. Doo suru tsumori desu ka.
That's a problem, isn't it? What do you intend to do?

Sono keikaku ni tsuite Watanabe san to hanasu tsumori deshita ga, dekimasendeshita.
I meant to talk to Mr. Watanabe about that project, but I couldn't.

Rainen no san-gatsu ni kuni e kaeru tsumori desu.
I intend to return home next March.

Takusan tabenai tsumori deshita ga, totemo oishii kara, zenbu tabemashita.
I didn't mean to eat much, but it was really delicious, so I ate all of it!

Donna kuruma o kau tsumori desu ka.
Which car do you intend to buy?

Katoo san wa kyuuryoo ni tsuite buchoo to hanasu tsumori da to iimashita.
Ms. Kato said she means to talk to the department manager about her salary.

Takahashi san wa rainen no natsu made ni kekkon suru tsumori da to iimashita.
Ms. Takahashi said she intends to get married by next summer.

7. ARIMASU VS. MOTTE IMASU – HAVING AND HOLDING

The verb motsu means "hold", but you will usually come across it in the -te iru form, when it means "possess, hold, have".

A. Takahashi san wa kuruma o motte imasu ka.
   Do you have a car, Ms. Takahashi?
B. Kyoonen made motte imashita ga, o-kane ga kakatta kara, urimashita.
   I had one until last year, but it cost (so much) money, so I sold it.

Dare no suutsukeesu o motte imasu ka.
Whose suitcase are you carrying?

Shachoo kara no memo o motte imasu ka.
Do you have that memo from the president?

O-kane o motte imasen.
I don't have any money.

Both aru and motsu can be translated into English as "have", but aru is used when something exists, whereas motsu includes the nuance of possession.

Denwa ga arimasu ka.   Denwa o motte imasu ka.
Do you have a phone?   Do you possess a phone?
[Lit: Is there a phone?]

A. Atarashii sukejuuru ga arimasu ka.
   Do you have the new schedule?
B. Hai, arimasu.
   Yes, I do.
A. Ima motte imasu ka.
   Do you have it (with you) now?
B. Iie, motte imasen. Tsukue no naka ni arimasu.
   No, I don't. It's in my desk.

VOCABULARY

aite imasu: be free, have no engagements [from aku]
buchoo: department head, manager
dashite kudasai: please submit [from dasu, to put out, send, show]
dekimashita: happened, be completed
emu pii surii pureeyaa: MP3 player
gaikoku: foreign country, abroad
hajimete: first time
hoshii: want
ichi-nichi: one day
iinkai: committee
ikitai: want to go [from iku]

kachoo: section head, assistant manager
kanojo: she, her
keikaku: plan, project, scheme
keiyaku: contract
kimemasu: decide [from kimeru]
koochoo: principal, head teacher
kotoshi: this year
kuukoo: airport
kyoo ka ashita: today or tomorrow
kyooiku: education
kyonen: last year
kyuuryoo: salary, wages
made ni: by [date or time]
memo: memo
messeeji: message
motte imasu: have, hold [from motsu]
mukae ni ikitai: want to go to meet
ni tsuite: concerning, regarding
o-kane: money
onegai shimasu: please (do that)
rainen: next year
shachoo: president
shinpai shinaide: don't worry
shinpai: worry, anxiety
soodan suru: consult, confer with, talk over
sono ato: after that
sukejuuru: schedule
tada: just, only, simply
tokubetsu no: special, particular
toritai: want to take [from toru]
tsumori: intention
uchiawase: meeting, consultation
urimasu: sell [from uru]
yasumitai: want to rest
yooshi: a form, a blank
yotei: plan, program, schedule

TEST YOURSELF

Read through the dialogue at the beginning of the lesson again, and then say if the following statements are true or false.

1. Nelson san wa, keiyaku ni tsuite chotto shitsumon ga arimasu. T/F
2. Nelson san no tomodachi wa onna no hito desu. T/F
3. Nelson san wa, kuukoo made tomodachi o mukae ni iku tsumori desu. T/F
4. Kare wa keiyaku ni tsuite koochoo sensei to hanashitai n desu. T/F
5. Koochoo sensei wa, ashita no asa wa aite imasu. T/F
6. Koochoo sensei to no uchiawase wa ashita desu. T/F

Keiko Takahashi and her boyfriend Kenji are back on speaking terms again. However, they're always arguing about what they want to do, as they have very different tastes, and rarely want to do the same thing. Look at the chart below, and make up sentences like the ones in the example about what they do and don't want to do. (Don't forget that in Japan, a circle is often used instead of a check mark to mean "yes/correct/positive".)

Example: Keiko san wa doyoobi no asa Tookyoo de kaimono o shitai n desu ga, Kenji san wa shitaku arimasen. Keiko san mo, Kenji san mo, doyoobi no gogo yakyuu o mi ni ikitai desu.

	Keiko	Kenji
do some shopping in Tokyo on Saturday morning	O	X
go to see baseball on Saturday afternoon	O	O
1. talk about the summer vacation	O	X
2. eat in an Italian restaurant	O	O

189

3. go to the beach on Sunday	O	X
4. join an English (language) class	O	X
5. see a movie tonight	X	O
6. get married next year	O	X

Exercise C

Mr. Watanabe is a little irritated by his daughter, Tomoko, who is not behaving well lately. He decides to tell her not to do certain things. How does he ask his daughter not to:

1. eat sandwiches in this room?

2. talk to her boyfriend on the phone?

3. use that printer?

4. write reports on Mr. Watanabe's computer?

5. read Mr. Watanabe's letters on his desk?

6. listen to her MP3 player at school?

Below is Mike's diary, showing some of the things he'll be doing during the next two weeks. Make sentences about his schedule like the one in the example, using yotei desu.

Example: (6th, evening, go for a drink with Mr. Watanabe)
Muika no yoru, Watanabe san to nomi ni iku yotei desu.

M, 6	evening: go for drink with Mr. Watanabe	M, 13	
T, 7	p.m.: meeting with Principal	T, 14	a.m.: submit report to Principal
W, 8		W, 15	p.m.: call Sue. Consult re: summer vacation
Th, 9	a.m.: attend meeting of education committee	Th, 16	
F, 10		F, 17	
Sa, 11	evening: bowling with staff from school	Sa, 18	a.m.: go to Tokyo, buy new suit

How would you say these sentences in Japanese?

1. Is it all right if I ask a question about my salary?

2. Are you free on Tuesday afternoon?

3. This summer, I intend to buy a new car.

4. There's a meeting in the next room, so please don't go in.

5. I'm hungry, so I want to eat a lot.

6. Next spring, I plan to go to America with my family.

先生 The first kanji (sen) means "prior/previous" and the other one (sei) means "to be alive, born". The whole word sensei means "teacher/professor", and is also used to refer to medical doctors, lawyers and sometimes politicians.

 Visit www.berlitzpublishing.com for a bonus internet activity—go to the downloads section and connect to the world in Japanese!

DAI JUU-SAN-KA KARA DAI JUU-GO-KA MADE NO FUKUSHUU.
REVIEW OF LESSONS 13 TO 15.

Read and listen again to Dialogues 13 to 15, and try to understand the meaning without referring back to the translations in previous lessons.

Dialogue 13: Ni-juu-ichi-nichi wa yasumi no hi desu.

Mike Nelson is still at the Watanabe's house, and Mrs. Watanabe is doing most of the talking now.

Watanabe	Neruson san wa sukii ga dekimasu ka.
Nelson	Hai, sukoshi dekimasu. Amari joozu ja nai desu kedo.
Mrs. Watanabe	Soo desu ka. Jitsu wa, watashitachi wa sangatsu ni sukii ni ikimasu ga, moshi yokattara, Neruson san mo issho ni ikimasen ka.

Nelson	Doomo arigatoo gozaimasu, sore wa ii desu ne. Nan-nichi ni ikimasu ka.
Mrs. Watanabe	Juu-hachi-nichi no yoru ni itte, ni-juu-ichi-nichi no gogo kaerimasu. Kin'yoobi kara getsuyoobi made desu. Ni-juu-ichi-nichi wa yasumi da kara, sukii-joo wa konde iru to omoimasu ga.
Nelson	Yasumi desu ka. Donna yasumi.
Mrs. Watanabe	San-gatsu ni-juu-ichi-nichi wa shunbun no hi desu.
Nelson	Shunbun no hi. "Shunbun" wa Eigo de nan to iimasu ka.
Mrs. Watanabe	Sa, eigo no kotoba ga wakarimasen ga, sono hi ni wa, yoru no jikan to hiruma no jikan ga onaji desu.
Nelson	Aa, hai, wakarimashita.
Mrs. Watanabe	Neruson san, biiru ga arimasen ne. Gomen nasai. Doozo. A, Hiro, sorosoro neru jikan desu yo.
Hiro	Moo sukoshi Neruson san to hanashitemo ii deshoo.
Mrs. Watanabe	Hiro, dame desu yo. Sonna koto ittewa ikemasen yo.
Hiro	O-kaasan. Neruson san ga kuru kara, osoku made okite ite mo ii to kinoo itta deshoo.
Mrs. Watanabe	Hai hai, soo itta kedo, moo osoi deshoo.
Nelson	Sa, watashi mo sorosoro shiturei shimasu.
Mrs. Watanabe	E? Moo? Mada ii deshoo.
Nelson	Sumimasen ne. Demo, ashita no asa mata yakyuu da kara.
Mrs. Watanabe	Soo desu ka. Yakyuu no geemu desu ka. Ja, ganbatte kudasai ne!
Nelson	Hai, ganbarimasu. Dewa, kore de shitsurei shimasu. Iroiro arigatoo gozaimashita. Konban wa taihen tanoshikatta desu.
Mrs. Watanabe	Iie, kochira koso. Mata doozo.

QUESTIONS:

1. Nelson san wa Watanabe san-tachi to issho ni sukii ni ikitai to omotte imasu ka.
2. Shunbun no hi" wa Eigo de nan to iimasu ka.

3. Hiro san wa moo sukoshi okite ite mo ii desu ka. Doo shite desu ka.
4. Nelson san wa dooshite kaeri masu ka.

Dialogue 14: Hanasanai hoo ga ii desu yo.

A group of the staff at Yokohama High School are going to see a movie together tonight. Mike Nelson and Ms. Takahashi agree to meet in a coffee shop for something to eat before going to meet the others. Ms. Takahashi is already waiting when Mike goes in.

Nelson   A, Takahashi san, konbanwa. Moo chuumon shita n desu ka.

Takahashi   Iie, mada desu. Menyuu o doozo.

Nelson   Arigatoo. Sa, nani ni shimashoo ka. (reading the menu) Hamu sando...tsuna sarada...supagetti... piza...aa, watashi wa piza ni shimasu. Piza to hotto koohii. Takahashi san wa?

Takahashi   O-naka ga suita kara, watashi mo piza desu. Sore kara, remon tii. (to waiter) Sumimasen. Piza futatsu to, hotto hitotsu to remon tii o hitotsu onegai shimasu.

Waiter   Piza futatsu, hotto hitotsu, remon tii o hitotsu desu ne. Kashikomarimashita.

Takahashi   (looking out of the window) Ara, Kenji san da. Are wa Kenji san desu.

Nelson   Booifurendo desu ka. Doko? Dono hito ga Kenji san desu ka.

Takahashi   Yuubinkyoku no mae ni imasu. Kooshuu denwa no tonari desu.

Nelson   Hai, hai. Aa, ima Takahashi san o mita deshoo. Ee. Doo shite mukoo e aruite iku n desu ka. Hen desu ne.

Takahashi   Jitsu wa, kinoo no yoru denwa de kenka shita n desu. Watashi wa konban gakkoo no sutaffu to issho ni, eiga o mi ni iku to itta n desu ne. Sooshitara, Kenji san ga okotta n desu yo. Okashii deshoo. Dakara watashi mo okotte, kore kara moo awanai hoo ga ii, to itta n desu. Sore de, kaiwa ga owarimashita.

Nelson   Soo desu ka. Doo shimasu ka. Ima Kenji san o yonda hoo ga ii deshoo.

Takahashi	Iie, kyoo wa Kenji san to hanasanai hoo ga ii to omoimasu.
Nelson	Soo desu ka. A, piza ga kimashita.
Waiter	Hai, hotto no o-kyaku sama wa?
Nelson	Watashi desu. Doomo.
Takahashi	Sa, jikan ga amari nai kara, hayaku tabeta hoo ga ii desu ne. Itadakimasu.

QUESTIONS:

1. Dare ga chuumon o shimasu ka.
2. Takahashi san no booifurendo wa Takahashi san o mita kedo, dooshite mukoo e aruite ikimashita ka.
3. Takahashi san wa, kyoo booifurendo to hanashitai to omotte imasu ka.
4. Nelson san to Takahashi san wa konban nani o shi ni ikimasu ka.

Dialogue 15: Watashi no keiyaku ni tsuite desu ga.

Mike Nelson is talking to Mr. Watanabe in the staff room at school.

Nelson	Watanabe san, chotto shitsumon ga aru n desu ga, ii desu ka.
Watanabe	Ii desu yo. Doozo. Nan deshoo ka.
Nelson	Watashi no keiyaku ni tsuite desu ga.
Watanabe	Keiyaku ni tsuite no shitsumon desu ka. Demo watashi wa keiyaku no koto wa yoku wakaranai n desu yo. Koochoo sensei to hanashita hoo ga ii to omoimasu. Nanika, mondai ga dekimashita ka.
Nelson	Iie, iie, mondai ja nai n desu. Jitsu wa, raigetsu watashi no tomodachi ga Nihon e kuru yotei na n desu ga, Nihon wa hajimete da kara, kuukoo made mukae ni ikitai to omotte iru n desu ga.
Watanabe	A, wakarimashita. Yasumi no koto desu ka.
Nelson	Ee, moshi mondai ja nakattara, ichi-nichi yasumi o toritai n desu.
Watanabe	Sore wa mondai nai to omoimasu yo. Tada, sono koto ni tsuite memo o kaite, watashi ni dashite kudasai. Saitoo san ga sono tokubetsu no yooshi o motte imasu kara, kanojo ni kiite kudasai.

Just then, Ms. Takahashi comes into the teachers' room to talk to Mike.

Takahashi	Neruson san, chotto ii desu ka. Koochoo sensei kara no messeeji desu ga, moshi yokattara, kyoo ka ashita Neruson san to uchiawase o shitai to itte imashita ga.
Nelson	Koochoo sensei to no uchiawase desu ka. Nanika...
Takahashi	Shinpai shinaide kudasai. Tada kore kara no keikaku ni tsuite soodan suru tsumori da to omoimasu.
Nelson	Soo desu ka. Jikan o ima kimemasu ka.
Takahashi	Hai, onegai shimasu. Koochoo sensei no sukejuuru o motte imasu kara, ima kimemashoo.
Nelson	Watashi wa, ashita no asa juu-ji made aite imasu ga.
Takahashi	Ashita no asa wa chotto. Koochoo sensei wa kyooiku iinkai ni yoru tsumori da to itte imashita kara. Gogo wa?
Nelson	Gogo wa, san-ji han made jugyoo ga arimasu ga, sono ato wa aite imasu.
Takahashi	Ja, yo-ji ni shimashoo.

QUESTIONS:

1. Dare ga keiyaku no koto ga yoku wakarimasu ka.
2. Nelson san wa nagai yasumi o toritai n desu ka.
3. Nelson san wa ashita nani ni tsuite koochoo sensei to hanasu yotei desu ka.
4. Doo shite ima Takahashi san to uchiawase no jikan o kimeru koto ga dekimasu ka.

TEST YOURSELF

Which is the odd man out in the following? Underline the word in each group which doesn't fit with the others.

1.	mittsu	itsu	kokonotsu	futatsu
2.	aki	fuyu	natsu	shunbun
3.	hamu	piza	sando	wain
4.	toki	hiruma	yoru	asa

Exercise A

5.	ushiro	shisha	shita	mae
6.	watashi	kare	onna	kanojo
7.	ikutsu	donna	dore	anna
8.	shutchoo	buchoo	kachoo	koochoo

Exercise B

Put these words into the correct order to make sentences. Be careful – there is one extra word in each group.

1. wa ashita asa desu rainen no yakyuu suru o Maiku yotei san

2. takusan dekiru nomanai ga ii konban omoimasu to hoo

3. no tsuite natsu gaikoku omoimasu ikitai e to kotoshi

4. shite desu shitsumon ka dare ii o mo

5. muzukashii nakatta omoimasen to konna deshita ni

6. tsumori tsuite hanasanaide kyuuryoo san ni ni koto no Takahashi kudasai

Exercise C

Imagine you have to call Mr. Wada at Takada Company to arrange an appointment, and fill in the missing lines.

Wada	Moshi moshi, Wada desu ga.
You	[Give your name.]
Wada	Aa, doomo.
You	[Say you're calling about the contract.]
Wada	Hai, hai. Sugu hanashita hoo ga ii desu ne.
You	[Ask him if he's free this afternoon.]
Wada	Kyoo wa chotto muzukashii desu ne. Iroiro-na uchiawase ga arimasu kara. Ashita wa doo desu ka.
You	[Tell him you're scheduled to attend a meeting from 10:00 tomorrow morning.]
Wada	Ja, ashita no gogo wa doo desu ka.
You	[Tell him yes, the afternoon is free.]
Wada	Ni-ji ni shimashoo ka.
You	[Agree with him.]
Wada	Ja, ashita no ni-ji desu ne. Dewa, shitsurei shimasu.

Complete the crossword puzzle by finding words which fill the blanks in the sentences below.

Across

1. Neruson san no apaato no _____ ni dare ga sunde imasu ka.

5. Sumimasen, kono denwa o tsukatte _____ ii desu ka.

7. Sono keikaku ni _____ hanashitai n desu ga.

9. Kissaten wa yuubinkyoku no _____ ni arimasu.

10. Nihongo no tesuto wa _____ ni muzukashii to omoimasen deshita.

12. Tanjoobi wa nan-_____ desu ka.

13. Tesuto wa hajimarimasu kara, kore kara hanashite wa _____.

Down

2. Kotoshi no natsu yasumi ni doko e _____ n desu ka.

3. "Autumn" wa Nihongo de _____ to iimasu.

4. Kanojo wa _____ takai kyuuryoo ga hoshii to iimashita.

6. Hotto o _____ kudasai.

8. Takahashi san to Saitoo san no _____ ni dare ga suwarimasu ka.

9. Sono _____ o yonde wa ikemasen yo.

11. Nihon no _____ wa atsui desu ka.

Exercise E

Answer these questions about yourself.

1. Sukii wa dekimasu ka. O-joozu desu ka.
   _____

2. Tanjoobi wa nan-gatsu, nan-nichi desu ka.
   _____

3. O-kuni de wa, yasumi no hi ga takusan arimasu ka.
   _____

4. Donna supootsu ga suki desu ka.
   _____

5. Anata wa ashita yasumi o totte mo ii desu ka.
   _____

6. Ima ikutsu desu ka.
   _____

7. Kinoo, nan-ji made okite imashita ka.
   _____

8. O-kuni de wa, ichiban atsui toki wa nan-gatsu desu ka.
   _____

9. Kekkon shite imasu ka. Booifurendo ka gaarufurendo ga imasu ka.
   _____

10. Yoku okorimasu ka.
    _____

11. Anata no uchi ka apaato ni wa, heya ga ikutsu arimasu ka.
    _____

12. Gaikoku e iku yotei ga arimasu ka.
    _____

 **Fukushuu** meaning "review", combines characters for "repeat" and "learn".

 Visit www.berlitzpublishing.com for a bonus internet activity—go to the downloads section and connect to the world in Japanese!

17

KAMAKURA E ITTA KOTO GA ARIMASU KA.
HAVE YOU EVER BEEN TO KAMAKURA?

 It's Friday, and Mike Nelson is chatting with Ms. Takahashi during the lunch break.

Takahashi **Neruson san wa Kamakura e itta koto ga arimasu ka.**
Have you ever been to Kamakura, Mr. Nelson?

Nelson **Iie, arimasen. Ikitai n desu kedo.**
No, I haven't. I'd like to go though.

Takahashi **Ja, nichiyoobi ni watashitachi to issho ni Kamakura e ikimasen ka. Saitoo san mo Wada san mo issho ni iku to itte imasu ga. Tenki ga yokattara, pikunikku o suru tsumori desu.**
Well, would you like to go to Kamakura with us on Sunday? Ms. Saitoo and Ms. Wada say they're coming too. If the weather's nice, we plan to have a picnic.

Nelson	Ii desu ne. Demo, tenki ga yoku nakattara, doo shimasu ka. Konban ame ga furu to kikimashita ga. Sounds good. But what will we do if the weather's not good? I heard that it's going to rain tonight.
Takahashi	Sonna koto o kangaenaide kudasai. Nichiyoobi wa kitto ii tenki desu yo. Don't even think about that! It'll definitely be nice weather on Sunday.
Nelson	Wakarimashita. Densha de iku n desu ka. I see. Will we go by train?
Takahashi	Soo desu. Densha no hoo ga hayai to omoimasu. Sore dake ja nakute, dare mo kuruma o motte imasen kara, shikata ga nai n desu. Yes. I think the train's quicker. And not only that, no one owns a car, so we have no choice.

The four are now in Kamakura, standing in front of the daibutsu, or great statue of Buddha, for which Kamakura is famous.

Nelson	Konna ni ookii daibutsu wa mita koto ga arimasen ne. I've never seen such a big statue of Buddha.
Takahashi	Naka ni haitte, atama no naka made noboru koto mo dekimasu yo. Watashi wa haitta koto ga nai kedo. You can go inside, and climb up inside the head too. I've never been in it though.
Nelson	Jaa, hairimashoo ka. Well, shall we go in?
Takahashi	Chotto matte. Sono mae ni, minna no shashin o toritai kara. Hai, mina san, daibutsu no mae ni tatte kudasai yo. Aa, dame desu. Soko ni tattara, daibutsu ga shashin ni hairimasen. Hold on. Before that, I want to take a picture of everyone. Okay, everybody, stand in front of the Buddha. No, that's no good. If you stand there, the Buddha isn't in the picture.
Nelson	Sono kaidan no ue ni suwattara, doo desu ka. How about if we sit at the top of those steps?
Takahashi	Soo ne. Sono hoo ga ii desu ne. Hai, mina san, soko ni suwatte kudasai. Ii desu ka. Hai, chiizu. Doomo arigatoo. Sa, daibutsu ni hairimashoo. Yes, that'd be better. Right, everyone, sit over there. Okay? Cheese! Thanks. Right, let's go into the statue of the Buddha now.

> Nelson Mite. Daibutsu no ushiro ni sugoi hito ga narande
> imasu ne. Jikan ga kakaru deshoo.
> Hey, look. There's an incredible number of people lining
> up behind the statue. It'll take ages.
>
> Takahashi Saki ni hiru-gohan o tabetara, doo deshoo.
> How about if we have lunch first?
>
> Nelson Soo desu ne. Demo ne, chotto samuku natte, sora
> mo kuraku natte irukara, pikunikku wa chotto…Are.
> Ame ja nai desu ka.
> Yes, okay. But, it's gotten a little cold, and the sky is
> getting dark so I'm afraid that it's not good to have a
> picnic. Oh, isn't that rain?
>
> Takahashi Soo desu yo. Ara, sugoi ame da. Dareka kasa o
> motte imasu ka. Dare mo kasa o motte inai n desu
> ka. Jaa, ichiban chikai resutoran made hashitte
> ikimashoo yo. Hayaku, hayaku.
> Yes, it is. Aargh, incredible rain. Does anyone have an
> umbrella? No one has an umbrella? Then let's run to the
> nearest restaurant. Quickly!

STRUCTURE AND USAGE NOTES

1. -TA KOTO GA ARIMASU KA – "HAVE YOU EVER…?"

This phrase using the plain past form of the verb (e.g. tabeta, "ate", itta,
"went") followed by koto ga arimasu ka is used when you are asking
someone about their experiences, so it is the equivalent of the English
"Have you ever…?" You have already come across the word koto to
mean "thing/event", and coupled with the past form of a verb you can think
of it as "experience", so tabeta koto is "experience of eating", and itta
koto is "experience of going". A literal translation of Sushi o tabeta koto
ga arimasu ka would therefore be "Do you have experience of eating
sushi?" or more colloquially, "Have you ever eaten sushi?"

Fuji san ni nobotta koto ga arimasu ka.
Have you ever climbed Mt. Fuji?

Kamakura no daibutsu o mita koto ga arimasu kedo, Nara no daibutsu
o mita koto wa arimasen.
I've seen the great statue of Buddha at Kamakura, but I haven't seen the
one at Nara.

Sonna koto o kangaeta koto ga nai n desu yo.
I've never considered such a thing!

Sugoi hito da to kikimashita ga, atta koto ga nai kara, yoku wakarimasen.
I hear that he's an amazing person, but I've never met (him), so I don't really know.

Sashimi o tabeta koto ga arimasu ka.
Have you ever eaten raw fish?

A positive answer to the last question would be Hai, arimasu, "Yes, I have" (or Hai, tabeta koto ga arimasu, "Yes, I have eaten it"), and a negative answer would be Iie, arimasen, "No, I haven't" (or Iie, tabeta koto ga arimasen, "No, I haven't eaten it").

A. Amerika e itta koto ga arimasu ka.
   Have you ever been to the USA?
B. Iie, arimasen. Kyonen Kanada e itta kedo, Amerika wa mada desu.
   No, I haven't. I went to Canada last year, but I haven't been to the USA yet [Lit: ... but the USA is not yet].

A. Onsen ni haitta koto ga arimasu ka.
   Have you ever been in a hot spring bath?
B. Arimasu yo. Dai-suki desu.
   I certainly have. I love them.

A. Densha no naka ni kasa o wasureta koto ga arimasu ka.
   Have you ever forgotten your umbrella on the train?
B. Mochiron arimasu yo.
   Of course I have!

---

2. -TARA – "IF..." AND "WHEN"

To make this kind of "if" sentence in Japanese, just add -ra to the plain past tense of the verb (e.g. tabeta, itta, etc.). Hence tabetara means "if you eat", ittara means "if you go", and denwa shitara means "if you call". In practice this is often called the -tara form, as all verbs end in -tara (or occasionally -dara).

Plain form	Plain past	-tara form	Meaning
taberu	tabeta	tabetara	if I/you, etc., eat
iku	itta	ittara	if you go
kuru	kita	kitara	if you come
suru	shita	shitara	if you do
aru	atta	attara	if there is

naru	natta	nattara	if it becomes
hanasu	hanashita	hanashitara	if you speak
nomu	nonda	nondara	if you drink
da	datta	dattara	if it is

Ame ga futtara, uchi ni ite, diibiidii o mimashoo.
If it rains, let's stay home and watch a DVD.

O-kanemochi dattara, doko e ikitai to omoimasu ka.
If you were rich, where do you think you'd like to go?

Yukkuri hanashitara, wakaru to omoimasu.
If you speak slowly, I think I'll understand.

Soko o migi ni magattara, eki ni demasu.
If you turn right there, you'll come out at the station.

Kaigi ga san-ji made ni owattara, shisha no Nagai san ni denwa shite kudasai.
If the meeting finishes by 3:00, please call Mr. Nagai at the branch office.

Sono kaidan ni nobottara, o-tearai wa migi-gawa ni arimasu.
If you go up the stairs, you'll find the restrooms on your right.

Moo sugu Yamada-san ga kimasu yo. Yamada-san ga kitara, tabemashoo.
Mr. Yamada is coming soon. When he comes, let's eat.

Eiga ga owattara, denwa shimasu ne.
I'll call you when the movie ends.

Do the same thing with the negative when you want to talk about if something *doesn't* happen, that is, add -ra to the negative of the plain past tense (the one that ends in -nakatta). The ending then becomes -nakattara.

Plain form	Negative past	Negative	-tara form	Meaning
kuru	konai	konakatta	konakattara	if you don't come
iku	ikanai	ikanakatta	ikanakattara	if you don't go
suru	shinai	shinakatta	shinakattara	if you don't do
nomu	nomanai	nomanakatta	nomanakattara	if you don't drink

| toru | toranai | toranakatta | toranakattara | if you don't take |
| aru | nai | nakatta | nakattara | if there isn't |

Wada san ga sugu konakattara, doo shimasu ka.
If Ms. Wada doesn't come soon, what will we do?

Watashi wa shashin o takusan toranakattara, yasumi no koto o sugu wasuremasu.
If I don't take lots of photos, I soon forget vacations.

Jikan ga nakattara, shinakute mo ii desu yo.
If you don't have time, it's all right if you don't do it.

Hayaku nenakattara, hayaku okiru koto mo dekimasen yo.
If you don't go to sleep early, you won't be able to get up early either.

Ashita no asa jikan ga attara, iinkai no kaigi ni dete kudasai.
If you have time tomorrow morning, please attend the committee meeting.

The word moshi, or "if", can be added to the beginning of a sentence to alert the listener early on that this is going to be an "if" sentence, and it also adds emphasis. However, it is still necessary to have the -tara verb ending.

Moshi Wada san kara denwa ga attara, atarashii yotei o oshiete kudasai.
If there's a call from Ms. Wada, please tell her about the new plan.

Moshi mondai ga attara, oshiete kudasai.
If there are any problems, please let me know.

The -tara ending can also be added to -i adjectives. Once again, find the past tense -katta ending, and add -ra.

Takakattara, mochiron kaimasen.
If it's expensive, of course I won't buy it.

Kibun ga warukattara, konakute mo ii desu yo.
If you're feeling bad, you don't need to come.

Chikakattara, aruku koto ga dekiru deshoo.
If it's close, we can walk, right?

Moshi yokattara, kore o tsukatte kudasai.
If you'd like to, please use this.

You can use the -tara form for making suggestions, in which case it can be translated as "How about -ing?" or "Why don't we…?"

Konshuu no nichiyoobi ni pikunikku o shitara doo desu ka.
How about a picnic this Sunday?

Soko de mattara doo desu ka.
Why don't we wait over there?

Kotoshi no natsu yasumi ni, gaikoku e ittara doo desu ka.
How about going abroad this summer vacation?

Sometimes the doo desu ka ending is left off, and the meaning is merely implied.

Koko de suwattara?
How about if we sit here?

Saki ni ittara?
How about if you go on ahead?

The -tara form can only be used for sentences where the two events mentioned take place one after the other. Therefore, you can use it for the equivalent of "If we go to Tokyo, let's visit Michiko", but not for "If we go to Tokyo, we should call Michiko beforehand". Another way of making "if" sentences is with the verb ending -eba, which will be explained in the next lesson.

---

3. DARE MO, DOKO MO, NANI MO – "NOBODY", "NOWHERE", "NOTHING"

When question words like dare, nani, or doko are followed by mo and a negative verb, the meanings change from "who", "what" and "where" to "not anyone", "not anything" and "not anywhere".

A. Tonari no heya ni dare ga imasu ka.
   Who's in the next room?
B. Dare mo imasen.
   No one.

O-kane ga nakattara, nani mo dekimasen.
If you don't have money, you can't do anything.

Kyoo wa kibun ga amari yoku nai kara, doko e mo ikitaku nai n desu.
I don't really feel well today, so I don't want to go anywhere.

Hoka ni nani mo nakattara, kore de kaigi o owarimashoo.
If there isn't anything else, let's finish the meeting here.

Dare mo konakattara, doo shimashoo ka.
If no one comes, what shall we do?

Kooshuu denwa wa, doko ni mo arimasen ne.
There isn't a public telephone anywhere, is there?

4. DENSHA NO HOO GA HAYAI – "THE TRAIN'S FASTER" AND OTHER COMPARATIVES

When making a comparison between two things, imagine they're on two sides (hoo) of a pair of scales, being measured against each other. Then you just need to ask the equivalent of "Which side is fast/slow/expensive?": Dochira no hoo ga hayai/osoi/takai desu ka. The word dotchi can be used in place of dochira. Dotchi is a casual version of dochira.

If you want to answer that "this one" or "that one" is faster (or slower), then use kochira (kotchi) or sochira (sotchi): Kochira no hoo ga hayai/osoi/takai desu.

A. Takushii to densha to, dochira no hoo ga hayai desu ka.
Which is faster, a taxi or the train?
B. Kono jikan wa, densha no hoo ga hayai to omoimasu.
At this time, I think the train is faster.

A. Kamakura to Yokohama to, dochira no hoo ga koko kara tooi desu ka.
Which is further from here, Kamakura or Yokohama?
B. Soo desu ne. Kamakura no hoo ga tooi to omoimasu.
Hmmm. I think Kamakura is further.

A. Kore to kore to, dochira no hoo ga ii desu ka.
Which is the better of these two?
B. Yasui hoo o kaimashoo.
Let's buy the cheaper one.

A. Oosaka to Nagoya to, dochira no hoo ga hiroi desu ka.
Which is bigger (in area), Osaka or Nagoya?
B. Mochiron Oosaka no hoo ga hiroi desu yo.
Of course Osaka is bigger!

You might also hear this pattern without no hoo.

O-sake to biiru to, dochira ga suki desu ka.
Which do you like, sake or beer?

Doyoobi to nichiyoobi to, dotchi ga ii desu ka.
Which is better, Saturday or Sunday?

---

5. SAMUKU NATTE – "IT'S GETTING COLD"

The verb naru means "become/get" so it can be used with adjectives to make phrases such as "get late", "get more expensive", "grow old", "become dark", and with nouns for phrases like "become a teacher", "become president", "become an adult". With -i adjectives, first drop the final -i and add -ku.

Samuku narimashita ne. Moo sugu fuyu desu yo.
It's gotten cold, hasn't it! It'll soon be winter!

Shichi-gatsu ni nattara, atsuku narimasu yo.
Come July, it's going to get hotter.

Wada san wa, kibun ga waruku natta to itte iru kara, moo kaetta hoo ga ii deshoo.
Since Ms. Wada says she's feeling bad, it would be better if she went home, wouldn't it?

Osoku natte, sumimasen.
I'm sorry I'm late.

With -na adjectives and with nouns, add ni.

Nihongo ga taihen o-joozu ni narimashita ne.
You've gotten really good at Japanese, haven't you!

Kare wa kitto yuumei ni narimasu yo.
He's definitely going to become famous.

Ookiku nattara, nani ni naritai n desu ka.
When you grow up, what do you want to be?

Sonna ni takusan tabetara, byooki ni narimasu yo.
If you eat that much food, you'll get sick.

Keiyaku ga kin'yoobi made ni dekinakattara, ooki-na mondai ni naru to omoimasu.
If the contract isn't done by Friday, I think there'll be big problems.

---

6. DAREKA – "SOMEONE"

Adding -ka to the end of question words such as dare, itsu, nani and doko is a bit like putting "some" in front of equivalent words in English (or in the case of questions and negatives, "any").

A. Shuumatsu ni, dokoka e ikimashita ka.
   Did you go anywhere on the weekend?
B. Iie, o-kane ga nai kara, doko e mo ikimasen deshita.
   No, I don't have any money, so I didn't go anywhere!

Gomen kudasai. Dareka imasu ka.
Excuse me. Is there anyone there?

Nanika tabemashita ka.
Have you eaten anything?

Itsuka nomi ni ikimashoo.
Let's go for a drink sometime.

Kasa wa doko kana. Dokoka de wasureta kamoshirenai.
I wonder where my umbrella is? I might have left it somewhere.

Dareka saki ni itte, narandara doo desu ka.
How about someone going ahead of us and standing in line?

Itsuka Hokkaidoo e ikitai.
I want to go to Hokkaido sometime.

Daijoobu desu ka. Nanika atta n desu ka.
Are you okay? Did something happen?

Note that the particles o and ga are usually dropped after these words.

CULTURAL NOTE

THE WEATHER

The Japanese are very conscious of nature and the seasons, and so the weather is a common topic of conversation. Comments on the weather are used as greetings, as small talk, and frequently as opening paragraphs in letters. Here are some of the phrases you are most likely to hear.

Dandan samuku natte imasu ne.
It's gradually getting colder, isn't it?

Kinoo, sugoi ame deshita ne.
That was incredible rain yesterday, wasn't it?

Kyoo wa atatakai desu ne.
It's warm today, isn't it?

Mushiatsukute, iya desu ne.
It's horrible and humid, isn't it?

Kaze ga tsuyoi desu ne. Ki o tsuketa hoo ga ii desu yo.
The wind is strong, isn't it? You'd better take care.

Suzushiku narimashita ne. Moo sorosoro aki desu ne.
It's gotten cooler, hasn't it? It's going to be autumn soon.

Sora o mite kudasai. Kitto yuki ga furu deshoo.
Just look at the sky. It's definitely going to snow.

VOCABULARY

ame ga furu: it rains [Lit: the rain falls]
ame: rain
Are.: Look!, Listen!
atatakai: warm
byooki: ill
Chiizu!: Cheese! [when taking a photograph]
chikai: close, nearby
daibutsu: large statue of Buddha
dandan: gradually, little by little
dare mo: no one
dareka: someone
diibiidii: DVD
dochira/dotchi: Which one? [of two]
furu: fall, drop
hiroi: large (in area), spacious, extensive
hoo: direction, side
hoka ni: other, another, else
Hokkaidoo: the northernmost of the four main islands of Japan
kaidan: steps, stairs
Kamakura: city close to Yokohama, famous for its large statue of Buddha
kasa: umbrella
kaze: wind
kibun ga ii: feel good
kibun ga warui: feel bad
kitto: definitely, without fail
kochira/kotchi: this side, this one (of two)
koto ga arimasu ka: Have you ever…?
kuraku: dark [from kurai]
mita koto wa arimasen: I've never seen [from miru]
mochiron: of course, naturally
moshi: if
mushiatsui: hot and humid
narande imasu: are lined up, lining up [from narabu]
naru: become, get
noboru: climb, go up
o-kanemochi: rich person
okiru: get up, get out of bed
o-tearai: restroom
pikunikku: picnic
saki ni: in advance, ahead, before
samuku natte…: getting cold and…
shashin: photograph
Shikata ga arimasen.: It can't be helped.
sochira/sotchi: that side, that one [of two]

Sono hoo ga ii.: That would be best.
sore dake ja nakute: not only that
sugoi: amazing, incredible
suwattara: if you sit [from suwaru]
suzushii: cool
tabetara: if we eat [from taberu]
tattara: if you stand [from tatsu]
tatte kudasai: please stand [from tatsu]
tooi: far, distant
tsuyoi: strong
yokattara: if it's all right
yoku nakattara: if it's not all right
yuki: snow

TEST YOURSELF

Read through the dialogue at the beginning of the lesson again, and then say if the following statements are true or false.

1. Takahashi san mo, Saitoo san mo, Wada san mo, nichiyoobi ni Kamakura e iku tsumori desu. T/F

2. Takahashi san wa, nichiyoobi wa ii tenki da to omotte imasu. T/F

3. Takahashi san wa kuruma o motte imasu. T/F

4. Daibutsu no naka ni hairu koto ga dekimasu ga, atama made hairu koto ga dekimasen. T/F

5. Minna kaidan no ue ni suwattara, daibutsu mo shashin ni hairimasu. T/F

6. Tenki ga dandan waruku narimashita. T/F

Exercise A

While waiting in the restaurant for the rain to stop, Mike chats with the others about various things they've done in their past. In the following table, you can see some of the things that Ms. Wada and Ms. Saitoo have and haven't done. Make up sentences like the ones in the example, using koto ga arimasu.

Examples: Wada san wa gaikoku e itta koto ga arimasu ga, Saitoo san wa arimasen.
Wada san mo Saitoo san mo Eigo o benkyoo shita koto ga arimasu.

Exercise B

-ta koto ga arimasu ka.	Ms. Wada	Ms. Saitoo
traveled abroad?	O	X
studied English?	O	O
1. owned a car?	O	X
2. climbed Mt. Fuji?	O	O
3. lived in Tokyo?	X	O
4. been to Hokkaido?	X	X
5. met Mr. Watanabe's wife?	O	X
6. taken a video?	O	O

Exercise C

Choose which of the two alternatives in each case is most appropriate to finish the sentence.

1. Wada san wa kaigi ni denakattara,
   a. hiru-gohan o tabemasen.
   b. keiyaku no koto o soodan suru koto wa dekimasen.

2. Kibun ga warukattara,
   a. hayaku neta hoo ga ii deshoo.
   b. hayaku okita hoo ga ii deshoo.

3. Wada san ga konakattara,
   a. doo shimashoo ka.
   b. byooki desu.

4. Tookattara,
   a. denwa shimasen.
   b. arukimasen.

5. Moshi yokattara,
    a. mita koto ga nai to omoimasu.
    b. shashin o toritai n desu ga.

6. O-sake o takusan nondara,
    a. byooki ni naru to omoimasu yo.
    b. wakaku naru to omoimasu yo.

How's your general knowledge? Using the cues below, make up questions and then see if you know the answers, as in the example.

Example: Children's Day, Respect for the Aged Day – first?
       Q. Kodomo no hi to Keiroo no hi to, dochira (no hoo) ga saki desu ka.
       A. Kodomo no hi no hoo ga saki desu.

1. Amazon, Nile – longer?
   Q. _____
   A. _____

2. Mt. Fuji, Mt. McKinley – higher?
   Q. _____
   A. _____

3. Hong Kong, Taiwan – further from Japan?
   Q. _____
   A. _____

4. Japan, Philippines – big?
   Q. _____
   A. _____

5. Tokyo, New York – has most people?
   Q. _____
   A. _____

And now some questions about you:

6. mountains, sea – like?
   Q. _____
   A. _____

7. telephone, fax – often use?
   Q. _____
   A. _____

Exercise D

8. Mexican food, Chinese food – often eat?

    Q. _____

    A. _____

9. study, work – like?

    Q. _____

    A. _____

10. newspapers, books – often read?

    Q. _____

    A. _____

Exercise E

How would you say these sentences in Japanese?

1. If it doesn't rain, shall we go somewhere on Sunday?

    _____

2. Have you ever eaten in that restaurant?

    _____

3. Which do you like better, the summer or the winter?

    _____

4. I have a stomachache, so I don't want anything to eat.

    _____

5. It's gradually getting warmer, isn't it? It'll soon be spring.

    _____

6. If you have time, could you call Mr. Fukuda and tell him about the meeting time?

    _____

天気 Tenki (weather) is a combination of the kanji characters for "heaven/sky" and "sprit".

Visit www.berlitzpublishing.com for a bonus internet activity—go to the downloads section and connect to the world in Japanese!

SOO SUREBA...
IF YOU DO THAT...

Mike Nelson is going to the theater this afternoon to see Kabuki with Mr. Kato, a teacher from his school. He's just talking to him on the phone now.

Nelson **Sa, nan-ji ni, doko de aimashoo ka.**
So what time and where shall we meet?

Kato **Watashi ga saki ni Nelson sensei no apaato ni ikimashoo ka. Soo sureba, issho ni eki made aruite iku koto ga dekimasu ne.**
Shall I come to your apartment first? If I do that, we can walk to the station together, right?

Nelson **Jitsu wa, watashi wa yooji ga iroiro aru n desu. Dakara sugu uchi o dete, Katoo san ni au mae ni yooji o sureba ii to omotte ita n desu ga.**
The fact is, I have various things to do. So I was thinking it would be better if I went out soon and did the errands before we met up.

217

Kato   Watashi mo issho ni ikimasu yo. Soo sureba, yooji ga owatte kara, dokoka de ranchi o taberu koto mo dekiru deshoo. Kabuki wa nagai kara, hairu mae ni nanika tabeta hoo ga ii to omoimasu. Ii desu ka.
I'll come with you. If I do that, after the errands are done we can have some lunch somewhere, right? Kabuki is long, so I think it's better if we have something to eat before we go in. Is that okay?

Nelson   Mochiron ii desu kedo, Katoo san ni wa zenzen omoshiroku nai to omoimasu yo. Mazu, haha no tanjoobi no purezento o okuru tame ni yuubinkyoku e itte, sore kara, gasu-dai to denki-dai o harau tame ni ginkoo e ikimasu. Sono ato...
Of course it's okay, but I think it'll be completely uninteresting for you. First I'm going to the post office to mail a present for my mother's birthday. Then I'm going to the bank to pay the gas and electricity bills. After that...

Kato   Daijoobu desu yo. Ja, juu-ji-han goro Maiku san no tokoro ni ikeba, jikan ga juubun arimasu ka.
It's okay. So if I come to your place at 10:30, will there be enough time?

Nelson   Hai hai, ii desu. Ja, matte imasu yo.
Yes, it's fine. I'll be waiting.

Later, at the post office.

Nelson   Kono kozutsumi o Amerika made okuritai n desu ga, ikura deshoo ka.
I'd like to send this package to the USA. How much is it, please?

Clerk   EMS desu ne. (She weighs the package) Hai, hassen nihyaku en desu. Kono yooshi ni kakikonde kudasai.
EMS (Express Mail Service), right? That's 8,200 yen. Please fill in this form.

Nelson   Sore kara, hyaku-juu en kitte o yon-mai kudasai.
And four 110-yen stamps, please.

Clerk   Hyaku-juu en kitte o yon-mai desu ne. Zenbu de hassen roppyaku yon-juu en desu. Hai, ichi-man-en o-azukari shimasu. O-tsuri wa sen-san-byaku-roku-juu en desu. Doozo.
Four 110-yen stamps. That's 8,640 yen altogether. Thank you, 10,000 yen. Here's the change of 1,360 yen.

Nelson	Arigatoo. *(to Mr. Kato)* Sugoi oozei no hito ga ushiro ni narande imasu ne. Ginkoo mo konna ni konde itara, yamemashoo.
	Thank you. There's an incredible number of people lining up behind us, aren't there? If the bank is this crowded, let's not bother.
Kato	Demo, gasu-dai to denki-dai o harawanakereba…
	But if you don't pay your gas and electricity…
Nelson	Ii n desu yo. Shinpai shinaide. Jikan wa mada juubun arimasu.
	It's okay. Don't worry. There's still enough time.

STRUCTURE AND USAGE NOTES

1. AU MAE NI – "BEFORE MEETING"

In order to talk about one event happening before another, use mae ni ("before") after the plain form of the verb. You can use the present tense of the plain form (iku, taberu, suru, etc.), whether you're talking about two events in the past, present or future.

Sono memo o Nagoya shisha ni okuru mae ni, misete kudasai.
Before you send that note to the Nagoya branch, please show it to me.

Watashi wa neru mae ni, itsumo hon o yomimasu.
Before I go to sleep, I always read a book.

Kissaten ni hairu mae ni, watashi wa ginkoo ni yoru kara, doozo saki ni itte kudasai.
Before we go into the coffee shop, I have to drop in at the bank, so please go on ahead.

Okane o harau mae ni, kono yooshi ni kakikonde kudasai.
Before you pay the money, please fill in this form.

Sono repooto o buchoo ni dasu mae ni, kopii o torimashita ka.
Before you gave that report to the department head, did you take a copy?

2. YOOJI GA OWATTE KARA – "AFTER THE ERRANDS ARE FINISHED"

When you want to talk about one event happening *after* another, use the -te form of the verb with kara. This is the equivalent of the English "after -ing", and can be used whether the second part of the sentence is in the past, present or future. (Be careful not to confuse this with kara after the plain form of the verb, when it means "because". See Lesson 11, Structure and Usage Note 6.)

Gasu-dai to denwa-dai to denki-dai o haratte kara, yuubinkyoku ni iku yotei desu.
After I pay the gas bill, the telephone bill and the electricity bill, I plan to go to the post office.

Kabuki o mite kara, dokoka e nomi ni ikimashoo ka.
After we've seen Kabuki, shall we go for a drink somewhere?

Kaigi ga owatte kara, watashi wa kaette mo ii desu ka. Kibun ga chotto warui n desu.
After the meeting finishes, is it all right if I go home? It's that I don't feel very well.

Sono shukudai o shite kara, sugu neta hoo ga ii to omoimasu.
After you finish your homework, I think you should go straight to bed.

Nihon e kite kara Nihongo no benkyoo o hajimemashita.
I started to learn Japanese after I came to Japan.

---

3. SOO SUREBA – "IF WE DO SO"

The verb ending -eba shows another way of making "if" sentences. Generally, -eba means "only if", so the condition being presented with -eba is stronger than that of -tara. To make the -eba form, start with the plain form of the verb, drop the final -u and replace it with -eba.

Plain form	-eba form	Meaning
sur-u	sur-eba	if I (you, etc.) do
kur-u	kur-eba	if I come
kak-u	kak-eba	if I write
hara-u	hara-eba	if I pay
okur-u	okur-eba	if I send
ar-u	ar-eba	if I have
tsukur-u	tsukur-eba	if I make
dekir-u	dekir-eba	if I can

O-kane ga juubun areba, Amerika dake ja nakute, Kanada e mo ikitai desu.
If I have enough money, I want to go to Canada, as well as the USA.

Moshi dekireba, kotoshi gaikoku e ikitai n desu.
If I can, I want to go abroad this year.

Ame ga fureba, dekakeru yotei o yamemashoo.
If it rains, let's drop the plan to go out.

Minna de soodan sureba ii to omoimasu.
I think it's best if we discuss it altogether.

Ranchi ni wa, sando dake o tsukureba ii desu ka.
Is it all right if I just make sandwiches for lunch?

When you want to talk about a situation if something *doesn't* happen, then find the negative plain form (ending in -nai), drop the final -i and add -kereba.

Plain negative	-kereba form	Meaning
tsukawana-i	tsukawana-kereba	if I (you, etc.) don't use
ikana-i	ikana-kereba	if I don't go
wakarana-i	wakarana-kereba	if I don't understand
na-i	na-kereba	if there isn't
dekakena-i	dekakena-kereba	if we don't go out
kawana-i	kawana-kereba	if I don't buy
matte ina-i	matte ina-kereba	if he isn't waiting

Jisho o tsukawanakereba, kono Nihongo no shukudai ga dekimasen.
If I don't use a dictionary, I can't do this Japanese homework.

Shinkansen no kippu o kyoo kawanakereba, moo toru koto ga dekinai to omoimasu.
If we don't buy the Shinkansen tickets today, I don't think we'll be able to get any.

Satoo san ga eki no mae de matte inakereba, denwa shita hoo ga iidesu ne.
If Ms. Sato is not waiting in front of the station, it's better to call, isn't it?

Hoka ni shitsumon ga nakereba, kore de owarimashoo.
If there aren't any more questions, let's finish here.

Jikan ga nakereba, shikata ga arimasen.
If you don't have time, it can't be helped.

O-sake o yamenakereba, byooki ni narimasu yo.
If you don't quit drinking, you'll get sick.

With -i adjectives, drop the final -i and add -kereba. With negatives (atsuku nai, yoku nai, omoshiroku nai, etc.), do the same thing, that is, drop the final -i from the nai, and add -kereba.

-i adjective	-kereba form	Meaning
atsu-i	atsu-kereba	if it's hot
ii/yo-i	yo-kereba	if it's good
isogashi-i	isogashi-kereba	if you're busy
hoshi-i	hoshi-kereba	if you want
taka-i	taka-kereba	if it's expensive
samuku na-i	samuku na-kereba	if it's not cold
yasuku na-i	yasuku na-kereba	if it's not cheap
yoku na-i	yoku na-kereba	if it's not good
tooku na-i	tooku na-kereba	if it's not far

Ashita tenki ga yokereba, dokoka e ikimashoo ka.
If the weather's nice tomorrow, shall we go somewhere?

Hazukashikereba, jiko shookai o eigo de shite mo ii desu.
If you're shy, it's okay to introduce yourself in English.

Hontoo ni hoshikereba, doozo katte kudasai.
If you really want it, go on and buy it.

Kozutsumi ga sonna ni omoku nakereba, kookuubin de okutte mo ii desu.
If the package isn't too heavy, it's okay to send it by airmail.

Tooku nakereba, aruite ikimashoo ka.
If it's not far, shall we walk?

Takaku nakereba, kaimasu.
If it's not too expensive, I'll buy it.

The -ba forms for desu are de areba ("if it is") and de nakereba ("if it isn't"). However, de areba is fairly formal, and nara is used more often in everyday speech.

Kirai nara, tabenakute mo ii desu.
If you don't like it, you don't have to eat it.

Kaigi ga juu-ji nara, daijoobu desu.
If the meeting is at 10:00, it's okay.

Sensei nara, kore ga wakaru deshoo.
If he's a teacher, he'll probably understand this.

Kookuubin de nakereba, dame da to omoimasu.
If it's not airmail, I think it's impossible (for it to get there on time).

Nichiyoobi de nakereba, iku koto ga dekimasen.
If it's not a Sunday, I can't go.

4. MAZU – "FIRST OF ALL"

Use the word mazu ("first of all/to begin with") when you are beginning to describe a sequence of events, instructions, or directions. Other useful words to continue with are sore kara ("and then/after that"), soshite ("then"), sono ato ("after that"), sono tsugi ni ("next"), and saigo ni ("finally/at the end").

Mazu Igirisu ni itte, sore kara Furansu ni itte, saigo ni Itaria ni ikimashita. Totemo tanoshikatta desu.
First we went to Britain, then we went to France, and finally we went to Italy. It was really enjoyable.

Ashita isogashii desu. Mazu Ginza no depaato e itte, chichi no tanjoobi no purezento o kaimasu. Sore kara ginkoo to yuubinkyoku e ikimasu. Sono ato, tomodachi ni atte, ranchi o tabemasu. Sono tsugi ni Tookyoo eki ni itte, Oosaka made no kippu o kaimasu. Sono ato, hoka no tomodachi no atarashii apaato ni yorimasu. Saigo ni, Yokohama e kaette, ane to eiga o mi ni ikimasu.
I'm busy tomorrow! First of all, I'm going to a department store in Ginza and buying a birthday present for my father. Then, I'm going to the bank and the post office. After that, I'll meet a friend and have lunch. Next, I'm going to Tokyo station to buy a ticket to Osaka. After that, I'll drop in at the new apartment of another friend. Finally, I'll go back to Yokohama and go to see a movie with my older sister.

5. TAME NI – "IN ORDER TO"

The phrase tame ni after a noun means "for the benefit of" or "for the sake of", showing purpose. The English equivalent is often simply "for".

Kore wa nihongo no gakusei no tame no jisho desu.
This is a dictionary for (the benefit of) students of Japanese.

Kare wa shigoto no tame ni raigetsu Yooroppa ni ikimasu.
He's going to Europe next month on business.

Nan no tame ni Nihon e kita n desu ka.
Why did you come to Japan?

It can also come after the plain form of the verb, in which case it is very often expressing a reason, meaning "for the purpose of" or "in order to". Note that in Japanese, the reason is given in the first part of the sentence, whereas in English it is usually in the last part.

Keeki o tsukuru tame ni, tamago o kaimasu.
I'm going to buy some eggs to make a cake.

Kitte o kau tame ni yuubinkyoku e ikimasu.
I'm going to the post office (in order) to buy some stamps.

Takahashi san wa, Eigo o benkyoo suru tame ni eikaiwa no kurasu ni hairimashita.
Ms. Takahashi has joined an English conversation class in order to study English.

Taberu tame ni, shigoto o shimasu.
I work in order to eat.

Kono kaigi wa rainen no yasumi no hi o kimeru tame desu.
This meeting is for the purpose of deciding next year's vacation days.

Watashi no keiyaku no koto o soodan suru tame ni, buchoo to hanashitai n desu.
I want to talk to the department manager in order to discuss my contract.

Kore o miseru tame ni kimashita.
I came to show you this.

---

6. YON-MAI – "FOUR (FLAT THINGS)"

Here is another way of counting, this time for flat things such as stamps, records, compact discs, pizzas, pieces of paper, envelopes and tickets. Use ichi, ni, san, etc. followed by -mai.

Kyooto made ni-mai kudasai.
Two (tickets) to Kyoto, please.

Kono hagaki wa, ichi-mai ikura desu ka.
How much is one of these postcards?

Sumimasen, hyaku-juu en kitte san-mai to, hyaku nana-juu en kitte o yon-mai kudasai.
Excuse me, could I have three 110-yen stamps and four 170-yen stamps, please?

Shii dii o takusan motte imasu ne. Nan-mai aru n desu ka.
You have a lot of CDs! However many are there?

Ookii fuutoo san-mai to chiisai fuutoo juu-mai kudasai.
Three large envelopes and ten small envelopes, please.

VOCABULARY

au mae ni: before meeting
dekakeru: go out
denki-dai: electricity charges
denki: electricity
denwa-dai: telephone charges
eikaiwa: English conversation
fuutoo: envelope
gasu-dai: gas charges
gasu: gas (petrol)
hagaki: postcard
harau: pay
ikeba: if we go
jisho: dictionary
juubun: enough, sufficient
kabuki: Japanese classical play
kakikonde: please fill in/out [from kakikomu]
kippu: ticket
kitte: stamp
kookuubin: airmail
kozutsumi: package, parcel
-mai: [counter for flat objects]
mazu: first of all, to begin with
miseru: show
o-azukari shimasu: receive, be entrusted with [from azukaru]
okuru: send
purezento: present
ranchi: lunch
saigo ni: finally, at the end
sono ato: after that
soshite: then
sureba: if I do
tamago: egg
tame ni: for the purpose of, benefit of
-te kara: after -ing
tsukuru: make
yameru: quit, stop, cease, drop (idea or plan)
yooji: errand, chore, something to do
yon-mai: four [flat objects]

TEST YOURSELF

Exercise A

Read through the dialogue at the beginning of the lesson again, and then say if the following statements are true or false.

1. Katoo san to Neruson san wa eki no mae de aimasu. T/F
2. Katoo san wa Neruson san to issho ni yuubinkyoku made ikimasu. T/F
3. Neruson san wa ginkoo e iku mae ni, yuubinkyoku e iku yotei desu. T/F
4. Neruson san wa juu-ichi-ji han ni uchi o demasu. T/F
5. Neruson wa kozutsumi o kookuubin de okurimasu. T/F
6. Ginkoo wa konde imasu ga, yuubinkyoku wa amari konde imasen. T/F

Exercise B

It's a school holiday tomorrow, but it'll be a busy day for Mike, as he has lots of things to do. Look at the list he's made, and make sentences about the things he's going to do, using -te kara, as in the example.

Example: Ku-ji han ni Kawasaki de tenisu o shimasu.
Tenisu o shite kara, denki-dai o harau tame ni ginkoo e ikimasu.
Denki-dai o haratte kara,...

9:30	play tennis in Kawasaki
	go to bank to pay electricity bill
	go to department store to buy father's birthday present
	_____
	_____
	_____
12.00	meet Mr. Itoo in coffee shop
	_____
1.30	go to see movie
	buy Shinkansen tickets to Kyoto
	_____
	_____

4.30	go back home
	write letter to Susan
	study Japanese
	_____
	_____
	_____
9.00	go for a drink with Mr. Kato
	_____

Now imagine it's the next day, and you're talking about what Mike did in the daytime yesterday. Beginning with his return home, describe his day, but this time working backwards, using mae ni, as in the example.

Example: Uchi e kaeru mae ni, Kyooto made no Shinkansen no kippu o kaimashita.
Shinkansen no kippu o kau mae ni, ...

_____
_____
_____
_____
_____
_____

Imagine you're at the post office, and complete your part of the conversation below.

Exercise C

You (I'd like to send this package to Britain. How much is it, please? By EMS.)

_____

Clerk Igirisu desu ka. Kyuu-sen yon-hyaku en desu. Kono yooshi ni kakikonde kudasai.

You (And, how much is a postcard to Australia?)

_____

Clerk Nana-juu en desu.

You (Three 70-yen stamps, please.)

_____

Clerk Hai, doozo.

You   (And, how much is this letter?)

_____

Clerk   Doko desu ka.
You   (The USA.)

_____

Clerk   Hyaku-juu en desu. Hai, zenbu de kyuu-sen nana-hyaku ni-juu en desu.

Exercise D

Match up the questions or statements from the column on the left with the most appropriate responses from the list on the right.

1. Doo shite Nihon e kita n desu ka.

2. Amerika e iku to kikimashita ga, ryokoo desu ka.

3. Nan no tame no kaigi desu ka.

4. Benkyoo suru n desu ka.

5. Kaimono ni iku n desu ka.

6. Nan no tame ni shigoto o yameta n desu ka.

a. Ee, Nihongo no tesuto no tame desu.

b. Iie, shigoto no tame iku n desu.

c. Ee, nihongo no gakusei no tame no desu.

d. Rainen no keikaku o soodan suru tame desu.

e. Hai, atarashii kutsu o kau tame ni ikimasu.

f. Kuni he kaeru n desu.

g. Nihongo o benkyoo suru tame desu.

Exercise E

How would you say these sentences in Japanese?

1. Tomorrow I'm going to Tokyo to buy tickets for Kabuki.

_____

2. If you don't understand, please ask Ms. Saitoo.

_____

3. Let's have lunch before we go out.

_____

4. If you don't have enough time, you don't need to come.

_____

5. Are you going to send this package by airmail?

_____

6. Mr. Takeda said he'd like to quit his job.

_____

銀行 These two characters mean "silver" and "go", but when combined into one compound word, they mean "a bank". The word is pronounced "ginkoo".

Visit www.berlitzpublishing.com for a bonus internet activity—go to the downloads section and connect to the world in Japanese!

19

KI O TSUKENAKEREBA NARIMASEN.
WE MUST BE CAREFUL.

Mike Nelson and the Watanabe family are just settling themselves down on the train as they set off for their skiing weekend. The train is packed full with people, luggage and skis.

Nelson **Sugoi nimotsu desu ne.**
What a lot of luggage!

Mr. Watanabe **Soo deshoo. Demo san-nin no kodomo mo iru deshoo. Dakara zenbu de go-nin-bun no yoo-fuku, go-nin-bun no sukii-uea nado o motte konakereba naranaikara, taihen na n desu yo.**
Yes, it's true. But we have three children, right? So altogether we have to bring clothes for five people, ski-wear for five people, and so on. It's tough, you know?

Nelson **Aa, wakarimashita. Densha wa sugoku konde imasu ne. Shiteiseki no kippu o katte, yokatta desu ne.**
Ah, I see! The train's incredibly crowded, isn't it? I'm glad we bought tickets for reserved seats.

Mr. Watanabe	Soo desu ne. Kodomo ga suwaru koto ga dekinakereba, motto urusaku narimasu kara. Yes, if the children can't sit down, they get even noisier, so…
Nelson	Densha no kippu to ieba, watashi wa mada haratte inai n desukedo, ikura deshita ka. Speaking of train tickets, I haven't paid yet, but how much were they?
Mr. Watanabe	Ichi-man ni-sen en desu. Doomo sumimasen. Kodomo wa hontoo ni urusai desu ne. (to the children) Ii kagen ni shi nasai. 11,000 yen. Thank you. The children are really noisy, aren't they? That's enough!
Nelson	Koofun shite iru n deshoo. Watashi mo totemo tanoshimi desu. Ashita no asa hayaku okite, ichi-nichi-juu sukii shitai to omotte iru n desu. They must be excited. I'm really looking forward to it too. I'd like to get up early tomorrow morning and ski all day long.
Ms. Watanabe	Soo desu ka. Ja, minna konban hayaku nenakereba narimasen ne. Tokorode, Neruson san wa sukii ga yoku dekiru to kikimashita kedo. I see. Well, everyone must go to bed early tonight, right? By the way, I heard that you are good at skiing, Mr. Nelson.
Nelson	Daigakusei no toki yoku yatte, sore kara Kanada ni sunde ita toki mo, ik-kagetsu ni ni-kai gurai yarimashita. Demo saikin wa amari yatte inai kara, ki o tsukenakereba naranai to omoimasu. Toshi o torimashita kara. When I was a university student, I often skied, and when I was living in Canada, I did it about twice a month. But I haven't done much recently, so I think I have to be careful. I've gotten old, you know?
Ms. Watanabe	Sonna koto nai desuyo. No, that's not so, not at all!
Mr. Watanabe	A, shanai hanbai ga kimashita. Neruson sensei biiru demo nomimashoo. Miho mo nomu. Ah, here comes someone selling (food and drink). Mr. Nelson, let's have a beer or something. (to Ms. Watanabe) Would you like to have some?
Ms. Watanabe	Watashi wa juusu de ii. Juice is fine with me.

231

Mr. Watanabe	(to the person with the cart) Ja, juusu o yon-hon to biiru o ni-hon kudasai. Sa, mina san, tanoshii ryokoo ni, kanpai.
	Four juices and two beers, please. Right everyone, here's to an enjoyable trip.
All	Kanpai.
	Cheers!
Nelson	Chotto shitsurei shimasu. O-tearai wa doko deshoo.
	Please excuse me. I wonder where the bathroom is.
Ms. Watanabe	Kotchi da to omoimasu. A, Neruson sensei, abunai. Sono sukii ni ki o tsukete.
	I think it's this way. Oh, Mr. Nelson, look out! Be careful of those skis!
Nelson	(There is the sound of a crash.) Itai. Ashi ga…
	Ouch! My leg…
Ms. Watanabe	Neruson sensei, daijoobu desu ka.
	Mr. Nelson, are you all right?
Nelson	Iie, dame desu. Tatsu koto ga dekimasen. Itai.
	No, it's no good. I can't stand up. Ouch!

STRUCTURE AND USAGE NOTES

1. -NAKEREBA NARIMASEN – "MUST" OR "HAVE TO"

In the previous lesson, you learned that the verb ending -eba is the equivalent of "if", and that the negative -nakereba is the equivalent of "if not". Another use of this -nakereba form is to make a pattern which means "must/have to". To do this, add narimasen, which means "it's no good/it won't do". You then have -nakereba narimasen, a pretty cumbersome pattern which literally means "If you don't…, it's no good", or in other words "you must/you have to".

Ashita wa o-kyaku ga takusan kuru kara, kyoo ichi-nichi-juu ryoori o tsukuranakereba narimasen.
Tomorrow we have a lot of guests coming, so I have to spend all day today making food.

Jiko shookai wa Nihongo de nakereba narimasen.
Your self-introduction must be in Japanese.

Ashita Narita kuukoo made tomodachi o mukae ni iku kara, densha no jikan o shirabenakereba narimasen.
I have to go to Narita Airport tomorrow to meet a friend, so I have to check up on the train times.

Chichi wa shigoto no tame ni Yooroppa e ikanakereba narimasen.
My father has to go to Europe on business.

Sono koto ni tsuite kimeru mae ni, buchoo to soodan shinakereba
narimasen.
Before I decide that, I have to consult the department manager.

Kyoo wa kaigi no repooto o kakanakereba naranai kara, osoku made
kaisha ni iru to omoimasu.
Today I have to write up the meeting report, so I think I'll be at the office
until late.

Heya ga kitanai kara, sooji shinakereba narimasen.
Because the room is dirty, I must clean it.

The negative "don't have to..." is expressed with -nakute mo ii desu
(see Lesson 13, Structure and Usage Note 6).

Kyoo owaranakute mo ii desu.
You don't have to finish it today.

Ashita wa nichiyoobi dakara, konban hayaku nenakute mo ii desu.
Tomorrow's Sunday, so you don't have to go to bed early tonight.

You may also come across the verb endings -nakereba ikemasen and
-nakereba dame desu, which can also be translated as "must/have to".

Sono shukudai o jibun de shinakereba ikemasen yo.
You must do your homework by yourself.

Sore o Ogawa san ni misenakereba dame desu yo.
You must show that to Mr. Ogawa.

---

2. FORMING ADVERBS FROM ADJECTIVES

To make an adverb (describing how something is done, such as "incredibly",
"cheaply" or "quickly") from an -i adjective, drop the final -i and add -ku.

-i adjective	Meaning	Adverb	Meaning
sugoi	incredible	sugoku	incredibly
yasui	cheap	yasuku	cheaply
hayai	quick, early	hayaku	quickly, early
ii/yoi	good, fine	yoku	well, often
isogashii	busy	isogashiku	busily

Koora o sonna ni hayaku nomanai hoo ga iidesu yo.
It's good not to drink your cola so quickly.

Moo natsu dakara, ima sukii-uea o totemo yasuku kau koto ga dekimasu.
It's summer now, so you can buy ski-wear really cheaply.

Watanabe san wa Eigo ga yoku dekinai to itte imasu ga, sonna ni waruku nai to omoimasu.
Mr. Watanabe says he can't speak English well, but I don't think he's that bad.

Shinkansen ni hayaku notte kudasai. Ip-pun dake eki ni tomarimasu kara.
Get on the Bullet Train quickly. It stops in the station only for a minute.

With -na adjectives, you don't need the -na, but follow the word up with ni instead.

joozu	skillful	joozu ni	skillfully
shinsetsu	kind	shinsetsu ni	kindly, gently
genki	energetic	genki ni	energetically
kantan	simple	kantan ni	simply
kirei	pretty, neat	kirei ni	prettily, neatly

Nihongo no jiko shookai o totemo joozu ni shimashita.
He introduced himself very well in Japanese.

Kantan ni setsumei shite kudasai.
Please explain it simply.

Kanji o mada kirei ni kaku koto ga dekimasen.
I can't write kanji characters neatly yet.

---

3. KATTE, YOKATTA – "I'M GLAD WE BOUGHT…"

The phrase katte, yokatta actually means "we bought, and it was good", but this -te yokatta ending can usually be thought of as "I'm glad that/it's lucky that/it's good that".

Densha no jikan o shirabete, yokatta ne.
It's lucky that we checked up on the train schedule, isn't it!
Sono kozutsumi o kookuubin de okutte, yokatta desu.
It's good that you sent that package by airmail.

Kasa o wasurenakute, yokatta desu.
I'm glad I didn't forget my umbrella.

Saikin tenki ga yoku natte, yokatta desu ne.
I'm glad that the weather has gotten better recently.

The opposite meaning can be expressed with -te, zannen desu, or "it's a shame/pity that…"

Shiteiseki o toru koto ga dekinakute, zannen desu ne.
It's a shame we couldn't get reserved seats, isn't it?

Kyoo wa Tanaka san ga kuru koto ga dekinakute, zannen desu ne.
It's a pity that Ms. Tanaka couldn't come today, isn't it?

4. TO IEBA – "SPEAKING OF..."

The word ieba comes from iu, "to talk", and so to ieba means "if you're talking about...". This phrase is used at the beginning of a sentence when you've just been reminded of something you want to talk about.

A. Saitoo san no tanjoobi no paatii ni ikimasu ka.
Are you going to Ms. Saitoo's birthday party?
B. Hai, ikimasu yo. A, tanjoobi to ieba, raishuu wa haha no tanjoobi desu. Purezento o kawanakereba narimasen.
Yes, I am. And speaking of birthdays, next week it's my mother's birthday. I must buy her a present.

A. Ano kuruma wa taka-soo desu ne. Ikeda san no deshoo.
That car looks really expensive, doesn't it. It's Mr. Ikeda's, isn't it?
B. Hai, soo da to omoimasu. Ikeda san to ieba, saikin atte inai n desu yo. Genki desu ka.
Yes, I think so. Speaking of Mr. Ikeda, I haven't seen him for a long time. Is he well?

5. ICHI-MAN – "TEN THOUSAND"

Japanese has a unit in counting, man, or "ten thousand". Ni-man is therefore "twenty thousand", and go-man is "fifty thousand". When you get up into the hundreds of thousands (which is very likely when talking about the price of airline tickets, or a few nights in a large hotel), things can get pretty confusing. Here are some examples of large numbers.

30,000	san-man
37,000	san-man nana-sen
83,500	hachi-man san-zen go-hyaku
100,000	juu-man
500,000	go-juu man
1,000,000	hyaku-man
1,200,000	hyaku-ni-juu-man
10,000,000	sen-man
100,000,000	ichi-oku

When reading large numbers, it might help to separate the digits into groups of four, instead of groups of three. Then if you temporarily ignore the right-hand group, what remains is the number of man. For example:

170,000 =	17,0000 =	17 man =	juu-nana-man
3,500,000 =	350,0000 =	350 man =	san-byaku go-juu-man

---

6. TOKI – "THE TIME WHEN…"

The word toki by itself means "time/occasion" but it also often occurs in cases where English uses "when/whenever" to talk about what is or was happening during a certain period (for example, "Whenever it rains…", "When I was a student…").

Ame no toki, kibun ga waruku narimasu.
Whenever it rains, I feel miserable.

Gakusei no toki, yoku Eigo no benkyoo o shimashita.
When I was a student, I studied English a lot.

Nimotsu ga ooi toki, itsumo takushii ni norimasu.
Whenever I have a lot of luggage, I take a taxi.

Tesuto no toki, atama ga itsumo itaku narimasu.
When I have a test, I always get a headache.

It can also be used after a verb or verb phrase. Remember that the verb should be in the plain form.

Densha ga konde iru toki, yoku takushii ni norimasu.
When the trains are crowded, I often take a taxi.

Amerika ni ryokoo shite iru/ita toki, hagaki o san-juu-mai gurai okurimashita.
When I was traveling in the USA, I sent about thirty postcards.

Koofun shite iru toki, kao ga akaku narimasu.
When I get excited, my face turns red.

Shiteiseki no kippu o kau koto ga dekinai toki, itsumo shinpai shimasu.
When I can't get a reserved seat ticket, I always worry.

Apaato o sooji suru toki, itsumo ongaku o kikimasu.
Whenever I clean the apartment, I always listen to music.

Asa-gohan o tabete iru/ita toki, ani kara denwa ga arimashita.
When I was eating breakfast, there was a call from my older brother.

Sukii ni iku toki, minna jibun no nimotsu o motanakereba narimasen.
When we go skiing, we all have to carry our own luggage.

Compare the following sentences:

Nihon ni iku toki, suutsukeesu o kaimasu.
When I go to Japan, I buy a suitcase.

Nihon ni iku toki, suutsukeesu o kaimashita.
When I went to Japan, I bought a suitcase.

Nihon ni itta toki, Kamakura e ikimasu.
When I go to Japan, I'll visit Kamakura.

Nihon ni itta toki, Kamakura e ikimashita.
When I went to Japan, I visited Kamakura.

Also, in the case of action verbs, whether or not you use a past tense or not depends on whether the action is completed or not.

Densha ni noru toki yamadasan o mimashita.
When I was getting on the train, I saw Yamada-san. (The action of getting on the train is incomplete.)

Densha ni notta toki yamadasan o mimashita.
When I got on the train, I saw Yamada-san. (The action of getting on the train is complete.)

---

7. PHRASES OF FREQUENCY

This is the pattern you need when you want to talk about the frequency with which something happens, as ik-kai means "once", ni-kai means "twice", and san-kai means "three times", etc. Here are some more examples of phrases you can use to indicate frequency.

ichi-nichi ni yon-kai	four times a day
ni-shuukan ni ik-kai	once every two weeks
ik-kagetsu ni ni-kai	twice a month
san-kagetsu ni ik-kai	once in three months
ichi-nen ni san-kai	three times a year
go-nen ni ik-kai	once in five years

Is-shuukan ni ik-kai gurai Oosaka shiten ni ikanakereba naranai kara, itsumo shiteiseki no kippu o kaimasu.
I have to go to the Osaka branch about once a week, so I always buy a reserved seat ticket.

Wakai toki ni yoku ryokoo shimashita ga, ima toshi o totta kara, ichi-nen ni-kai gurai ni narimashita.
When I was young, I often used to go on trips, but now I'm old, so it has become twice a year.

Nihongo no kurasu wa is-shuukan ni nan-kai desu ka.
How many times a week is the Japanese class?

Atarashii kaisha de wa, rok-kagetsu ni ik-kai Yooroppa e shutchoo ni ikimasu.
At my new company, I'll be going on a business trip to Europe once every six months.

---

8. YON-HON – "FOUR (LONG, THIN THINGS)"

Here's another type of counter, this time for counting long, thin objects such as pens, rolled umbrellas, bottles and cans of drink, flowers and bananas. The numbers up to ten are:

ip-pon	rop-pon
ni-hon	nana-hon/shichi-hon
san-bon	hap-pon/hachi-hon
yon-hon	kyuu-hon
go-hon	jup-pon

Biiru o moo ip-pon kudasai.
Another (bottle of) beer, please.

Tako wa ashi ga nan-bon arimasu ka.
How many legs does an octopus have?

Kotoshi kasa o yon-hon mo densha no naka de wasuremashita yo.
This year I've forgotten four umbrellas on the train.

Sono akai hana o go-hon kudasai.
Five of those red flowers, please.

VOCABULARY

abunai: dangerous, look out!
ashi: leg, foot
-bun: quantity, share, portion
daigakusei no toki: when I am/was a university student
demo: or something
gurai: about, approximately
hanbai: sales, selling
-hon: [counter for long, thin objects]
ichi-man: ten thousand
ichi-nichi-juu: all day long
Ii kagen ni shi nasai.: That's enough.

ik-kagetsu: one month
ik-kai: once, one time
jibun no: one's own, my own, your own
jibun: self, oneself
koofun shite imasu: is/are excited
-man: [unit of ten thousand]
motte konakereba narimasen: have to bring [from motte kuru]
nenakereba narimasen: have to sleep [from neru]
nimotsu: luggage
noru: to get on/in (transportation)
oku: hundred million
ongaku: music
ryokoo: trip, journey
saikin: recently
shanai: inside the train
shiraberu: investigate, look into
shiteiseki: reserved seat
sooji suru: do the cleaning
sukii-uea: ski-wear
sunde ita toki: when I was living [from sumu]
tako: octopus
tanoshimi desu: I'm looking forward to (it)
to ieba: speaking of...
toshi o totta: old [from toshi o toru, to get older]
toshi: age
urusai: noisy
urusaku narimasu: get noisy
yarimashita: did, tried [from yaru]
yoofuku: clothes
yoku dekiru: can do well
yon-hon: four [long, thin objects]

TEST YOURSELF

Read the dialogue at the beginning of the lesson again, and then say if the following statements are true or false.

1. Watanabe san no kazoku wa go-nin desu. T/F

2. Watanabe san to okusan to Nelson san wa suwaru koto ga dekimasu ga, san-nin no kodomo wa tatanakereba narimasen. T/F

3. Nelson san wa densha ni noru mae ni, kippu no o-kane o haraimashita. T/F

4. Nelson san wa ashita no asa hayaku okiru tsumori desu. T/F

Exercise A

5. Nelson san wa Kanada ni sunda koto ga arimasu. T/F

6. Minna koora o nomimasu. T/F

Exercise B

It's only a few weeks now before Sue arrives on her visit to Japan, and although Mike is still finding it hard to get around with a sprained ankle, he has lots of things to do in preparation. Look at the list he's made, and make sentences about what he has to do, using -nakereba narimasen.

Example: - ask Watanabe about vacation days
Yasumi no hi ni tsuite Watanabe san ni kikanakereba narimasen.

Things to do:

- ask Mr. Watanabe about vacation days

  _____

- clean the apartment

- pay telephone bill

  _____

- buy 2 tickets for Kabuki

- buy new clothes

  _____

- call Shirazawa ryokan

  _____

- check up on train times to Narita airport

  _____

Exercise C

Answer these questions about how often you do certain things, using phrases such as is-shuukan ni ni-kai, ichi-nen ni ik-kai, etc.

Example: Tenisu o yoku shimasu ka.
Hai, is-shuukan ni san-kai gurai shimasu.
or
Iie, ichi-nen ni ni-kai gurai dake desu.
or
Iie, zenzen shimasen.

1. Nihongo no benkyoo o yoku shimasu ka.

_____

2. Yoku kaimono ni ikimasu ka.

_____

3. Resutoran de yoku tabemasu ka.

_____

4. Tokidoki gaikoku e ikimasu ka.

_____

5. Jibun no heya o yoku sooji shimasu ka.

_____

6. Atarashii yoofuku o yoku kaimasu ka.

_____

7. Shashin o yoku torimasu ka.

_____

8. Umi e tokidoki ikimasu ka.

_____

9. Yoku densha ni norimasu ka.

_____

10. Tokidoki keeki o tsukurimasu ka.

_____

Read the questions below, and then use the pictures to help you
answer them. Use toki in your answers, as in the example.

Exercise D

Example: Q. Itsu Nihongo no benkyoo o hajimemashita ka.

A. Nihon ni sunde ita
toki, Nihongo no benkyoo
o hajimemashita.

1. Itsu sono nyuusu
   o kikimashita ka.

_____

_____

2. Atama wa itsu itaku
   narimashita ka.

_____

_____

_____

_____

3. Itsu okusan ni hajimete atta n desu ka.

4. Itsu takushii ni norimasu ka.

_____

_____

5. Watanabe san wa
   itsu uchi ni
   yorimashita ka.

_____

_____

6. Itsu kare to sono koto ni tsuite hanashimashita ka.

How would you say these sentences in Japanese?

1. You all have to buy your own tickets.

2. A ticket from Tokyo to Osaka is about 13,500 yen.

3. He speaks quickly, so I don't understand him very well.

4. I'm glad we took the Shinkansen.

5. Speaking of London, have you ever been there, Mr. Wada?

6. When I was in Japan last year, I climbed Mt. Fuji.

Exercise E

切符
The characters for "cut" and "tally/sign" together make up the word kippu, which means "ticket".

Visit www.berlitzpublishing.com for a bonus internet activit—go to the downloads section and connect to the world in Japanese!

20

DAI JUU-NANA-KA KARA DAI JUU-KYUU-KA MADE NO FUKUSHUU.
REVIEW OF LESSONS 17 TO 19

Read and listen again to Dialogues 17 to 19, and try to understand the meaning without referring back to the translations in previous lessons.

Dialogue 17: Kamakura e itta koto ga arimasu ka.

It's Friday, and Mike Nelson is chatting with Ms. Takahashi during the lunch break.

Takahashi	**Neruson san wa Kamakura e itta koto ga arimasu ka.**
Nelson	**Iie, arimasen. Ikitai n desu kedo.**
Takahashi	**Ja, nichiyoobi ni watashitachi to issho ni Kamakura e ikimasen ka. Saitoo san mo Wada san mo issho ni iku to itte imasu ga. Tenki ga yokattara, pikunikku o suru tsumori desu.**
Nelson	**Ii desu ne. Demo, tenki ga yoku nakattara, doo shimasu ka. Konban ame ga furu to kikimashita ga.**

Takahashi	Sonna koto o kangaenaide kudasai. Nichiyoobi wa kitto ii tenki desu yo.
Nelson	Wakarimashita. Densha de iku n desu ka.
Takahashi	Soo desu. Densha no hoo ga hayai to omoimasu. Sore dake ja nakute, dare mo kuruma o motte imasen kara, shikata ga nai n desu.

The four are now in Kamakura, standing in front of the daibatsu, or great statue of Buddha, for which Kamakura is famous.

Nelson	Konna ni ookii daibutsu wa mita koto ga arimasen ne.
Takahashi	Naka ni haitte, atama no naka made noboru koto mo dekimasu yo. Watashi wa haitta koto ga nai kedo.
Nelson	Jaa, hairimashoo ka.
Takahashi	Chotto matte. Sono mae ni, minna no shashin o toritai kara. Hai, mina san, daibutsu no mae ni tatte kudasai yo. Aa, dame desu. Soko ni tattara, daibutsu ga shashin ni hairimasen.
Nelson	Sono kaidan no ue ni suwattara, doo desu ka.
Takahashi	Soo ne. Sono hoo ga ii desu ne. Hai, mina san, soko ni suwatte kudasai. Ii desu ka. Hai, chiizu. Doomo arigatoo. Sa, daibutsu ni hairimashoo.
Nelson	Mite. Daibutsu no ushiro ni sugoi hito ga narande imasu ne. Jikan ga kakaru deshoo.
Takahashi	Saki ni hiru-gohan o tabetara, doo deshoo.
Nelson	Soo desu ne. Demo ne, chotto samuku natte, sora mo kuraku natte irukara, pikunikku wa chotto... Are. Ame ja nai desu ka.
Takahashi	Soo desu yo. Ara, sugoi ame da. Dareka kasa o motte imasu ka. Dare mo kasa o motte inai n desu ka. Jaa, ichiban chikai resutoran made hashitte ikimashoo yo. Hayaku, hayaku.

QUESTIONS:

1. Zenbu de nan-nin Kamakura e ikimasu ka.
2. Nan de ikimasu ka.
3. Shashin o toru tame ni, minna doko ni suwarimasu ka.
4. Hiru-gohan o tabete kara, minna nani o suru tsumori desu ka.

Dialogue 18: Soo sureba...

Mike Nelson is going to the theater this afternoon to see Kabuki with Mr. Kato, a teacher from his school. He's just talking to him on the phone now.

Nelson Sa, nan-ji ni, doko de aimashoo ka.

Kato Watashi ga saki ni Nelson sensei no apaato ni ikimashoo ka. Soo sureba, issho ni eki made aruite iku koto ga dekimasu ne.

Nelson Jitsu wa, watashi wa yooji ga iroiro aru n desu. Dakara sugu uchi o dete, Katoo san ni au mae ni yooji o sureba ii to omotte ita n desu ga.

Kato Watashi mo issho ni ikimasu yo. Soo sureba, yooji ga owatte kara, dokoka de ranchi o taberu koto mo dekiru deshoo. Kabuki wa nagai kara, hairu mae ni nanika tabeta hoo ga ii to omoimasu. Ii desu ka.

Nelson Mochiron ii desu kedo, Katoo san ni wa zenzen omoshiroku nai to omoimasu yo. Mazu, haha no tanjoobi no purezento o okuru tame ni yuubinkyoku e itte, sore kara, gasu-dai to denki-dai o harau tame ni ginkoo e ikimasu. Sono ato...

Kato Daijoobu desu yo. Ja, juu-ji-han goro Maiku san no tokoro ni ikeba, jikan ga juubun arimasu ka.

Nelson Hai hai, ii desu. Ja, matte imasu yo.

Later, at the post office...

Nelson Kono kozutsumi o Amerika made okuritai n desu ga, ikura deshoo ka.

Clerk EMS desu ne. (She weighs the package) Hai, hassen nihyaku en desu. Kono yooshi ni kakikonde kudasai.

Nelson Sore kara, hyaku-juu en kitte o yon-mai kudasai.

Clerk Hyaku-juu en kitte o yon-mai desu ne. Zenbu de hassen roppyaku yon-juu en desu. Hai, ichi-man-en o-azukari shimasu. O-tsuri wa sen-san-byaku-roku-juu en desu. Doozo.

Nelson Arigatoo. (to Mr. Kato) Sugoi oozei no hito ga ushiro ni narande imasu ne. Ginkoo mo konna ni konde itara, yamemashoo.

| Kato | Demo, gasu-dai to denki-dai o harawanakereba... |
| Nelson | Ii n desu yo. Shinpai shinaide. Jikan wa mada juubun arimasu. |

QUESTIONS:

1. Nelson san wa doo shite uchi o hayaku demasu ka.
2. Nelson san wa doo shite ginkoo e iku tsumori desu ka.
3. Yuubinkyoku de, Nelson san wa nani o kakanakereba narimasen ka.
4. Yuubinkyoku wa konde imasu ka.

Dialogue 19: Ki o tsukenakereba narimasen.

Mike Nelson and the Watanabe family are just settling themselves down on the train as they set off for their skiing weekend. The train is packed full with people, luggage and skis.

Nelson	Sugoi nimotsu desu ne.
Mr. Watanabe	Soo deshoo. Demo san-nin no kodomo mo iru deshoo. Dakara zenbu de go-nin-bun no yoofuku, go-nin-bun no sukii-uea nado o motte konakereba naranaikara, taihen na n desu yo.
Nelson	Aa, wakarimashita. Densha wa sugoku konde imasu ne. Shiteiseki no kippu o katte, yokatta desu ne.
Mr. Watanabe	Soo desu ne. Kodomo ga suwaru koto ga dekinakereba, motto urusaku narimasu kara.
Nelson	Densha no kippu to ieba, watashi wa mada haratte inai n desukedo, ikura deshita ka.
Mr. Watanabe	Ichi-man ni-sen en desu. (Mike gives him the money.) Doomo sumimasen. Kodomo wa hontoo ni urusai desu ne. (to the children) Ii kagen ni shi nasai.
Nelson	Koofun shite iru n deshoo. Watashi mo totemo tanoshimi desu. Ashita no asa hayaku okite, ichi-nichi-juu sukii shitai to omotte iru n desu.
Ms. Watanabe	Soo desu ka. Ja, minna konban hayaku nenakereba narimasen ne. Tokorode, Neruson san wa sukii ga yoku dekiru to kikimashita kedo.

Nelson	Daigakusei no toki yoku yatte, sore kara Kanada ni sunde ita toki mo, ik-kagetsu ni ni-kai gurai yarimashita. Demo saikin wa amari yatte inai kara, ki o tsukenakereba naranai to omoimasu. Toshi o torimashita kara.
Ms. Watanabe	Sonna koto nai desuyo.
Mr. Watanabe	A, shanai hanbai ga kimashita. Neruson sensei biiru demo nomimashoo. Miho mo nomu.
Ms. Watanabe	Watashi wa juusu de ii.
Mr. Watanabe	(to the person with the cart) Ja, juusu o yon-hon to biiru o ni-hon kudasai. Sa, mina san, tanoshii ryokoo ni, kanpai.
All	Kanpai.
Nelson	Chotto shitsurei shimasu. O-tearai wa doko deshoo.
Ms. Watanabe	Kotchi da to omoimasu. A, Neruson sensei, abunai. Sono sukii ni ki o tsukete.
Nelson	(There is the sound of a crash.) Itai. Ashi ga...
Ms. Watanabe	Neruson sensei, daijoobu desu ka.
Nelson	Iie, dame desu. Tatsu koto ga dekimasen. Itai.

QUESTIONS:

1. Nelson san to Watanabe san-tachi wa ima doko ni imasu ka.
2. Watanabe san wa doo shite nimotsu ga ooi desu ka.
3. Watanabe san wa donna kippu o kaimashita ka.
4. Densha no naka de nani o kaimashita ka.

TEST YOURSELF

Exercise A

Which is the odd man out in the following groups of words?

1. ik-kagetsu, ichi-mai, ichi-nichi, is-shuukan

2. hyaku, man, sen, hayaku

3. kozutsumi, denki-dai, tegami, hagaki

4. doo shite, mazu, saigo ni, soshite

5. yuki, kaze, tooi, ame

6. samuku, ookiku, waruku, keiyaku

How would you say the following in Japanese?

1. 36,500 yen _____
2. 5 stamps _____
3. 7 bottles of beer _____
4. 6 months _____
5. 12:45 _____
6. August 10th _____

Test yourself on these common phrases or sayings – what are they in Japanese?

1. It can't be helped. _____
2. Behave yourself! _____
3. How do you do? _____
4. Enjoy your meal. _____
5. Cheers! _____
6. Excuse me for disturbing you. _____
7. Good night. _____
8. Watch out! _____
9. Please take care. _____
10. That's a pity. _____

Using the clues below, fill in the crossword puzzle to find out where Mike is planning to go with Sue when she comes to Japan.

1. Biiru o ni-_____ kudasai.

2. Fuji san ni _____ koto ga arimasu ka.

3. Watashi wa hazukashii toki, kao ga _____ narimasu.

4. Kabuki no _____ o ni-mai motte imasu ga, issho ni ikimasen ka.

5. Raishuu shigoto de Amerika e ikanakereba

   _____.

6. _____ ga warui kara, sugu uchi e kaeru to omoimasu.

7. Kyooto _____ ja nakute, Nara e mo ikitai n desu.

8. O-sake o sonna ni takusan nomeba, _____ ni narimasu yo.

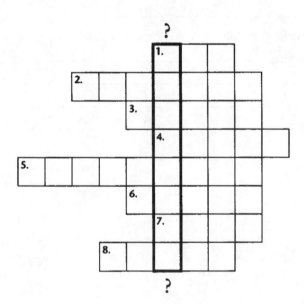

Mike Nelson is chatting with Ms. Takahashi at school. Put the lines of their dialogue in the correct order by writing the numbers 1–8 next to the appropriate line.

_____ a. *Nelson*   Hai, mokuyoobi ni Hokkaidoo e iku yotei desu.

_____ b. *Nelson*   Hai, ikimasu. Demo asa totemo hayaku okinakereba narimasen ne.

_____ c. *Takahashi* Suuzan san wa ashita kuru deshoo.

_____ d. *Nelson*   Hontoo? Ja, e-hagaki o okurimasu yo.

_____ e. *Takahashi* Ii desu ne. Watashi wa itta koto ga nai n desu.

_____ f. *Nelson*   Soo desu. Ashita no asa juu-ji han ni.

_____ g. *Takahashi* Tanoshimi ni shite iru deshoo. Kuukoo made mukae ni ikimasu ka.

_____ h. *Takahashi* Ryokoo wa? Dokoka e ikimasu ka.

Answer these questions about yourself.

1. Nihon e itta koto ga arimasu ka.

   _____

2. Kodomo no toki, doko ni sunde imashita ka.

   _____

3. O-kane ga takusan attara, nani o kaitai n desu ka.

   _____

4. Nihongo to Furansugo to, dochira no hoo ga muzukashii to omoimasu ka.

   _____

5. Anata no kuni de wa, nan-gatsu ni samuku narimasu ka.

   _____

6. Ashita nani o shinakereba narimasen ka.

   _____

7. Shii dii o nan-mai motte imasu ka.

   _____

8. Is-shuukan ni nan-kai gurai Nihongo no benkyoo o shimasu ka.

   _____

最後

These are the characters for saigo which means "last/final", as this is the last lesson of the book. The word combines the characters for "most" and "after/behind".

Visit www.berlitzpublishing.com for a bonus internet activity—go to the downloads section and connect to the world in Japanese!

ANSWER KEY

Lesson 1

A. 1-T, 2-T, 3-T

B. Free answers

C. 1. Hajimemashite.
   2. Amerikajin desu.
   3. Nihon no kuruma desu ka.
   4. Hai, soo desu.
   5. Iie, chigaimasu.

D. 1. *A.* Maiku san no suutsukeesu desu ka.
      B. Hai, soo desu.
   2. *A.* Gakusei desu ka.
      B. Hai, soo desu.
   3. *A.* Sensei desu ka.
      B. Iie, chigaimasu.
   4. *A.* Watanabe san no kuruma desu ka.
      B. Hai, soo desu.
   5. *A.* Enjinia desu ka.
      B. Iie, chigaimasu.
   6. *A.* Amerikajin desu ka.
      B. Hai, soo desu.

E. You   Shitsurei desu ga, Tanaka san desu ka.
   Tanaka Hai, soo desu.
   You   Hajimemashite, [your company or school name] no [your name] desu.
   Tanaka Hajimemashite, Fujimura no Tanaka desu.
   You   Watashi no meishi desu. Doozo.

Lesson 2

A. 1-T, 2-T, 3-F

B. 1. Hai, arimasu. OR Iie, arimasen.
   2. [Place name] ni arimasu (e.g. Nyuu Yooku ni arimasu).
   3. b OR Iie, ookii uchi ja arimasen.
   4. Hai, arimasu. OR Iie, arimasen.
   5. [Country name or city name] desu (e.g. Nyuu Yooku desu).

C. 1-hito 2-meishi 3-tsukue 4-denwa 5-paato 6-purintaa
   7-konpyuutaa

D. 1. O-kuni wa doko desu ka.
2. (Watashi no) kaisha wa Nyuu Yooku ni arimasu.
3. Sumimasen ga, ginkoo wa doko desu ka. OR ... doko ni arimasu ka.
4. Denwa wa asoko ni arimasu. Doozo. OR ... asoko desu.
5. Sore wa watashi no uchi ja arimasen.

E. 1-ni 2-arimasen 3-asoko 4-ja 5-no 6-namae 7-wa 8-X

Lesson 3

A. 1-T, 2-F, 3-F, 4-T, 5-F

B. 1. Mizu o onegai shimasu/ kudasai.
2. O-cha o onegai shimasu/ kudasai.
3. Yaki-zakana teishoku o onegai shimasu/ kudasai.
4. Wain o onegai shimasu/ kudasai.
5. Sashimi o onegai shimasu/ kudasai.
6. Sore o onegai shimasu/ kudasai.

C. 1. Q: Ashita eiga o mimasu ka.
A: Iie, (ashita eiga o) mimasen.
2. Q: Mainichi o-cha o nomimasu ka.
A: Hai, (mainichi o-cha o) nomimasu.
3. Q: Kyoo kaisha e ikimasu ka.
A: Iie, (kyoo kaisha e) ikimasen.
4. Q: Tokidoki sakana o tabemasu ka.
A: Hai, (tokidoki sakana o) tabemasu.
5. Q: Mainichi rajio o kikimasu ka.
A: Iie, (mainichi rajio o) kikimasen.

D. 1. wa, o
2. wa, ga
3. no, o
4. ga
5. wa, e
6. wa, no

E. 1. Eigo ga wakarimasu ka.
2. Konban nani o shimasu ka.
3. (Watashi wa) sashimi ga amari suki ja arimasen.
4. Tanaka san wa nani o oshiemasu ka.
5. Konban dono eiga o mimasu ka.
6. Kono daigaku wa ookii desu ne.

Lesson 4

A. 1-F 2-F 3-T 4-T 5-T 6-T

B. 1. yo-ji
2. ni-ji han
3. ku-ji yon-juu-go-fun
4. juu-ichi-ji yon-jup-pun
5. ichi-ji han
6. roku-ji juu-go-fun

C. 1. Shichi-ji juu-go-fun ni koohii o nomimasu.

2. Shichi-ji han kara shichi-ji yon-juu-go-fun made rajio no nyuusu o kikimasu.

3. Hachi-ji ni eki e ikimasu.

4. Hachi-ji yon-juu-go-fun kara yo-ji yon-juu-go-fun made shigoto o shimasu.

5. Roku-ji ni shinbun o yomimasu.

6. Shichi-ji kara hachi-ji han made Nihongo o benkyoo shimasu. OR Nihongo no benkyoo o shimasu.
7. Ku-ji han kara juu-ichi-ji made terebi o mimasu.

D. 1. Shichi-ji han ni aimashoo.
2. Ashita kara Nihongo o benkyoo shimasu. OR Nihongo no benkyoo o shimasu.
3. Terebi de nyuusu o mimashoo ka. OR Terebi no nyuusu o mimashoo ka.
4. Ashita no kaigi wa nan-ji kara desu ka.
5. Takushii de eki e ikimashoo.
6. Wain wa mada arimasu ka.

E. Moshi moshi
Moshi moshi
konbanwa
konbanwa
eiga ga suki desu ne
Hai, suki desu
jikan ga arimasu ka
Sore wa ii eiga desu ne
Hai, soo desu
nan-ji ni aimashoo ka
Eiga wa roku-ji han ni hajimarimasu
aimashoo
mata ashita
mata ashita

Lesson 5

A. 1-T, 2-T, 3-T, 4-F, 5-F

B. Gomen kudasai.
Shitsurei shimasu. OR O-jama shimasu.
Shitsurei shimasu.
Itadakimasu. OR Onegai shimasu.

C. 1. Sumimasen ga, Yokohama Gakuin Kookoo wa doko desu ka.
Tsugi no shingoo de migi ni magatte kudasai. Hidari-gawa ni arimasu.
2. Sumimasen ga, Oosaka Daigaku wa doko desu ka.
Massugu itte kudasai. Hidari-gawa ni arimasu.
3. Sumimasen ga, Yamate eki wa doko desu ka.
Tsugi no kado de hidari ni magatte kudasai. Migi-gawa ni arimasu.

D. 1. Sumimasen ga, kono hon wa ikura desu ka.
Ni-sen go-hyaku roku-juu en desu.
2. Sumimasen ga, kono surippa wa ikura desu ka.
San-zen san-byaku nana-juu-go en desu.
3. Sumimasen ga, kono rajio wa ikura desu ka.
Kyuu-sen go-hyaku ni-juu en desu.
4. Sumimasen ga, kono terebi wa ikura desu ka.
Go-man hap-pyaku en desu.
5. 8,255
6. 1,120
7. 5,093
8. 7,303

E. 1. Tsugi no shingoo de hidari ni magatte kudasai.
2. Ashita uchi de terebi o mimasu.
3. Mondai ga arimasu ka.
4. Koko ni namae to juusho o kaite kudasai.
5. Sumimasen ga, sono hon wa ikura desu ka.
6. Hidari-gawa ni ookii gakkoo ga arimasu ne.
7. Tokorode, ashita nani o shimasu ka.
8. Koohii wa ikaga desu ka.

Lesson 6

Dialogue 1   1. Watanabe san wa sensei desu.
2. Gakkoo wa Yokohama desu/ni arimasu.
3. Maiku san wa Amerikajin desu.

Dialogue 2   1. Jimu desu.
2. Hai, arimasu.
3. Atarashii paato no namae wa Saitoo san desu.

Dialogue 3   1. Iie, sakana ga suki desu.
               2. Hai, sashimi teishoku ni shimasu.
               3. "Kiku" wa hana desu.
               4. Mizu o nomimasu.

Dialogue 4   1. Uchi ni imasu.
               2. Eiga wa hachi-ji-han ni hajimarimasu.
               3. Sakana o tabemasu.
               4. Takushii de ikimasu.

Dialogue 5   1. Hidari-gawa ni arimasu.
               2. Sen ni-hyaku en desu.
               3. Hai, soo desu.
               4. Koohii o nomimasu.

A. migi – hidari, kono – sono, kirai – suki, e – kara, itadakimasu – go-chisoo sama, koko – soko, iie – hai, ikimasu – kimasu, konbanwa – ohayoo gozaimasu, oshiemasu – benkyoo shimasu, sensei – gakusei, takusan – sukoshi, anata – watashi

B. 1. go-sen rop-pyaku go-juu en
     2. san-byaku juu doru
     3. juu-ni-ji ni-juu-go-fun
     4. san-zen kyuu-hyaku kyuu-juu go en
     5. yon-sen go-hyaku doru
     6. juu-ji yon-jup-pun

C. 1. koko (the only one that isn't a question word)
     2. ano (the only one that isn't a number)
     3. inu (the only one that isn't a time word)
     4. hashi (the only one that isn't a kind of food)
     5. daigaku (the only one that isn't a person)

D. 1. hanashimasu
     2. eki made ikimasu
     3. arimasu ka/takusan arimasu
     4. aimashoo ka
     5. takusan arimasu/arimasu ka
     6. e ikimashoo ka
     7. suwatte kudasai
     8. ni shimasu
     9. desu ka
    10. suki desu ne

E. 1. Watashi no namae wa _____ desu.
     2. Hai, suki desu./Iie, amari suki ja arimasen./Iie, kirai desu.
     3. Hai, ikimasu./Iie, ikimasen.
     4. Hai, tokidoki shimasu./Iie, tenisu o shimasen.
     5. _____ desu./_____ ni arimasu.
     6. Hai, sukoshi wakarimasu. /Iie, wakarimasen.
     7. Hai, imasu. /Iie, imasen.
     8. Hai, mainichi mimasu. /Tokidoki mimasu./Iie, mimasen.

Lesson 7

A. 1-T, 2-F, 3-F, 4-T, 5-T, 6-T

B. sushi-takai/oishii, shukudai-muzukashii,
densha-hayai, kaisha-ookii/chiisai, inu-ookii/chiisai,
tatemono-takai

C. 1. Iie, amari muzukashiku arimasen yo.
   2. Iie, amari atarashiku arimasen yo.
   3. Iie, amari oishiku arimasen yo.
   4. Iie, amari yoku arimasen yo.
   5. Iie, amari samuku arimasen yo.

D. Itoo san wa hiru-gohan o tabete imasu.
Sakai san wa gakusei no shukudai o yonde imasu.
Neruson san wa Eigo o oshiete imasu.
Takahashi san wa Eigo o benkyoo shite imasu.
Ogawa san wa yakyuu no renshuu o shite imasu.

E. 1. Kyoo no Nihongo no shukudai wa muzukashii desu ne.
   2. Haha no tanjoobi wa ashita desu. OR Ashita wa haha no tanjoobi desu.
   3. Juu-ni-ji mae ni kaerimasu.
   4. O-niisan wa doko ni sunde imasu ka.
   5. Maiku san wa kyoo Kawasaki de Eigo o oshiete imasu.
   6. Sumimasen ga, Keiko wa ima imasen. Tonari no uchi de, terebi no eiga o mite imasu. Yobimashoo ka.

Lesson 8

A. 1-T, 2-T, 3-F, 4-F, 5-F, 6-T

B. akai, no, ja arimasen, doo shite, kau, miru, ga, aimasu, kono, deshoo, takaku

C. 1. Kirei-na hana desu ne.
   2. Genki-na kodomo desu ne.
   3. Takai tatemono desu ne.
   4. Yuumei-na hon desu ne.
   5. Hen-na eiga desu ne.

D. 1. a+c 2. c+b 3. a+b 4. c+a 5. b+a

E. 1. Asoko no hito wa Saitoo san deshoo ka.
   2. Motto kantan-na repooto o kaite kudasai.
   3. Kuroi jaketto wa chotto chiisai deshoo.
   4. Kyoo (no) densha wa totemo konde imasu ne.
   5. Tookyoo wa amari suki ja arimasen ga, Yokohama wa ii desu.
   6. Haha wa Tookyoo no yuumei-na depaato de hataraite imasu.

Lesson 9

A. 1-T, 2-T, 3-F, 4-F, 5-T, 6-F

B. 1. Kayoobi no yoru nani o shimashita ka.
Roku-ji han kara shichi-ji han made tenisu no renshuu o shimashita.
2. Suiyoobi no yoru nani o shimashita ka.
Haha ni denwa o shimashita.
3. Mokuyoobi no yoru nani o shimashita ka.
Roku-ji kara hachi-ji made Nihongo no kurasu ga arimashita.
4. Kin'yoobi no yoru nani o shimashita ka.
Takahashi san to issho ni resutoran ni ikimashita.
5. Doyoobi to nichiyoobi (OR shuumatsu) ni nani o shimashita ka.
Umi ni/e ikimashita.

C. 1. Kayoobi no yoru, roku-ji han kara shichi-ji han made tenisu no renshuu o shimashita kedo, heta deshita. OR joozu ja arimasen deshita.
2. Suiyoobi no yoru, haha ni denwa shimashita kedo, imasen deshita.
3. Mokuyoobi no yoru, roku-ji kara hachi-ji made Nihongo no kurasu ga arimashita kedo, watashi dake deshita.
4. Kin'yoobi no yoru, Takahashi san to issho ni resutoran ni ikimashita kedo, oishiku arimasen deshita.
5. Shuumatsu ni umi e ikimashita kedo, taihen samukatta desu.

D. 1. Maiku san ni atte, Ginza e itte, eiga o mimashita.
2. Sono eiga wa SF de, omoshiroku arimasen deshita.
3. Kissaten ni haitte, koohii o nomimashita.
4. Eigo de hanashite ite, muzukashikatta desu.
5. Watashi wa Eigo ga heta de, hazukashikatta desu.
6. Takushii de kaette, takakatta desu.

E. 1. Itsu Amerika kara kaerimashita ka.
2. Nan-nin ga yama no onsen e ikimashita ka.
3. Hontoo ni iya-na tenki deshita.
4. Kinoo no yoru sushi o takusan tabete, sake mo takusan nomimashita.
5. Kesa shinbun o yomimashita kedo, moo nyuusu o wasuremashita.
6. Shuumatsu ni, dokoka e ikimashita ka.

Lesson 10

A. 1-T, 2-F, 3-T, 4-F, 5-T, 6-T

B. mooshimasu
kara kimashita
o oshiete imasu
Furansugo o benkyoo shimashita OR Furansugo no benkyoo o shimashita
itte
no daigaku de
Furansugo o benkyoo shimashita OR Furansugo no benkyoo o shimashita
eiga to supootsu desu

C. 1. Wada san wa, tomodachi wa eki no mae de matte iru to omotte imasu.
2. Fukuda san wa, kono gakkoo wa hen-na gakkoo da to omotte imasu.
3. Itoo san wa, koohii wa amari oishiku nai to omotte imasu.
4. Maiku san wa, Ogawa san no Nihongo wa yoku wakaranai to omotte imasu.
5. Katoo san wa, Watanabe san wa nete iru to omotte imasu.
6. Nakayama san wa, konban Tomoko san ni au koto ga dekinai to omotte imasu.

D. 1. Nagakute, omoshiroku arimasen ne.
2. Yasukute, oishii desu ne.
3. Muzukashikute, suki ja arimasen ne.
4. Atama ga yokute, kirei desu ne.
5. Atsukute, ii tenki desu ne.
6. Hayakute, yasui desu ne.

E. 1. Tanaka san wa itsumo shigoto no koto o kangaete imasu.
2. Tsugi no jugyoo wa ni-ji han ni hajimatte, san-ji ni-jup-pun ni owaru to omoimasu.
3. Sakana ga oishikute, takusan tabemashita.
4. Suugaku wa suki ja nai kedo, kagaku wa suki desu.
5. Densha wa sugu kuru deshoo.
6. Nihon no shinbun o yomu koto ga dekimasu ka.

Lesson 11

A. 1-T, 2-T, 3-T, 4-F, 5-T, 6-F

B. 1. moo ichido
2. tsukatta
3. kekkon
4. ichiban
5. nonda
6. iroiro
7. taka-soo
8. shitsumon
9. setsumei
10. katta
11. senshuu
= MAE NO OKUSAN ("ex-wife")

C. 1. Fuji san to Eberesuto to Makkinrii no naka de, dore ga ichiban takai desu ka.
Eberesuto san ga ichiban takai to omoimasu.
2. Tookyoo to Rondon to Manira no naka de, dore ga ichiban atsui desu ka.
Manira ga ichiban atsui to omoimasu.
3. Eigo to Nihongo to Doitsugo no naka de, dore ga ichiban muzukashii desu ka.
(free choice) ga ichiban muzukashii to omoimasu.
4. Sake to biiru to wain no naka de, dore ga ichiban suki desu ka.
(free choice) ga ichiban suki da to omoimasu.

5. Eiga to supootsu to kaimono no naka de, dore ga ichiban tanoshii desu ka.
   (free choice) ga ichiban tanoshii to omoimasu.
6. Aka to shiro to kuro no naka de, dore ga ichiban suki desu ka.
   (free choice) ga ichiban suki da to omoimasu.

D. 1. Doo shite kaigi ga san-ji ni owaranakatta n desu ka.
      Shitsumon ga takusan atta kara desu.
      OR Shitsumon ga ookatta kara desu.
   2. Doo shite shitsumon ga takusan atta n desu ka.
      Setsumei ga amari yoku nakatta kara desu.
   3. Doo shite setsumei wa amari yoku nakatta n desu ka.
      Repooto no koto o amari benkyoo shinakatta kara desu.
   4. Doo shite repooto no koto o amari benkyoo shinakatta n desu ka.
      Atama ga itakatta kara desu.
   5. Doo shite atama ga itakatta n desu ka.
      Kinoo no ban takusan nonda kara desu.
   6. Doo shite kinoo no ban takusan nonda n desu ka.
      Tomodachi no tanjoobi datta kara desu.

E. 1. Fukuda san wa san-nen mae ni kekkon shimashita.
   2. Takahashi san no booifurendo wa hansamu de, shinsetsu-soo desu ne.
   3. Ichiban suki-na supootsu wa nan desu ka.
   4. Ni-ji han ni denwa shita to omoimasu.
   5. Tanaka san wa kesa atama ga itai kara, kaisha ni ikanai to omoimasu.
   6. Kuruma wa san-nen mae ni katta kedo, mada atarashi-soo desu.

Lesson 12

Dialogue 7: 1. Iie, genki ja arimasen. Atama ga itai n desu.
             2. Iie, mada desu.
             3. Fumiko san ga imasu.
             4. Okaasan no tanjoobi desu kara (ikimasu).

Dialogue 8: 1. Ginza no depaato de kaimono o shite imasu.
             2. Suutsu o mite imasu.
             3. Takai kara desu.
             4. Iie, suki ja nai to omoimasu.

Dialogue 9: 1. Getsuyoobi desu.
             2. Iie, tomodachi to issho ni ikimashita.
             3. Hazukashikatta kara desu.
             4. Hai, suki da to omoimasu.

Dialogue 10: 1. San-shuukan mae kara Nihon ni imasu.
             2. Hai, dekimasu.
             3. Yakyuu no chiimu no koto o yoku kangaete imasu.
             4. Yakyuu o suru to omoimasu.

Dialogue 11:   1. Hai, Nihon ryoori ya Chuukka ryoori no resutoran de tsukaimasu.
2. Iie, soo omotte imasen./Iie, joozu ja nai to omotte imasu.
3. Ni-nen mae kara Eigo no benkyoo o shite imasu.
4. Iie, rikon shite imasu.

A. ban - yoru, buraun - chairo, chotto - sukoshi, dame - warui, hataraku - tsutomeru, heta - joozu ja nai, jugyoo - kurasu, kangaeru - omou, minna de - issho ni, nan-sai - ikutsu, haha - o-kaasan, takusan - ooi, hontoo - uso ja nai

B. A-6, B-5, C-2, D-4, E-1, F-7, G-3

C. 1-shumi, 2-uso, 3-owaru, 4-kao, 5-au, 6-atta, 7-kesa, 8-neru, 9-kara, 10-asa, 11-dekita, 12-zenzen, 13-itai, 14-itsu, 15-aoi, 16-akai, 17-ani, 18-kedo, 19-genki, 20-kangaeru, 21-kau, 22-dake, 23-takai

D. [country name] desu.
Senshuu no kayoobi ni kita n desu.
Ashita made desu.
Tookyoo wa, hito ga ooi desu ne.
[age]-sai desu.
Hai, soo desu./Iie, kekkon shite imasu.
Hai, muzukashii desu./Chotto muzukashii desu.
Hai, dekimasu./Iie, dekimasen.

E. 1. [day] yoobi desu.
2. Hai, tokidoki tsukaimasu./Iie, amari tsukaimasen.
3. [food] desu.
4. Hai, kekkon shite imasu./Iie, hitori desu./Iie, rikon shite imasu.
5. [place name] ni sunde imasu.
6. Hai, muzukashii to omoimasu./Iie, muzukashiku nai to omoimasu.
7. Hai, mainichi benkyoo shimasu./Iie, mainichi benkyoo shimasen.
8. [hobby] desu.
9. Hai, dekimasu./Iie, dekimasen.
10. Hai, yoku wakarimasu./Iie, amari wakarimasen.

Lesson 13

A. 1-T, 2-T, 3-F, 4-F, 5-T, 6-F

B. 1. San-gatsu ni-juu-hachi-nichi ni Kawasaki de tenisu o shimasu.
2. San-gatsu san-juu-ichi-nichi ni Takahashi san no paatii ga arimasu.
3. Shi-gatsu yokka ni Suu san wa Nihon e kimasu.
4. Shi-gatsu juu-yokka ni Nihongo no koosu ga owarimasu.
5. Shi-gatsu ni-juu-ku-nichi ni "Golden Week" ga hajimarimasu.

C. 1. Akai denwa mo kuroi denwa mo tsukatte mo ii desu.
2. Ni-ji no kaigi ni denakute mo ii desu.
3. Yo-ji han ni kaette mo ii desu.
4. Kono heya de koohii o nonde mo ii desu.
5. Neruson san ni Nihongo de hanashite mo ii desu.
6. Minna no mae de, jiko shookai o shinakute mo ii desu.

D. Neruson san wa, kyoo no kaigi wa nan-ji ni hajimaru ka to kikimashita.
Watashi wa ni-ji da to kotaemashita.
Neruson san wa dono heya ni aru ka to kikimashita.
Watashi wa wakaranai to kotaemashita.
Neruson san wa hiru-gohan no jikan da to iimashita. Obata san mo iku ka to kikimashita.
Watashi wa mada ikanai to iimashita.

E 1. "Kochira koso" o Eigo de nan to iimasu ka.
2. Tanaka san wa roku-ji made kaisha ni iru to iimashita.
3. Sonna kotoba o tsukatte wa ikemasen.
4. Raigetsu no shutchoo wa mikka kara nanoka made desu.
5. Kono tsukue o tsukatte mo ii desu ka.
6. Iroiro arigatoo gozaimashita. Taihen/Totemo tanoshikatta desu.

Lesson 14

A. 1-T, 2-T, 3-F, 4-T, 5-F, 6-F

B. Sports: bowling, golf, basketball, ice skating, hiking, surfing, windsurfing
Countries: Ireland, Australia, India, New Zealand, Brazil, Italy, Austria

C. 1. Osoi kara, takushii de kaetta hoo ga ii desu.
2. Moo sugu kaetta hoo ga ii desu.
3. Supagetti ya piza o tabeta hoo ga ii desu.
4. Atarashii no o katta hoo ga ii desu.
5. Rikon shita hoo ga ii desu.
6. Chokoreeto o sonna ni takusan tabenai hoo ga ii desu.

D. 1. Kinoo, shinbun wa teeburu no ue ni arimashita kedo, ima wa tsukue no shita ni arimasu.
2. Kinoo, ranpu wa tsukue no tonari/soba ni arimashita kedo, ima wa tsukue no ue ni arimasu.
3. Kinoo, rajio wa waapuro to hon no aida ni arimashita kedo, ima wa teeburu no ue ni arimasu.
4. Kinoo, suutsukeesu wa teeburu no mae ni arimashita kedo, ima wa teeburu no ushiro ni arimasu.
5. Kinoo tenki wa yokatta desu kedo, kyoo wa warui desu.
6. Kinoo, kaaten wa arimasendeshita kedo, kyoo wa arimasu.

E. 1. Hotto o futatsu to hambaagaa o hitotsu to supagetti o hitotsu onegai shimasu/kudasai.
2. Atama ga itai kara, uchi ni ite, terebi o mita hoo ga ii to omoimasu.
3. Kono eiga ga omoshiro-soo desu ne. Konban mi ni ikimashoo ka.
4. Yuubinkyoku no tonari no ookii uchi ni dare ga sunde imasu ka.
5. Wada san ni denwa shinai hoo ga ii to omoimasu ka.
6. Watanabe san wa gakkoo no naka ni tsukue ga zenbu de ikutsu aru ka to kikimashita.

Lesson 15

A. 1-T, 2-T, 3-T, 4-F, 5-F, 6-T

B. 1. Keiko san wa natsu yasumi no koto ni tsuite hanashitai n desu ga, Kenji san wa hanashitaku arimasen.
2. Keiko san mo Kenji san mo Itaria ryoori no resutoran de tabetai n desu.
3. Keiko san wa nichiyoobi ni umi e ikitai n desu ga, Kenji san wa ikitaku arimasen.
4. Keiko san wa Eigo no kurasu ni hairitai n desu ga, Kenji san wa hairitaku arimasen.
5. Keiko san wa konban eiga o mitaku nai n desu ga, Kenji san wa mitai desu.
6. Keiko san wa rainen kekkon shitai n desu ga, Kenji san wa kekkon shitaku arimasen.

C. 1. Kono heya de sando o tabenaide.
2. Denwa de booifurendo to hanasanaide.
3. Sono purintaa o tsukawanaide.
4. Watashi no konpyuutaa de repooto o kakanaide.
5. Tsukue no ue no watashi no tegami o yomanaide.
6. Gakkoo de emu-pii pureeyaa o kikanaide.

D. 1. Nanoka no gogo, koochoo sensei to uchiawase o suru yotei desu.
2. Kokonoka no asa, kyooiku iinkai no kaigi ni deru yotei desu.
3. Juu-ichi-nichi no yoru, gakkoo no sutaffu to booringu ni iku (OR o suru) yotei desu.
4. Juu-yokka no asa, koochoo sensei ni repooto o dasu yotei desu.
5. Juu-go-nichi no gogo, Suu san ni denwa shite, natsu yasumi ni tsuite soodan suru yotei desu.
6. Juu-hachi-nichi no asa, Tookyoo ni itte, atarashii suutsu o kau yotei desu.

E. 1. Watashi no kyuuryoo ni tsuite shitsumon shite mo ii desu ka.
2. Kayoobi no gogo wa aite imasu ka.
3. Kotoshi no natsu, atarashii kuruma o kau tsumori desu.
4. Tonari no heya de kaigi ga aru kara, hairanaide kudasai.
5. O-naka ga suita kara, takusan tabetai desu.
6. Rainen no haru (ni), kazoku to issho ni Amerika e iku yotei desu.

Lesson 16

Dialogue 13: 1. Hai, ikitai to omotte imasu.
2. "Spring equinox" to iimasu.
3. Iie, okite itewa ikemasen. Moo osoi kara desu.
4. Ashita no asa yakyuu ga aru kara desu.

Dialogue 14: 1. Takahashi san ga chuumon o shimasu.
2. Kinoo kenka shita kara desu.
3. Iie, kyoo Kenji san to hanashitaku nai to omimasu.
4. Gakkoo no sutaffu to issho ni eiga o mi ni ikimasu.

Dialogue 15: 1. Koochoo sensei ga yoku wakarimasu.
2. Iie, ichi-nichi dake yasumi o toritai n desu.
3. Kore kara no keikaku ni tsuite hanasu yotei desu.
4. Takahashi san wa ima koochoo sensei no sukejuuru o motte iru kara desu.

A. 1. itsu (the others are all numbers)
2. shunbun (the others are all seasons)
3. wain (the others are all foods)
4. toki (the others all refer to parts of the day)
5. shisha (the others all show location)
6. onna (the others are all personal pronouns)
7. anna (the others are all question words)
8. shutchoo (the others are all people)

B. 1. Maiku san wa ashita no asa yakyuu o suru yotei desu. (rainen)
2. Konban takusan nomanai hoo ga ii to omoimasu. (dekiru)
3. Kotoshi no natsu gaikoku e ikitai to omoimasu. (tsuite)
4. Shitsumon o shite mo ii desu ka. (dare)
5. Konna ni muzukashii to omoimasen deshita. (nakatta)
6. Takahashi san ni kyuuryoo no koto ni tsuite hanasanaide kudasai. (tsumori)

C. Moshi moshi, [your name] desu.
Keiyaku ni tsuite desu ga.
Kyoo no gogo wa aite imasu ka.
Asa juu-ji kara kaigi ni deru yotei desu.
Hai, ii desu ne. Gogo wa aite imasu.
Hai, ni-ji ni shimashoo.

D. Across: 1-shita, 5-mo, 7-tsuite, 9-tonari, 10-sonna, 12-gatsu, 13-ikemasen
Down: 2-ikitai, 3-aki, 4-motto, 6-futatsu, 8-aida, 9-tegami, 11-natsu

E. 1. Hai, dekimasu./Iie, dekimasen. Hai, joozu desu./Iie, amari joozu ja arimasen.
2. Tanjoobi wa _____-gatsu _____-nichi desu.
3. Hai, takusan arimasu./Iie, sonna ni takusan arimasen.
4. _____ ga suki desu./Supootsu ga suki ja arimasen.
5. Hai, totte mo ii desu./Iie, totte wa ikemasen.
6. _____-sai desu.
7. _____-ji made okite imashita.
8. Ichiban atsui toki wa _____-gatsu desu.
9. Hai, kekkon shite imasu./Iie, kekkon shite imasen./Iie, rikon shite imasu.
Hai, imasu./Iie, imasen.
10. Hai, yoku okorimasu./Iie, amari okorimasen.
11. _____ [number] arimasu.
12. Hai, _____ e iku yotei ga arimasu./Iie, arimasen.

Lesson 17

A. 1-T, 2-T, 3-F, 4-F, 5-T, 6-T

B.
1. Wada san wa kuruma o motta koto ga arimasu ga, Saitoo san wa arimasen.
2. Wada san mo Saitoo san mo Fuji san ni nobotta koto ga arimasu.
3. Wada san wa Tookyoo ni sunda koto ga arimasen ga, Saitoo san wa arimasu.
4. Wada san mo Saitoo san mo Hokkaidoo e itta koto ga arimasen.
5. Wada san wa Watanabe san no okusan ni atta koto ga arimasu ga, Saitoo san wa arimasen.
6. Wada san mo Saitoo san mo bideo o totta koto ga arimasu.

C. 1-b, 2-a, 3-a, 4-b, 5-b, 6-a,

D.
1. Amazon to Nairu to, dochira (no hoo) ga nagai desu ka.
   Amazon (no hoo) ga nagai desu.
2. Fuji san to Makkinrii to, dochira (no hoo) ga takai desu ka.
   Makkinrii (no hoo) ga takai desu.
3. Honkon to Taiwan to, Nihon kara dochira (no hoo) ga tooi desu ka.
   Honkon (no hoo) ga tooi desu.
4. Nihon to Firipin to, dochira (no hoo) ga hiroi desu ka.
   Nihon (no hoo) ga hiroi desu.
5. Tookyoo to Nyuu Yooku to, dochira (no hoo) ga hito ga ooi desu ka.
   Tookyoo (no hoo) ga hito ga ooi desu.
6. Yama to umi to, dochira (no hoo) ga suki desu ka.
7. Denwa to fakkusu to, dochira (no hoo) o yoku tsukaimasu ka.
8. Mekishiko ryoori to Chuuka ryoori to, dochira (no hoo) o yoku tabemasu ka.
9. Benkyoo to shigoto to, dochira (no hoo) ga suki desu ka.
10. Shinbun to hon to, dochira (no hoo) o yoku yomimasu ka.
    (Free answers)

E.
1. Ame ga furanakattara, nichiyoobi ni dokoka e ikimashoo ka.
2. Sono resutoran de tabeta koto ga arimasu ka.
3. Natsu to fuyu to, dochira (no hoo) ga suki desu ka.
4. O-naka ga itai kara, nani mo tabetaku arimasen.
5. Dandan atatakaku natte imasu ne. Moo sorosoro haru deshoo.
6. Jikan ga attara, Fukuda san ni denwa shite, kaigi no jikan o oshiete kudasai.

Lesson 18

A. 1-F, 2-T, 3-T, 4-F, 5-T, 6-F

B. Denki-dai o haratte kara, chichi no tanjoobi no purezento o kau tame ni depaato e ikimasu.
Chichi no tanjoobi no purezento o katte kara, kissaten de Itoo san ni aimasu.

Itoo san ni atte kara, eiga o mi ni ikimasu.
Eiga o mite kara, Kyooto made no Shinkansen no kippu o kaimasu.
Shinkansen no kippu o katte kara, uchi e kaerimasu.
Uchi e kaette kara, Suuzan san ni tegami o kakimasu.
Tegami o kaite kara, Nihongo o benkyoo shimasu.
Nihongo o benkyoo shite kara, Katoo san to issho ni nomi ni ikimasu.
Shinkansen no kippu o kau mae ni, eiga o mi ni ikimashita.
Eiga o mi ni iku mae ni, kissaten de Itoo san ni aimashita.
Itoo san ni au mae ni, chichi no tanjoobi no purezento o kau tame ni depaato e ikimashita.
Chichi no tanjoobi no purezento o kau mae ni, denki-dai o harau tame ni ginkoo e ikimashita.
Ginkoo e iku mae ni, Kawasaki de tenisu o shimashita.

C. Kono kozutsumi o Igirisu made okuritai n desu ga, ikura deshoo ka.
Kookuubin de.
Sore kara, Oosutoraria made no hagaki wa ikura desu ka.
Hyaku-go-juu en kitte o san-mai kudasai.
Kono tegami wa ikura desu ka.
Amerika desu.

D. 1-g, 2-b, 3-i, 4-a, 5-h, 6-f, 7-d

E. 1. Ashita kabuki no kippu o kau tame ni Tookyoo e ikimasu.
2. (Moshi) wakaranakereba, Saitoo san ni kiite kudasai.
3. Dekakeru mae ni, ranchi o tabemashoo.
4. Jikan ga juubun nakereba, konakute mo ii desu.
5. Kono kozutsumi o kookuubin de okurimasu ka.
6. Takeda san wa shigoto o yametai to iimashita.

Lesson 19

A. 1-T, 2-F, 3-F, 4-T, 5-T, 6-F

B. Apaato o sooji shinakereba narimasen.
Denwa-dai o harawanakereba narimasen.
Kabuki no kippu o ni-mai kawanakereba narimasen.
Atarashii yoofuku o kawanakereba narimasen.
Shirazawa ryokan ni denwa shinakereba narimasen.
Narita kuukoo e no densha no jikan o shirabenakereba narimasen.

C. Free answers.

D. 1. Asa-gohan o tabete ita toki, sono nyuusu o kikimashita.
2. Terebi o mite ita toki, atama wa itaku narimashita.
3. Ginkoo ni tsutomete ita toki, kanai ni hajimete atta n desu. OR Ginkoo de hataraite ita toki, ...
4. Densha ga konde iru toki, takushii ni norimasu.
5. Watashi ga sooji o shite ita toki, Watanabe san ga uchi ni yorimashita.
6. Eki no mae de atta toki, kare to sono koto ni tsuite hanashimashita.

E. 1. Minna jibun no kippu o kawanakereba narimasen.
2. Tookyoo kara Oosaka made no kippu wa ichi-man san-zen go-hyaku en gurai desu.
3. Kare wa hayaku hanasu kara, yoku wakarimasen.
4. Shinkansen ni notte, yokatta desu.
5. Rondon to ieba, Wada san wa itta koto ga arimasu ka.
6. Kyonen Nihon ni ita toki, Fuji san ni noborimashita.

Lesson 20

Dialogue 17: 1. Yo-nin ikimasu.
2. Densha de ikimasu.
3. Kaidan no ue ni suwarimasu.
4. Daibutsu no naka ni hairu tsumori desu.

Dialogue 18: 1. Iroiro-na yooji ga arimasu kara.
2. Gasu-dai to denki-dai o harau tame ni ikimasu.
3. Yooshi ni kakikomanakereba narimasen.
4. Hai, konde imasu.

Dialogue 19: 1. Densha no naka ni imasu.
2. Kodomo ga san-nin iru kara desu.
3. Shiteiseki no kippu o kaimashita.
4. Biiru ni-hon to koora yon-hon o kaimashita.

A. 1. ichi-mai
2. hayaku
3. denki-dai
4. doo shite
5. tooi
6. keiyaku

B. 1. san-man roku-sen go-hyaku en
2. kitte go-mai/go-mai no kitte
3. biiru nana-hon/nana-hon no biiru
4. rok-kagetsu
5. juu-ni-ji yon-juu-go-fun
6. hachi-gatsu tooka

C. 1. Shikata ga arimasen.
2. Ii kagen ni shi nasai.
3. Hajimemashite.
4. Itadakimasu.
5. Kanpai.
6. O-jama shimasu/shimashita.
   O-yasumi nasai.
7. Abunai.
8. Ki o tsukete kudasai.
9. Sore wa zannen desu ne.

D. 1-hon 2-nobotta 3-akaku 4-kippu 5-narimasen 6-kibun 7-dake 8-byooki

E. 1-c, 2-f, 3-g, 4-b, 5-h, 6-a, 7-e, 8-d

F. 1. Hai, arimasu/Iie, arimasen.
2. [place name] ni sunde imashita.
3. _____ o kaitai n desu.
4. _____ no hoo ga muzukashii to omoimasu.
5. _____-gatsu ni samuku narimasu.
6. _____-nakereba narimasen.
7. _____-mai motte imasu.
8. Is-shuukan ni _____-kai gurai Nihongo no benkyoo o shimasu.

APPENDIX 1
VERBS

This is a list of all verbs which have appeared in *Essential Japanese*, showing the -masu form and the -te form.

Dictionary form	-masu form	-te form	Meaning
agaru	agarimasu	agatte	go/come up
aku	akimasu	aite	be open, free
aru	arimasu	atte	be, exist, have
aruku	arukimasu	aruite	walk
au	aimasu	atte	meet
azukaru	azukarimasu	azukatte	receive, be entrusted with
chigau	chigaimasu	chigatte	differ, be mistaken
dasu	dashimasu	dashite	put out, send, submit
dekakeru	dekakemasu	dekakete	go out
dekiru	dekimasu	dekite	can, be able to
deru	demasu	dete	go out, appear
furu	furimasu	futte	fall, drop
ganbaru	ganbarimasu	ganbatte	try hard, do one's best
hairu	hairimasu	haitte	go in, enter
hajimaru	hajimarimasu	hajimatte	begin
hanasu	hanashimasu	hanashite	speak, talk
harau	haraimasu	haratte	pay
hashiru	hashirimasu	hashitte	run
hataraku	hatarakimasu	hataraite	work, labor
iku	ikimasu	itte	go
irassharu	irasshaimasu	irasshatte	be [formal]
iru	imasu	ite	be, exist
itadaku	itadakimasu	itadaite	receive
iu	iimasu	itte	say, relate
kaeru	kaerimasu	kaette	return, go/come home
kakaru	kakarimasu	kakatte	take (time), last
kakikomu	kakikomimasu	kakikonde	fill in/out (a form)
kaku	kakimasu	kaite	write
kangaeru	kangaemasu	kangaete	think about, consider
kau	kaimasu	katte	buy
ki o tsukeru	ki o tsukemasu	ki o tsukete	take care
kiku	kikimasu	kiite	hear, ask
kimeru	kimemasu	kimete	decide

komu	komimasu	konde	be crowded
kotaeru	kotaemasu	kotaete	answer, reply
kuru	kimasu	kite	come
magaru	magarimasu	magatte	turn
matsu	machimasu	matte	wait
miru	mimasu	mite	see, watch
miseru	misemasu	misete	show
moosu	mooshimasu	mooshite	be called/named
narabu	narabimasu	narande	line up, queue
naru	narimasu	natte	become, get
neru	nemasu	nete	sleep, go to bed
noboru	noborimasu	nobotte	climb, go up
nomu	nomimasu	nonde	drink
noru	norimasu	notte	get in/on, ride
oboeru	oboemasu	oboete	remember, recall
okiru	okimasu	okite	get up
okoru	okorimasu	okotte	get angry
okuru	okurimasu	okutte	send
omou	omoimasu	omotte	think
oshieru	oshiemasu	oshiete	teach, tell
owaru	owarimasu	owatte	end, finish
shiraberu	shirabemasu	shirabete	investigate, look into
suku	sukimasu	suite	become empty
sumu	sumimasu	sunde	live, reside
suru	shimasu	shite	do
suwaru	suwarimasu	suwatte	sit down
taberu	tabemasu	tabete	eat
tatsu	tachimasu	tatte	stand up
tomaru	tomarimasu	tomatte	stay over
tomeru	tomemasu	tomete	stop, halt
toru	torimasu	totte	take
tsukareru	tsukaremasu	tsukarete	become tired
tsukau	tsukaimasu	tsukatte	use
tsutomeru	tsutomemasu	tsutomete	be employed
uru	urimasu	utte	sell
wakaru	wakarimasu	wakatte	understand
wasureru	wasuremasu	wasurete	forget
yameru	yamemasu	yamete	quit, stop
yaru	yarimasu	yatte	do, try
yobu	yobimasu	yonde	call, summon
yomu	yomimasu	yonde	read
yoru	yorimasu	yotte	call in, drop by

APPENDIX 2
THE JAPANESE WRITING SYSTEMS

As we explained in the Introduction, written Japanese is made up of three quite different writing systems, kanji, hiragana and katakana characters, which are used in combination.

As there is not enough space in this book to teach the written language, we have instead used the Roman alphabet.

Kanji characters were developed in China over three thousand years ago, and were first introduced into Japan in the third century. Where the letters of our Roman alphabet represent sounds, kanji represent meanings. Each kanji is rather like a picture or symbol, representing just one thing or idea, so it follows that thousands and thousands of individual kanji must be learned in order to be able to read a newspaper, or write a letter. In everyday life it is necessary to know around three thousand different kanji, although specialists need to know far more for their particular field.

An added complication of kanji characters is that they may be pronounced in several completely different ways, depending on which other characters they are combined with in compound words. For example, the kanji character for "east", when by itself, is pronounced higashi, and the character for "capital city" is pronounced kei, but when the two are combined in a compound word meaning "eastern capital", they are pronounced too and kyoo – Tokyo. Some examples of kanji characters and the way they are pronounced have been given in each lesson.

In addition to kanji, there are two sets of phonetic characters, hiragana and katakana. These are two separate ways of representing the same sounds. There are 46 characters in each set, and apart from the five vowels and a single "n" sound, all the rest represent syllables made up of a consonant and a vowel. In other words, there is no character for the sound "k", but there are characters for the sounds ka, ki, ku, ke and ko. When you say Japanese words slowly, you will see that most of them can be split easily into syllables, and each of these would be written with one hiragana or katakana character. For example hi-ra-ga-na would be written with four characters, ki-mo-no with three, and su-shi with two.

Hiragana characters are used in a number of ways. They are joined to the end of words written in kanji to indicate grammatical function, such as different verb endings to show past or present tense. Hiragana characters are also used for small words such as those meaning "in", "at" or "to", which do not have kanji equivalents, and for words whose kanji characters are very complex, or which have become obsolete over the years.

Katakana characters represent exactly the same sounds as hiragana, so in principle, all words can be written in katakana, but in fact, they are used in much the same way as we use italics, that is, to show stress, and to write foreign words which have been imported into Japanese. There are a great number of such words, mostly taken from American English, and it is easy to recognize them in written form as they are always written in katakana. Hiragana are cursive and flowing characters, whereas katakana tend to be squarer, with more straight lines and corners.

Here is an example of how kanji, hiragana and katakana are used together in a sentence. The sentence means "Mike's school is in Yokohama."

Ma	I	ku	sa	n	no	gak	koo	wa
マ	イ	ク	さ	ん	の	学	校	は
{ katakana }			{ hiragana }			{ kanji }		{hiragana}

yoko	hama	ni	a	ri	ma	su
横	浜	に	あ	り	ま	す。
{ kanji }		{	hiragana			}

The complete set of hiragana and katakana characters are shown in the following table.

Hiragana					Katakana				
あ a	い i	う u	え e	お o	ア a	イ i	ウ u	エ e	オ o
か ka	き ki	く ku	け ke	こ ko	カ ka	キ ki	ク ku	ケ ke	コ ko
さ sa	し shi	す su	せ se	そ so	サ sa	シ shi	ス su	セ se	ソ so
た ta	ち chi	つ tsu	て te	と to	タ ta	チ chi	ツ tsu	テ te	ト to
な na	に ni	ぬ nu	ね ne	の no	ナ na	ニ ni	ヌ nu	ネ ne	ノ no
は ha	ひ hi	ふ hu	へ he	ほ ho	ハ ha	ヒ hi	フ hu	ヘ he	ホ ho
ま ma	み mi	む mu	め me	も mo	マ mo	ミ mi	ム mu	メ me	モ mo
や ya		ゆ yu		よ yo	ヤ ya		ユ yu		ヨ yo
ら ra	り ri	る ru	れ re	ろ ro	ラ ra	リ ri	ル ru	レ re	ロ ro
わ wa				を o	ワ wa				ヲ o
ん n					ン n				

about, approximately: gurai (19)
above, on: ue (14)
academy, school: gakuin (1)
address: juusho (5)
after: ato (15); kara (18)
afternoon: gogo (7)
again, once more: mata (4)
ahead, before: saki ni (17)
air conditioner: eakon (14)
airmail: kookuubin (18)
airport: kuukoo (15)
all: zenbu (10)
all day long: ichi-nichi-juu (19)
all kinds of: iroiro(-na) (11)
already, (not) any longer: moo (5)
always: itsumo (8)
amazing, incredible: sugoi (17)
American person: Amerikajin (1)
among, within: naka (11)
and: to (1); ya (10)
answer, respond: kotaeru (13)
answer, response: kotae (10)
apartment (flat): apaato (14)
April: shi-gatsu (13)
argument: kenka (14)
as far as: made (5)
at: ni [with time] (4)
at, in: de [place where action occurs] (5)
attend a meeting: kaigi ni deru (13)
August: hachi-gatsu (13)
Australia: Oosutoraria (14)
Austria: Oosutoria (14)
autumn/fall: aki (13)
Autumnal Equinox Day: shuubun no hi (13)

bad, wrong: warui (7)
bank: ginkoo (2)
baseball: yakyuu (7)
basketball: basukettobooru (10)
be, exist: aru [inanimate objects] (2); iru [animate objects] (4)
be called, named: moosu (10)
be crowded: komu (8)
be employed: tsutomeru (10)
be excited: koofun suru (19)
be incorrect, wrong: chigau (1)
be married: kekkon suru (11)
be open, free, have no engagements: aku (15)
because: kara (11)

become, get: naru (17)
become empty: suku (14)
become hungry: o-naka ga suku (14)
become tired: tsukareru (9)
bed: beddo (14)
beer: biiru (9)
before, in front of: mae (7)
behave yourselves: ii kagen ni shi nasai (19)
behind, in back of: ushiro (14)
below, under: shita (14)
belt: beruto (8)
between: aida (14)
big: ookii (2)
birthday: tanjoobi (7)
black: kuro(i) (8)
blue: buruu (8)
blue-green: ao(i) (8)
book: hon (5)
both...and...: ...mo...mo (9)
bowling: booringu (14)
boyfriend: booifurendo (10)
branch office: shisha (14)
Brazil: Burajiru (14)
brief, simple: kantan(-na) (8)
bring: motte kuru (19)
brown: buraun (8); chaiiro (8)
building: tatemono (5)
Bullet Train: Shinkansen (11)
bus: basu (10)
business card: meishi (1)
business trip: shutchoo (13)
busy: isogashii (13)
but: ga (1)
but, although: kedo (8)
buy: kau (8)
by: de [means by which something is done] (4); made ni [date or time] (15)
by the way: tokorode (5)

cake: keeki (14)
call, summon: yobu (7)
call in, drop by: yoru (15)
can, be able to: dekiru (10)
Canada: Kanada (1)
Canadian person: Kanadajin (1)
can't be helped: shikata ga arimasen (17)
car: kuruma (1)
carpet: kaapetto (14)
CD, compact disc: shii dii (14)
certainly, very good: kashikomarimashita [formal] (14)
chance, opportunity: chansu (9)
change [money]: o-tsuri (5)
cheap: yasui (7)

cheese: chiizu (17)
child: kodomo (8)
children: kodomotachi (11)
Children's Day: kodomo no hi (13)
Chinese cuisine: Chuuka ryoori (11)
Chinese written characters: kanji (9)
chocolate: chokoreeto (14)
chopsticks: hashi (4)
city, town: machi (9)
class: kurasu (9)
clerk, office worker: jimu no hito (2)
climb, go up: noboru (17)
close, nearby: chikai (17)
clothes: yoofuku (19)
coat: kooto (8)
coffee shop: kissaten (9)
cola: koora (14)
cold: samui (7)
come: kuru (3)
Coming-of-Age Day: seijin no hi (13)
committee: iinkai (15)
company, office: kaisha (1)
computer: konpyuutaa (2)
concerning, regarding: ni tsuite (15)
Constitution Day: kenpoo kinenbi (13)
consult, talk over: soodan suru (15)
contract: keiyaku (15)
conversation: kaiwa (14)
conversation, chat: hanashi (4)
cook: ryoori suru (4)
cooking, cuisine: ryoori (4)
cool: suzushii (17)
corner: kado (5)
Could I speak to…?: …-san onegai shimasu. (4)
country: kuni (10)
course [of study]: koosu (13)
Culture Day: bunka no hi (13)
curtain: kaaten (14)
cushion: kusshon (14)

dangerous: abunai (19)
dark: kurai (17)
date [of the month]: -nichi (13)
day: hi (13)
day after tomorrow: asatte (3)
day off, vacation: yasumi no hi (13)
daytime: hiruma (13)
December: juu-ni-gatsu (13)
decide: kimeru (15)
definitely, without fail: kitto (17)
department head: buchoo (15)
department store: depaato (8)

design: dezain (8)
designer: dezainaa (8)
desk: tsukue (2)
dictionary: jisho (18)
difficult: muzukashii (7)
direction, side: hoo (17)
dirty: kitanai (14)
dislike: kirai(-na) (3)
divorce: rikon (11)
do: suru (3); yaru (19)
do the cleaning: sooji suru (19)
dog: inu (4)
dollars: doru (5)
dress [noun]: wanpiisu (8)
drink [verb]: nomu (3)
DVD: diibiidii (17)

early: hayai (7)
eat: taberu (3)
education: kyooiku (15)
egg: tamago (18)
eight: hachi (1)
eight (objects): yattsu (14)
electricity: denki (18)
electricity charges: denki-dai (18)
eleven: juu-ichi (1)
embarrassed, shy: hazukashii (9)
Emperor's Birthday: tennoo tanjoobi (13)
engineer: enjinia (1)
England, Great Britain: Igirisu (2)
English conversation: Eikaiwa (18)
English language: Eigo (3)
English/British person: Igirisujin (2)
enjoyable, fun: tanoshii (9)
Enjoy your meal.: Itadakimasu. (3)
enough, sufficient: juubun (18)
entrance area [in a house]: genkan (5)
envelope: fuutoo (18)
errand, chore: yooji (18)
et cetera, and so on: nado (10)
Europe: Yooroppa (13)
evening: yoru (9), ban (11)
every day: mainichi (3)
everyone: mina san, minna (2)
everyone together: minna de (7)
exactly, precisely: choodo (11)
excuse me, I beg your pardon: gomen nasai (13)
excuse me for disturbing you: o-jama shimasu (5)
excuse me, goodbye: shitsurei shimasu (2)
expensive: takai (7)
explain: setsumei suru (11)
explanation: setsumei (11)

face: kao (10)
fall, drop: furu (17)
family: kazoku (7)
family (your): go-kazoku (7)
family computer: famikon (14)
famous: yuumei(-na) (8)
far, distant: tooi (17)
father (my): chichi (7)
father (your): o-toosan (7)
fax: fakkusu (8)
February: ni-gatsu (13)
females, women: josei (11)
fill in/out [a form]: kakikomu (18)
finally, at the end: saigo ni (18)
fine, all right: daijoobu(-na) (8)
finish, end [verb]: owaru (10)
first of all, to begin with: mazu (18)
first time: hajimete (15)
fish: sakana (3)
five: go (1)
five (objects): itsutsu (14)
floppy disk: furoppi (14)
flower: hana (3)
food: tabemono (10)
foreign country, abroad: gaikoku (15)
foreigner: gaijin (4)
forget: wasureru (9)
form, a blank: yooshi (15)
four: shi/yo/yon (1)
four (objects): yottsu (14)
France: Furansu (10)
French language: Furansugo (10)
frequently occurring: yoku aru (11)
Friday: kin'yoobi (9)
friend: tomodachi (3)
from: kara (2)

game: geemu (10)
gas (petrol): gasu (18)
gas charges: gasu-dai (18)
German language: Doitsugo (10)
get angry: okoru (14)
get up, get out of bed: okiru (13)
girlfriend: gaarufurendo (11)
go: iku (3)
go in, enter: hairu (9)
go out: dekakeru (18)
go out, appear: deru (13)
go skiing: sukii ni iku (13)
go to meet: mukae ni iku (15)
go up: agaru (5)
golf: gorufu (9)

good, fine: ii (3)
good evening: konbanwa (2)
good morning: ohayoo gozaimasu (2)
good night: oyasumi nasai (2)
gradually, little by little: dandan (17)
gray: guree (8)
green: guriin, midori (8)
green tea: o-cha (3)
Greenery Day: midori no hi (13)
grilled fish: yaki-zakana (3)
guest, customer: kyaku, o-kyaku san (14)
gym: jimu (8)

half past -: -han (4)
ham: hamu (14)
hamburger: hanbaagaa (14)
handsome: hansamu(-na): (11)
happen, be completed: dekiru (15)
happy: ureshii (11)
happy to meet you: doozo yoroshiku (2)
hate, loathe: dai-kirai(-na) (3)
have: gozaimasu [formal] (8)
have, hold: motsu (15)
have a headache: atama ga itai (7)
have a talk, chat: hanashi o suru (4)
have you ever...?: ...koto ga arimasu ka. (17)
he, him: kare (14)
head: atama (7)
healthy, energetic: genki(-na) (8)
hear, listen, ask: kiku (3)
hello: konnichiwa (2); [on the telephone] moshi moshi (4)
her, she: kanojo (15)
here: koko (2)
high: takai (7)
high school: kookoo [short for kootoo gakkoo] (1)
hiking: haikingu (14)
him, he: kare (14)
history: rekishi (10)
hobby: shumi (10)
homework: shukudai (7)
horrible: iya(-na) (8)
hot: atsui (7), hotto (14)
hot and humid: mushiatsui (17)
hot coffee: hotto (koohii) (14)
hot spring: onsen (9)
hotel: hoteru (8)
hour: jikan (9)
house, home: uchi (2)
how?: doo (3)
How about...?: ...doo desu ka. (3)
How are you?: O-genki desu ka. (8)
How do you do?: Hajimemashite. (1)

how many?: ikutsu (14)
how many people?: nan-nin (9)
how much (money)?: ikura (5)
how old?: ikutsu, nan-sai (11)
however, but: demo (4)
hundred: hyaku (5)
hundred million: oku (19)
husband (my): otto/shujin (7)
husband (your): go-shujin (7)

I, me: watashi (1); boku [used by boys and men] (11)
I wonder…: …kana, kashira (8)
ice skating: aisu sukeeto (14)
ill: byooki(-na) (17)
in, at [location]: ni (2)
in fact: jitsu wa (11)
India: Indo (14)
inside: naka (14)
inside the train: shanai (19)
intention: tsumori (15)
interest, hobby: shumi (10)
interesting, amusing: omoshiroi (9)
interference, obstruction: jama (5)
introduce: shookai suru (10)
investigate, look into: shiraberu (19)
Ireland: Airurando (14)
iron: airon (14)
is/are: desu (1); aru [inanimate objects] (2); iru [animate objects] (4); irassharu
    [polite form of iru] (4); de gozaimasu [formal] (8)
isn't/aren't: ja arimasen (2)
Italy: Itaria (14)

jacket: jaketto (8)
January: ichi-gatsu (13)
Japan: Nihon, Nippon (1)
Japan Alps: Nihon Arupusu (9)
Japanese language: Nihongo (1)
Japanese-style inn: ryokan (9)
jeans: Jiinzu,G-pan (8)
July: shichi-gatsu (13)
June: roku-gatsu (13)
just, only: tada (15)

keyboard: kiiboodo (14)
kind, gentle: shinsetsu(-na) (8)

Labor Thanksgiving Day: kinroo kansha no hi (13)
lamp: ranpu (14)
laptop: rapputoppu (14)
large [in area], spacious: hiroi (17)
last month: sengetsu (13)
last week: senshuu (9)

last year: kyonen (15)
late: osoi (7)
left (side): hidari (5)
left-hand side: hidari-gawa (5)
leg, foot: ashi (19)
lemon tea: remon tii (14)
lesson, class: jugyoo (10)
lesson one: dai ik-ka (1)
letter: tegami (13)
lie, untruth, story: uso (10)
life, living: seikatsu (10)
like: suki(-na) (3)
like very much, love: dai-suki(-na) (3)
line up, queue: narabu (17)
little, a bit: sukoshi (5), chotto (7)
lonely: sabishii (11)
long: nagai (10)
look forward to: tanoshimi ni suru (19)
Look out!: Abunai! (19)
luggage: nimotsu (19)
lunch: hiru-gohan (7), ranchi (18)

make: tsukuru (18)
males, men: dansei (11)
man: otoko no hito (9)
manager: maneejaa (10)
many, abundant: ooi (11)
many, much: takusan (4)
March: san-gatsu (13)
marriage: kekkon (11)
mathematics: suugaku (10)
May: go-gatsu (13)
meat: niku (4)
meet: au (4)
meeting: kaigi (3)
meeting, consultation: uchiawase (15)
memo: memo (15)
menu: menyuu (14)
message: messeeji (15)
minute: -fun/pun (4)
miso soup: miso shiru (3)
Monday: getsuyoobi (9)
money: o-kane (15)
monitor: monitaa (14)
mood, feeling: kibun (17)
more: motto (8)
morning: asa (9)
most, -est: ichiban (11)
mother (my): haha (7)
mother (your): o-kaasan (7)
Mount Fuji: Fuji san (11)
mountain: yama (9)

movie, film: **eiga** (3)
MP3 player: **Emu pii surii pureeyaa** (15)
Mr., Mrs., Ms., Miss: **san** (1); **sama** [very polite] (4)
music: **ongaku** (19)
my: **watashi no** (1)

name: **namae** (1)
National Foundation Day: **kenkoku kinenbi** (13)
near, close [adverb]: **chikaku** (14)
near, next to: **soba** (14)
necktie: **nekutai** (8)
neither…nor…: **…mo…mo** (9)
never: **zenzen** (8)
new: **atarashii** (2)
New Year's Day: **ganjitsu** (13)
New Zealand: **Nyuu Jiirando** (14)
news: **nyuusu** (4)
newspaper: **shinbun** (2)
next: **tsugi no** (5)
next month: **raigetsu** (13)
next to, by the side: **tonari** (7)
next week: **raishuu** (9)
next year: **rainen** (15)
nine: **kyuu/ku** (1)
nine (objects): **kokonotsu** (14)
no: **iie** (1)
no good, useless: **dame(-na)** (8)
no one: **dare mo** (17)
noisy: **urusai** (19)
noodles: **soba** (10)
not very: **amari** (3)
November: **juu-ichi-gatsu** (13)
now, at the moment: **ima** (4)

ocean: **umi** (9)
…o'clock: **-ji** (4)
October: **juu-gatsu** (13)
octopus: **tako** (19)
odd, strange: **hen(-na)** (8)
of course, naturally: **mochiron** (17)
office work: **jimu** (2)
often: **yoku** (8)
Ohio (state): **Ohaio-shu** (10)
older brother (my): **ani** (7)
older brother (your): **o-niisan** (7)
older sister (my): **ane** (7)
older sister (your): **o-neesan** (7)
on, on top, above: **ue** (14)
once, one time: **ichido** (11); **ik-kai** (19)
once more: **moo ichido** (11)
one: **ichi** (1)
one (object): **hitotsu** (14)

one day: ichi-nichi (15)
one month: ik-kagetsu (19)
one person: hitori : (9)
one-year period: ichi-nen-kan (11)
only: dake (9)
or: ka (15)
orange: orenji (8)
order, request [noun]: chuumon (14)
other, another, else: hoka ni : (17)
outside: soto (9)
over there: asoko (2)
over there, the other direction: mukoo (14)
own, my own, your own: jibun no (19)

package (parcel): kozutsumi (18)
painful: itai (7)
pardon me: gomen kudasai (4)
part-time worker: paato (2)
party: paatii (9)
past, after: sugi (7)
pay: harau (18)
people: hitotachi (9)
person, people: hito (2)
photocopy: kopii (14)
photograph: shashin (17)
physical education: taiiku (10)
piano: piano (10)
pickles: tsukemono (3)
picnic: pikunikku (17)
picture postcard: e-hagaki (19)
pink: pinku (8)
pity, unfortunate: zannen(-na) (9)
pizza: piza (14)
place: tokoro (9)
plan, schedule: yotei (15)
please: onegai shimasu (5)
pleased to meet you: yoroshiku onegai shimasu (2)
post office: yuubinkyoku (14)
postcard: hagaki (18)
practice: renshuu (7)
present, gift: purezento (18)
president [of a company]: shachoo (15)
pretty, clean: kirei(-na) (8)
principal, head teacher: koochoo (15)
printer: purintaa (2)
probably, must be: deshoo (8)
problem: mondai (5)
project, plan: keikaku (15)
public telephone: kooshuu denwa (14)
purple: murasaki (8)
purpose/benefit of: tame ni (18)

question: shitsumon (11)
quick: hayai (7)
quickly: hayaku (10)
quiet, peaceful: shizuka(-na) (8)
quit, cease: yameru (18)

radio: rajio (3)
rain: ame [noun], ame ga furu [verb] (17)
raw fish: sashimi (3)
raw fish on rice: sushi (10)
read: yomu (3)
really, truly: hontoo ni (9)
receive, be entrusted with: azukaru (18)
recently: saikin (19)
red: aka(i) (8)
remember, recall: oboeru (7)
report [noun]: repooto (8)
reserved seat: shiteiseki (19)
reside, live: sumu (7)
Respect for the Aged Day: keiroo no hi (13)
restaurant: resutoran (3)
restroom: o-tearai, tearai (17)
return, go/come home: kaeru (7)
review: fukushuu (6)
rice (cooked): gohan (3)
rich person: kanemochi (17)
right (side): migi (5)
right-hand side: migi-gawa (5)
room: heya (13)
run: hashiru (10)

sake, rice wine: o-sake, sake (9)
salad: sarada (14)
salary, wages: kyuuryoo (15)
sales, selling: hanbai (19)
same: onaji (13)
sandwich: sando (14)
Saturday: doyoobi (9)
say, relate: iu (13)
schedule: sukejuuru (15)
school: gakkoo (1)
science: kagaku (10)
science-fiction: SF (esu efu) (4)
sea: umi (9)
second floor, upstairs: ni-kai (7)
section head, assistant manager: kachoo (15)
see, watch: miru (3)
self, oneself: jibun (19)
self-introduction: jiko shookai (10)
sell: uru (15)
send: okuru (18)
September: ku-gatsu (13)

set meal: teishoku (3)
seven: nana/shichi (1)
seven (objects): nanatsu (14)
share, portion: -bun (19)
she, her: kanojo (15)
shirt: shatsu (8)
shoes: kutsu (8)
shop: mise (14)
shopping [noun]: kaimono (8)
show: miseru (18)
shy, embarrassed: hazukashii (9)
…side: -gawa (5)
single: o-hitori (11)
sit down: suwaru (5)
six: roku (1)
six (objects): muttsu (14)
size: saizu (8)
ski resort: sukii-joo (13)
skiing: sukii (13)
skillful, good at: joozu(-na) (9)
skirt: sukaato (8)
ski-wear: sukii-uea (19)
sky: sora (8)
sleep, go to bed: neru (7)
slippers: surippa (5)
slow: osoi (7)
slowly: yukkuri (5)
slowly, gradually: sorosoro (13)
small: chiisai (7)
smart, clever: atama ga ii (10)
snow: yuki (17)
so, therefore: dakara (9)
someone: dareka (17)
something, anything: nanika (9)
sometimes: tokidoki (3)
somewhere, anywhere: dokoka (9)
soon: sugu (4)
sorry: sumimasen (1)
sorry, I apologize: doomo sumimasen (1)
spaghetti: supagetti (14)
speak, talk: hanasu (3)
special, particular: tokubetsu no (15)
sport: supootsu (10)
Sports Health Day: taiiku no hi (13)
spring: haru (13)
Spring Equinox Day: shunbun no hi (13)
staff: sutaffu (14)
stamp: kitte (18)
stand: tatsu (17)
stay (overnight): tomaru (9)
steak: suteeki (14)
steps, stairs: kaidan (17)
still, (not) yet: mada (4)

stomach: o-naka (14)
stop, halt [transitive]: tomeru (5)
straight ahead: massugu (5)
strong: tsuyoi (17)
student: gakusei (1)
study : benkyoo [noun], benkyoo (o) suru [verb] (4)
suit: suutsu (8)
suitcase: suutsukeesu (1)
summer: natsu (13)
summer vacation: natsu-yasumi (13)
Sunday: nichiyoobi (9)
Supermarket: suupaa (14)
surfing: saafingu (14)
sweater: seetaa (8)

T-shirt: T-shatsu (8)
table: teeburu (14)
take: toru (15)
take (time), last: kakaru (9)
take care, be careful: ki o tsukeru (7)
talk, speak: hanasu (3)
tasty, delicious: oishii (3)
taxi: takushii (4)
teacher, professor: sensei (1)
team: chiimu (10)
telephone: denwa (2)
telephone charges: denwa-dai (18)
television, TV: terebi (4)
tell, teach: oshieru (3)
ten: juu (1)
ten (objects): too (14)
ten thousand: ichi-man (19)
tennis: tenisu (4)
terrible, awful: taihen(-na) (8), hidoi (14)
test [noun]: tesuto (4)
thank you: arigatoo gozaimasu (1)
Thank you very much.: Doomo arigatoo gozaimasu. (1)
Thank you for the meal.: Go-chisoo sama deshita. (3)
that [adjective]: sono (3)
that [noun]: sore (2)
that, over there [adjective]: ano (3)
that kind of: sonna, anna (13)
that one [of two]: sochira, sotchi (17)
that over there [noun]: are (2)
then: soshite (18)
there: soko (2)
thing, event, fact: koto (10)
think: omou (10)
think about, consider: kangaeru (10)
this [adjective]: kono (3)
this [noun]: kore (2)
this evening: konban (3)
this kind of: konna (13)

this month: kongetsu (13)
this morning: kesa (9)
this one [of two]: kochira, kotchi (17)
this year: kotoshi (15)
thousand: sen (5)
three: san (1)
three (objects): mittsu (14)
Thursday: mokuyoobi (9)
ticket: kippu (18)
time, hour: jikan (4)
time, period: toki (13)
to begin [intransitive]: hajimaru (4)
to get older [of people]: toshi o toru (19)
to get on/in [transportation]: noru (19)
to put out, send, submit: dasu (11)
to, towards: e (1), ni (9)
toast: toosuto (14)
today: kyoo (2)
together: issho ni (7)
tomorrow: ashita (3)
too, also: mo (8)
town, city: machi (9)
traffic signals: shingoo (5)
train: densha (4)
train station: eki (2)
trip, journey: ryokoo (19)
try hard, do one's best: ganbaru (10)
Tuesday: kayoobi (9)
tuna: tsuna (14)
turn [verb]: magaru (5)
twelve: juu-ni (1)
two: ni (1)
two (objects): futatsu (14)
two people: futari (9)

umbrella: kasa (17)
understand: wakaru (2)
United States: Amerika (1)
university: daigaku (2)
university student: daigakusei (5)
umarried: o-hitori (11)
unskillful, bad at: heta(-na) (9)
until: made (4)
us, we: watashitachi (9)
use: tsukau (11)

vacation, holiday, rest: yasumi (13)
various: iroiro(-na) (11)
very, extremely: totemo (8)
video: bideo (9)

wait: matsu (5)
walk: aruku (14)

want: **hoshii** (15)
warm: **atatakai** (17)
water: **mizu** (3)
weather: **tenki** (9)
Wednesday: **suiyoobi** (9)
week: **shuukan** (10)
weekend: **shuumatsu** (9)
welcome: **yookoso** (1)
well, in that case: **ja** (1)
What?: **Nan/nani?** (3)
What date?: **Nan-nichi?** (13)
What day?: **Nan-yoobi?** (9)
What kind of...?: **Donna?** (13)
What time?: **Nan-ji?** (4)
When?: **Itsu?** (9)
Where?: **Doko?** (2)
Which?: **Dono?** (3)
Which month?: **Nan-gatsu?** (13)
Which one?: **dore** (2); **Dochira?, Dotchi?** [of two] (17)
white: **shiro(i)** (8)
Who?: **Dare?** (2)
Why?: **Doo shite, naze?** (4)
wife (my): **kanai/tsuma** (7)
wife (your): **okusan** (7)
wind: **kaze** (17)
windsurfing: **uindo saafingu** (14)
wine: **wain** (3)
winter: **fuyu** (13)
without standing on ceremony: **go-enryo naku** (11)
woman: **onna no hito** (9)
women: **onna no hitotachi** (9)
word: **kotoba** (13)
work [verb]: **shigoto (o) suru** (4)
work, employment: **shigoto** (4)
work, labor [verb]: **hataraku** (7)
worry, anxiety: **shinpai** (15)
write: **kaku** (5)

year: **nen** (11)
year, age: **toshi** (19)
...years old: **-sai** (11)
yellow: **kiiro(i)** (8)
yen: **en** (5)
yes: **hai** (1); **ee** [informal] (9)
yes, please: **itadakimasu** [when offered food and drink] (5)
yesterday: **kinoo** (9)
yesterday evening: **kinoo no ban** (11)
you: **anata** (2)
young: **wakai** (9)
younger brother (my): **otooto** (7)
younger brother (your): **otootosan** (7)
younger sister (my): **imooto** (7)
younger sister (your): **imootosan** (7)

JAPANESE–ENGLISH GLOSSARY

abunai: dangerous, Look out! (19)
agaru: go up (5)
aida: between (14)
airon: iron (14)
Airurando: Ireland (14)
aisu sukeeto: ice skating (14)
aka(i): red (8)
aki: fall/autumn (13)
aku: be open, free, have no engagements (15)
amari: not very [+ negative verb] (3)
ame: rain [noun] (17)
ame ga furu: rain [verb] (17)
Amerika: the United States (1)
Amerikajin: an American (1)
anata: you (2)
ane: (my) older sister (7)
ani: (my) older brother (7)
anna: that kind of (13)
ano: that – over there [adjective] (3)
ao(i): blue-green (8)
apaato: apartment, flat (14)
appurupai: apple pie (14)
ara: oh! [used mostly by women] (14)
are: look! listen! (17); that over there [noun] (2)
arigatoo gozaimasu: thank you [more informal than doomo arigatoo gozaimasu] (1)
aru: be, exist, there is/are, have [used with inanimate objects] (2)
aruku: walk (14)
asa: morning (9)
asatte: the day after tomorrow (3)
ashi: leg, foot (19)
ashita: tomorrow (3)
asoko: over there (2)
atama: head (7)
atama ga ii: smart, clever (10)
atama ga itai: have a headache (7)
atarashii: new (2)
atatakai: warm (17)
ato: after (15)
atsui: hot (7)
au: meet (4)
azukaru: receive, be entrusted with (18)

ban: evening (11)
basu: bus (10)
basukettobooru: basketball (10)
beddo: bed (14)

benkyoo: study [noun] (4)
benkyoo (o) suru: study [verb] (4)
beruto: belt (8)
bideo: video (9)
biiru: beer (9)
booifurendo: boyfriend (10)
boku: I [used by boys and men](11)
booringu: bowling (14)
buchoo: department head, manager (15)
-bun: quantity, share, portion (19)
bunka no hi: Culture Day (13)
Burajiru: Brazil (14)
buraun: brown (8)
buruu: blue (8)
byooki(-na): ill (17)

chaiiro: brown (8)
chansu: chance, opportunity (9)
chichi: (my) father (7)
chigau: be incorrect, wrong (1)
chiimu: team (10)
chiisai: small (7)
chiizu: cheese (17)
chikai: close, nearby (17)
chikaku: near, close [adverb] (14)
choodo: exactly, precisely (11)
chokoreeto: chocolate (14)
chotto: a little, a bit (7)
Chuuka ryoori: Chinese cuisine (11)
chuumon: an order, request (14)

da: is/are [plain form of desu] (10)
dai ik-ka: lesson one (1)
dai-kirai(-na): hate, loathe (3)
dai-suki(-na): like very much, love (3)
daibutsu: large statue of Buddha (17)
daigaku: university (2)
daigakusei: university student (5)
daijoobu(-na): fine, all right (8)
dakara: so, therefore (9)
dake: only (9)
dame(-na): no good, useless (8)
dandan: gradually, little by little (17)
dansei: males, men (11)
dare: who? (2)
dare mo: no one (17)
dareka: someone (17)
dasu: to put out, send, submit (11)
de: at, in [particle indicating place where an action occurs] (5)
de: by [particle indicating means by which something is done] (4)
de gozaimasu: is, are [formal] (8)
dekakeru: go out (18)

dekiru: can, be able to (10); happen, be completed (15)
demo: - or something (19); however, but [at the beginning of a sentence] (4)
denki: electricity (18)
denki-dai: electricity charges (18)
densha: train (4)
denwa: telephone (2)
denwa-dai: telephone charges (18)
depaato: department store (8)
deru: go out, appear (13)
deshoo: I wonder if, probably, must be (8)
desu: am/is/are (1)
dezain: design (8)
dezainaa: designer (8)
diibiidii: DVD (17)
doo: how? (3)
doo shimashita ka.: What happened? (9)
doo shimashoo ka.: What shall I do? (5)
doo shite: why? (4)
dochira: where? [formal] (11); which one? [of two] (17)
Doitsugo: German language (10)
doko: where? (2)
dokoka: somewhere, anywhere (9)
doomo arigatoo gozaimasu: thank you very much (1)
doomo sumimasen: I'm sorry, I apologize (1)
Donna?: What kind of...? (13)
dono: which? [adjective] (3)
dore: which one? (2)
doru: dollars (5)
dotchi: which one? [of two] [short form of dochira] (17)
doyoobi: Saturday (9)
doozo: here you are [when giving something] (1)
doozo doozo: please do so, please go ahead (4)
doozo yoroshiku: happy to meet you (2)

e: to, towards (1)
ee: yes [informal] (9)
e-hagaki: picture postcard (20)
eakon: air conditioner (14)
eiga: movie, film (3)
Eigo: English language (3)
Eikaiwa: English conversation (18)
eki: train station (2)
Emu pii surii pureeyaa: MP3 player (15)
en: yen (5)
enjinia: engineer (1)

fakkusu: fax (8)
famikon: family computer (14)
Fuji san: Mount Fuji (11)
fukushuu: review (6)
-fun/pun: minute (4)
Furansu: France (10)

Furansugo: French language (10)
furoppi: floppy disk (14)
furu: fall, drop (17)
futari: two (people)(9)
futatsu: two (objects) (14)
fuutoo: envelope (18)
fuyu: winter (13)

G-pan: jeans (8)
ga: [particle indicating subject of verb] (3)
ga: but (1); but [when joining two sentences] (8)
gaijin: foreigner (4)
gaikoku: foreign country, abroad (15)
gairaigo: words borrowed from other languages (14)
gakkoo: school (1)
gakuin: academy, school, place of learning (1)
gakusei: student (1)
ganbaru: try hard, do one's best (10)
ganjitsu: New Year's Day (13)
gaarufurendo: girlfriend (11)
gasu: gas (petrol) (18)
gasu-dai: gas charges (18)
-gawa: the - side (5)
geemu: game (10)
genkan: entrance area [in a house] (5)
genki(-na): healthy, energetic (8)
getsuyoobi: Monday (9)
ginkoo: bank (2)
go: five (1)
Go-chisoo sama deshita.: Thank you for the meal. (3)
go-enryo naku: without standing on ceremony (11)
go-gatsu: May (13)
go-kazoku: (your) family (7)
go-shujin: (your) husband (7)
gogo: afternoon (7)
gohan: cooked rice (3)
Gomen kudasai.: Excuse me, is anyone there? (5); Pardon me for causing any inconvenience. (4)
gomen nasai: excuse me, I beg your pardon (13)
gorufu: golf (9)
gozaimasu: have [formal] (8)
gurai: about, approximately (19)
guree: gray (8)
guriin: green (8)

hachi: eight (1)
hachi-gatsu: August (13)
hagaki: postcard (18)
haha: (my) mother (7)
hai: yes (1)
haikingu: hiking (14)
hairu: go in, enter (9)

hajimaru: to begin [intransitive] (4)
Hajimemashite.: How do you do? (1)
hajimete: first time (15)
hamu: ham (14)
-han: half past - (4)
hana: flower (3)
hanashi: a talk, conversation, chat (4)
hanashi o suru: have a talk, chat (4)
hanasu: speak, talk (3)
hanbaagaa: hamburger (14)
hanbai: sales, selling (19)
hansamu(-na): handsome (11)
harau: pay (18)
haru: spring (13)
hashi: chopsticks (4)
hashiru: run (10)
hataraku: work, labor [verb] (7)
hayai: quick, early (7)
hazukashii: shy, embarrassed (9)
hen(-na): odd, strange (8)
heta(-na): bad at, unskillful (9)
heya: room (13)
hi: day (13)
hidari: the left (5)
hidari-gawa: the left-hand side (5)
hidoi: terrible, awful(14)
hiroi: large [in area], spacious, extensive (17)
hiru-gohan: lunch (7)
hiruma: daytime (13)
hisashiburi: it's been a long time (8)
hito: person, people (2)
hitori: one (person) (9)
hitotachi: people (9)
hitotsu: one (object) (14)
hoo ga ii: - would be best (14)
hoo: direction, side (17)
hoka ni: other, another, else (17)
Hokkaidoo: the northernmost of the four main islands of Japan (8)
hon: book (5)
-hon: [counter for long, thin objects] (19)
hontoo ni: really, truly (9)
hoshii: want (15)
hoteru: hotel (8)
hotto (koohii): hot (coffee) (14)
hyaku: hundred (5)

ichi: one (1)
ichi-gatsu: January (13)
ichi-man: ten thousand (19)
ichi-nen-kan: a one-year period (11)
ichi-nichi-juu: all day long (19)
ichi-nichi: one day (15)

ichiban: most, the first, number one (11)
ichido: once, one time (11)
Igirisu: England, Great Britain (2)
Igirisujin: an English/British person (2)
ii: good, fine (3)
ii kagen ni shi nasai: please behave yourselves (19)
iie: no (1)
iinkai: committee (15)
ik-kagetsu: one month (19)
ik-kai: once, one time (19)
ikaga: how about... [polite form of doo] (5)
iku: go (3)
ikura: how much (money)? (5)
ikutsu: how old? (11); how many? (14)
ima: now, at the moment (4)
imooto: (my) younger sister (7)
imootosan: (your) younger sister (7)
Indo: India (14)
inu: dog (4)
irassharu: is, are [very polite form of iru] (4)
iroiro(-na): all kinds of, various (11)
iru: am, is, are [used with animate objects] (4)
isogashii: busy (13)
issho ni: together (7)
itadakimasu: bon appetit (3); yes, please [when offered food or drink] (5)
itai: painful (7)
Itaria: Italy (14)
itsu: when?(9)
itsumo: always (8)
itsutsu: five (objects) (14)
iu: say, relate (13)
iya(-na): horrible (8)

ja: well, in that case (1)
ja arimasen: isn't, aren't (2)
jaketto: jacket (8)
jama: interference, obstruction (5)
-ji: - o'clock (4)
jibun: self, oneself (19)
jibun no: one's own, my own, your own (19)
Jiinzu: jeans (8)
jikan: time, hour (4)
-jikan: - hours (9)
jiko shookai: self-introduction (10)
jimu: office work (2)
jimu: gym (8)
jimu no hito: clerk, office worker (2)
-jin: person (of a country) (1)
jisho: dictionary (18)
jitsu wa: in fact (11)
josei: females, women (11)
joozu(-na): skillful, good at (9)

jugyoo: lesson, class (10)
juppun: 10 minutes (4)
juu: ten (1)
juu-gatsu: October (13)
juu-ichi-gatsu: November (13)
juu-ichi: eleven (1)
juu-ni-gatsu: December (13)
juu-ni: twelve (1)
juubun: enough, sufficient (18)
juusho: address (5)

ka: [sentence ending to indicate a question] (1)
ka: or (15)
kaaten: curtain (14)
kabuki: Japanese classical play (18)
kachoo: section head, assistant manager (15)
kado: corner (5)
kaeru: return, go/come home (7)
kagaku: science (10)
kaidan: steps, stairs (17)
kaigi: a meeting (3)
kaigi ni deru: attend a meeting (13)
kaimono: shopping [noun] (8)
kaisha: company, office (1)
kaiwa: conversation (14)
kakaru: take (time), last (9)
kakikomu: fill in/out [a form] (18)
kaku: write (5)
Kamakura: city close to Yokohama, famous for its large statue of Buddha (17)
...kana: I wonder...
Kanada: Canada (1)
Kanadajin: a Canadian (1)
kanai/tsuma: (my) wife (7)
kanemochi: rich person (17)
kangaeru: think about, consider (10)
kanji: Chinese written characters (9)
kanojo: she, her (15)
kantan(-na): brief, simple (8)
kao: face (10)
kaapetto: carpet (14)
kara: from (2); because (11); after (18)
kare: him, he (14)
kasa: umbrella (17)
kashikomarimashita: certainly, very good [formal] (14)
...kashira: I wonder... (8)
kau: buy (8)
Kawasaki: industrial city near Tokyo (7)
kayoobi: Tuesday (9)
kaze: wind (17)
kazoku: family (7)
kedo: but, although (8)
keikaku: plan, project, scheme (15)

keiroo no hi: Respect for the Aged Day (13)
keiyaku: contract (15)
keeki: cake (14)
kekkon: marriage (11)
kekkon suru: be married (11)
kenka: argument (14)
kenkoku kinenbi: National Foundation Day (13)
kenpoo kinenbi: Constitution Day (13)
kesa: this morning (9)
ki o tsukeru: take care, be careful (7)
kibun: mood, feeling (17)
kiiboodo: keyboard (14)
kiiro(i): yellow (8)
kiku: chrysanthemum (3); hear, listen, ask [verb] (3)
kimeru: decide (15)
kinoo: yesterday (9)
kinoo no ban: yesterday evening (11)
kinroo kansha no hi: Labor Thanksgiving Day (13)
kin'yoobi: Friday (9)
kippu: ticket (18)
kirai(-na): dislike (3)
kirei(-na): pretty, clean (8)
kissaten: coffee shop (9)
kitanai: dirty (14)
kitte: stamp (18)
kitto: definitely, without fail (17)
kochira: this way (1); this person [used with introductions] (2); this one [of two] (17)
kochira koso: the pleasure's mine (13)
koochoo: principal, head teacher (15)
kodomo no hi: Children's Day (13)
kodomo: child (8)
kodomotachi: children (11)
koofun suru: be excited (19)
koko: here (2)
kookoo: high school [short for kootoo gakkoo] (1)
kokonotsu: nine (objects) (14)
kookuubin: airmail (18)
komu: be crowded (8)
konban: this evening (3)
konbanwa: good evening (2)
kongetsu: this month (13)
konna: this kind of (13)
konnichiwa: good day, hello [not used early in the morning] (2)
kono: this [adjective] (3)
konpyuutaa: computer (2)
kopii: photocopy (14)
koora: cola (14)
kore: this [noun] (2)
kooshuu denwa: public telephone (14)
koosu: course [of study] (13)
kotae: answer, response (10)
kotaeru: answer, respond (13)

kotchi: this side, this one [of two] [from kochira] (17)
kooto: coat (8)
koto: thing, event, fact (10)
koto ga arimasu ka: have you ever...? (17)
kotoba: word (13)
kotoshi: this year (15)
kozutsumi: package, parcel (18)
ku-gatsu: September (13)
kuukoo: airport (15)
kuni: country (10)
kurai: dark (17)
kurasu: class (9)
kuro(i): black (8)
kuru: come (3)
kuruma: car (1)
kusshon: cushion (14)
kutsu: shoes (8)
kyaku: guest, customer (14)
kyoo: today (2)
kyooiku: education (15)
kyonen: last year (15)
kyuu/ku: nine (1)
kyuuryoo: salary, wages (15)

machi: town, city (9)
mada: still, (not) yet (4)
made: until (4); as far as (5)
made ni: by [date or time] (15)
mae: before, in front of (7)
magaru: turn [verb] (5)
-mai: [counter for flat objects] (18)
mainichi: every day (3)
-man: ten thousand (19)
maneejaa: manager (10)
massugu: straight ahead (5)
mata: again, once more, another time (4)
mata ashita: until tomorrow, see you tomorrow [informal] (4)
mata doozo: please come again (13)
matsu: wait (5)
mazu: first of all, to begin with (18)
meishi: business card (1)
memo: memo (15)
menyuu: menu (14)
messeeji: message (15)
midori: green (8)
midori no hi: Greenery Day (13)
migi: the right (5)
migi-gawa: right-hand side (5)
mina san, minna: everyone (2)
minna de: altogether, everyone together (7)
miru: see, watch (3)
mise: shop (14)

miseru: show (18)
miso shiru: miso soup (3)
mittsu: three (objects) (14)
mizu: water (3)
moo: already, (not) any longer, another, further (5)
mo: too, also (8)
moo ichido: once more (11)
…mo…mo: both…and…/neither…nor… (9)
mochiron: of course, naturally (17)
mokuyoobi: Thursday (9)
mondai: problem (5)
monitaa: a monitor (14)
moshi moshi: hello? [on the telephone] (4)
moshi yokattara: if it's all right (13)
moshi: if (17)
moosu: be called, named (10)
motsu: have, hold (15)
motte kuru: bring (19)
motto: more (8)
mukae ni iku: go to meet (15)
mukoo: the other direction, over there (14)
murasaki: purple (8)
mushiatsui: hot and humid (17)
muttsu: six (objects) (14)
muzukashii: difficult (7)

nado: and so on, et cetera (10)
nagai: long (10)
naka: among, within (11); inside (14)
namae: name (1)
nan/nani: what? (3)
nan-gatsu: which month? (13)
nan-ji: what time? (4)
nan-nichi: what date? (13)
nan-nin: how many people? (9)
nan-sai: how old? (11)
nan-yoobi: what day? (9)
nana/shichi: seven (1)
nanatsu: seven (objects) (14)
nanika: something, anything (9)
narabu: line up, queue (17)
naru: become, get (17)
natsu: summer (13)
natsu-yasumi: summer vacation (13)
naze: why (4)
ne: isn't it? aren't they? don't you? etc. (3)
nekutai: necktie (8)
nen: year (11)
neru: sleep, go to bed (7)
ni: in, at [location] (2); at [when giving the time] (4); to, towards (9)
ni: two (1)
-nichi: [added to numbers to give the date] (13)

ni-gatsu: February (13)
ni-kai: second floor, upstairs (7)
niku: meat (4)
ni tsuite: concerning, regarding (15)
nichiyoobi: Sunday (9)
Nihon: Japan (1)
Nihon Arupusu: Japan Alps, mountain range in central Japan (9)
Nihongo: Japanese language (1)
nimotsu: luggage (19)
-nin: [counter for people] (9)
Nippon: Japan (1)
no: [particle showing possession, similar to English "...'s"] (1)
noboru: climb, go up (17)
nomu: drink [verb] (3)
noru: to get on/in [transportation] (19)
Nyuu Jiirando: New Zealand (14)
Nyuu Yooku: New York (9)
nyuusu: the news (4)

o: [particle to indicate object of verb] (3)
...o kudasai: Could I have..., please? (3)
...o onegai shimasu: Could I have..., please? (3)
o-cha: green tea (3)
o-genki desu ka: How are you? (8)
o-hisashiburi: it's been a long time (8)
o-hitori: single, unmarried (11)
o-jama shimasu: excuse me for disturbing you (5)
o-kage sama de: thank you for asking [set phrase in response to
    o-genki desu ka] (8)
o-kake kudasai: please take a seat (5)
o-kane: money (15)
o-kanemochi: rich person (17)
o-kaasan: (your) mother [or when addressing one's own mother] (7)
o-kuni: (your) country (2)
o-kyaku san: guest, customer [formal] (14)
o-naka ga suku: become hungry (14)
o-naka: stomach (14)
o-neesan: (your) older sister [or when addressing one's own older sister] (7)
o-niisan: (your) older brother [or when addressing one's own older brother] (7)
o-sake: sake, rice wine (9)
o-tearai: restroom (17)
o-toosan: (your) father [or when addressing one's own father] (7)
o-tsuri: the change [money] (5)
oboeru: remember, recall (7)
Ohaio-shu: the state of Ohio (10)
ohayoo gozaimasu: good morning (2)
ooi: many, abundant, a lot of (11)
oishii: tasty, delicious (3)
ookii: big (2)
okiru: get up, get out of bed (13)
okoru: get angry (14)
oku: hundred million (19)

okuru: send (18)
okusan: (your) wife (7)
omoshiroi: interesting, amusing (9)
omou: think (10)
onaji: same (13)
onegai shimasu: please [Lit: I have a request/favor] (3); Could I speak to...? (4); please do that (15)
ongaku: music (19)
onna no hito: woman (9)
onna no hitotachi: women (9)
onsen: hot spring (9)
orenji: orange (8)
oshieru: tell, teach (3)
osoi: late, slow (7)
Oosutoraria: Australia (14)
Oosutoria: Austria (14)
otoko no hito: man (9)
otooto: (my) younger brother (7)
otootosan: (your) younger brother (7)
otto/shujin: (my) husband (7)
owaru: finish, end [verb] (10)
oyasumi nasai: good night (2)

paatii: party (9)
paato: part-time worker (2)
piano: piano (10)
pikunikku: picnic (17)
pinku: pink (8)
piza: pizza (14)
purezento: present (18)
purintaa: printer (2)

raigetsu: next month (13)
rainen: next year (15)
raishuu: next week (9)
rajio: radio (3)
ranchi: lunch (18)
ranpu: lamp (14)
rapputoppu: laptop (14)
rekishi: history (10)
remon tii: lemon tea (14)
renshuu: practice (7)
repooto: report [noun] (8)
resutoran: restaurant (3)
rikon: divorce (11)
roku: six (1)
roku-gatsu: June (13)
ryokan: Japanese-style inn (9)
ryokoo: trip, journey (19)
ryoori: cooking, cuisine (4)
ryoori suru: cook (4)

sabishii: lonely (11)
saafingu: surfing (14)
...-sai: ...years old (11)
saigo ni: finally, at the end (18)
saikin: recently (19)
saizu: size (8)
sakana: fish (3)
sake: sake, rice wine (9)
saki ni: in advance, ahead, before (17)
sama: Mr., Mrs., Ms., Miss [very polite] (4)
samui: cold
san: Mr., Mrs., Ms., Miss (1)
san: three (1)
san-gatsu: March (13)
sando: sandwich (14)
sarada: salad (14)
sashimi: raw fish (3)
seijin no hi: Coming-of-Age Day (13)
seikatsu: life, living (10)
sen: thousand (5)
sengetsu: last month (13)
sensei: teacher, professor [used instead of san as a term of address to teachers, professors and doctors] (1)
senshuu: last week (9)
seetaa: sweater (8)
setsumei: explanation (11)
setsumei suru: explain (11)
SF (esu efu): science-fiction (4)
shachoo: president (15)
shanai: inside the train (19)
shashin: photograph (17)
shatsu: shirt (8)
shi/yo/yon: four (1)
shi-gatsu: April (13)
shichi-gatsu: July (13)
shichi/nana: seven (1)
shigoto: work, employment (4)
shigoto suru: work [verb] (4)
shii dii: CD, compact disc (14)
shikata ga arimasen: it can't be helped (17)
shinbun: newspaper (2)
shingoo: traffic signals (5)
Shinkansen: Bullet Train (11)
shinpai: worry, anxiety (15)
shinsetsu(-na): kind, gentle (8)
shiraberu: investigate, look into (19)
shiro(i): white (8)
shisha: branch office (14)
shita: below, under (14)
shiteiseki: reserved seat (19)
shitsumon: question (11)
shitsurei desu ga: I'm sorry to trouble you, but ...; Excuse me, but ... (1)

shitsurei shimasu: excuse me (2); goodbye (4)
shizuka(-na): quiet, peaceful (8)
shookai suru: introduce (10)
shuubun no hi: Autumnal Equinox Day (13)
shuukan: week (10)
shukudai: homework (7)
shuumatsu: weekend (9)
shumi: interest, hobby (10)
shunbun no hi: Spring Equinox Day (13)
shutchoo: business trip (13)
soo desu: that's right, that's so (1)
soo desu ka: I see, is that so? (1)
soba: near, next to (14)
soba: noodles (10)
sochira: that side, that one [of two] (17)
soodan suru: consult, confer with, talk over (15)
sooji suru: do the cleaning (19)
soko: there (2)
sonna: that kind of (13)
sono: that [adjective] (3)
sono ato: after that (15)
sora: sky (8)
sore: that [noun] (2)
sore de: so, therefore, and then (14)
sore kara: and also (4)
sorosoro: slowly, gradually, soon (13)
soshite: then (18)
sotchi: that side, that one [of two] [from **sochira**] (17)
soto: outside (9)
suugaku: mathematics (10)
sugi: past, after (7)
sugoi: amazing, incredible (17)
sugu: soon (4), quickly (14)
suiyoobi: Wednesday (9)
sukaato: skirt (8)
sukejuuru: schedule (15)
suki(-na): like (3)
sukii: skiing (13)
sukii ni iku: go skiing (13)
sukii-joo: ski resort (13)
sukii-uea: ski-wear (19)
sukoshi: a little, a small amount (5)
suku: become empty (14)
sumimasen: excuse me, I'm sorry (1)
sumu: reside, live (7)
supagetti: spaghetti (14)
supootsu: sport (10)
surippa: slippers (5)
suru: do (3); **...ni suru:** I'll have/decide on... (3)
sushi: raw fish on rice (10)
sutaffu: staff (14)
suteeki: steak (14)

suupaa: supermarket (14)
suutsu: suit (8)
suutsukeesu: suitcase (1)
suwaru: sit down (5)
suzushii: cool (17)

T-shatsu: T-shirt (8)
tabemono: food (10)
taberu: eat (3)
-tachi: [plural ending for words associated with people] (9)
tada: just, only, simply (15)
taihen(-na): terrible, awful (8)
taiiku: physical education (10)
taiiku no hi: Sports Health Day (13)
takai: high, expensive (7)
tako: octopus (19)
takusan: a lot of, many, much (4)
takushii: taxi (4)
tamago: egg (18)
tame ni: for the purpose of, benefit of (18)
tanjoobi: birthday (7)
tanoshii: enjoyable, fun (9)
tanoshimi ni suru: look forward to (19)
tatemono: building (5)
tatsu: stand (17)
tearai: restroom (17)
teeburu: table (14)
tegami: letter (13)
teishoku: set meal (3)
tenisu: tennis (4)
tenki: weather (9)
tennoo tanjoobi: Emperor's Birthday (13)
tenpura: tempura [deep fried food] (11)
terebi: television, TV (4)
tesuto: a test (4)
to: and [to join nouns] (1)
too: ten (objects) (14)
to ieba: speaking of…, that reminds me (19)
tooi: far, distant (17)
toki: time, period (13)
tokidoki: sometimes (3)
tokoro: place (9)
tokorode: by the way (5)
tokubetsu no: special, particular (15)
tomaru: stay (overnight) (9)
tomeru: stop, halt [transitive verb] (5)
tomodachi: friend (3)
tonari: next to, by the side (7)
toru: take (15)
toshi: year, age (19)
toshi o toru: get older [of people] (19)
toosuto: toast (14)

totemo: very, extremely (8)
tsugi no: the next (5)
tsukareru: become tired (9)
tsukau: use (11)
tsukemono: pickles (3)
tsukue: desk (2)
tsukuru: make (18)
tsuma/kanai: (my) wife (7)
tsumori: intention (15)
tsuna: tuna (14)
tsutomeru: be employed (10)
tsuyoi: strong (17)

uchi: house, home (2)
uchiawase: meeting, consultation (15)
ue: above, on top (14)
uindo saafingu: windsurfing (14)
umi: sea, ocean(9)
ureshii: happy (11)
uru: sell (15)
urusai: noisy (19)
ushiro: behind, in back of (14)
uso: untruth, story, lie (10)

wa: [particle to indicate main topic of sentence] (2)
...wa doo desu ka.: How about...? (3)
wain: wine (3)
wakai: young (9)
wakarimashita: I see, I've got it, I understand [from wakaru] (5)
wakaru: understand (2)
wanpiisu: dress [noun] (8)
waapuro: word processor (14)
warui: bad, wrong (7)
wasureru: forget (9)
watashi: I, me (1)
watashi no: my (1)
watashitachi: us, we (9)

ya: and (10)
yaki-zakana: grilled fish (3)
yakyuu: baseball (7)
yama: mountain (9)
yameru: quit, stop, cease (18)
yaru: do, try (19)
yasui: cheap (7)
yasumi: holiday, rest, pause (13)
yasumi no hi: holiday, vacation, day off (13)
yattsu: eight (objects) (14)
yo: [sentence ending to show emphasis] (5)
yobu: call, summon (7)
yoofuku: clothes (19)
yooji: errand, chore, something to do (18)

yokattara: if it's allright (17)
yookoso: welcome (1)
yoku: often (8); well (10)
yoku aru: frequently occurring (11)
yomu: read (3)
yon/yo/shi: four (1)
Yooroppa: Europe (13)
Yoroshiku onegai shimasu.: Pleased to meet you. [Lit: Please treat me well.] (2); .
   Goodbye [on the phone] (4)
yoru: call in, drop by (15)
yoru: evening (9)
yooshi: a form, a blank (15)
yotei: plan, program, schedule (15)
yottsu: four (objects) (14)
yu: hot water (9)
yuubinkyoku: post office (14)
yuki: snow (17)
yukkuri: slowly (5)
yuumei(-na): famous (8)

zannen(-na): pity, unfortunate (9)
zenbu: all (10)
zenzen: never [+ negative verb] (8)